Peter Felten

PETER F. ✍ W9-DIH-584

PETER FELTEN

BETWEEN TWO ISLANDS

BETWEEN TWO ISLANDS

Dominican International Migration

SHERRI GRASMUCK
AND
PATRICIA R. PESSAR

UNIVERSITY OF CALIFORNIA PRESS
BERKELEY   LOS ANGELES   OXFORD

University of California Press
Berkeley and Los Angeles, California

University of California Press, Ltd.
Oxford, England

©1991 by
The Regents of the University of California

Library of Congress Cataloging-in-Publication Data

Grasmuck, Sherri.
   Between two islands : Dominican international migration /
Sherri Grasmuck, Patricia R. Pessar.
      p.   cm.
   Includes bibliographical references and index.
   ISBN 0-520-07149-2. — ISBN 0-520-07150-6 (pbk.)
      1. Dominican Republic—Emigration and immigration.
   2. United States—Emigration and immigration. 3. Return
   migration—Dominican Republic. 4. Dominican Republic—
   Rural conditions. 5. Dominicans (Dominican Republic)—
   United States. 6. Households—Dominican Republic. 7.
   Households—United States.   I. Pessar, Patricia R.   II.
   Title.
   JV7395.G7   1991
   304.8'097293—dc20   90-50924
                                                            CIP

Printed in the United States of America

9 8 7 6 5 4 3 2 1

The paper used in this publication meets the minimum
requirements of American National Standard for Information
Sciences—Permanence of Paper for Printed Library
Materials, ANSI Z39.48–1984. ∞

For our parents—
Wally and Gen Grasmuck
and
Henry and Irene Pessar

Contents

List of Tables   ix

List of Charts and Maps   xiii

Acknowledgments   xv

1. Introduction   1

2. The Dominican State, Social Classes, and Emigration   18

3. Research Design   51

4. Urban Emigration and Return Migration: Consequences
    for National Development   65

5. Dominican Rural Emigration   98

6. Households and International Migration: Dynamics of
    Generation and Gender   133

7. Dominican Workers in the New York City Labor Market   162

8. Conclusion   199

References   209

Index   239

List of Tables

1. Dominican Immigrants Legally Admitted to the United
    States   20
2. Dominican Non-Immigrants Admitted to the United
    States   21
3. Immigrants per 10,000 Population, 1981   22
4. Emigrant Children, 1981   25
5. Economically Active Population, Dominican Republic,
    1970–1981   37
6. Rates of School Enrollment by Age, Dominican Republic,
    1960 and 1980   37
7. Rates of Unemployment of Economically Active
    Population of Santo Domingo, by Level of Education,
    1979   39
8. Number of Dominican Republic State Employees by
    Category of Monthly Salary, 1966–1977   40
9. Minimum and Real Wages in the Dominican Republic,
    1966–1984   42
10. Changes in the Distribution of Family Income in Santo
    Domingo, 1969 to 1973   43
11. Dominican and United States Minimum Monthly Salaries
    Compared, 1974–1987   47
12. Relation of Outside Migrant to Remaining Head of
    Household in Santiago   69

ix

13. Previous Residence of Head of Household in Santiago, by
    Migratory Status   70

14. Regular Payments from Abroad Received by Households
    in Santiago, 1980   72

15. Household Income in Santiago, 1980, by Migratory Status   72

16. Possession of Household Consumer Items in Santiago,
    1980, by Migratory Status   73

17. Employment of Head of Household in Santiago, 1980, by
    Sex and Migratory Status   75

18. Employment, over a Five-Year Period, of Head of
    Household in Santiago, 1980, by Migratory Status   76

19. Educational Levels of New York–Based Migrants from
    Urban Communities Compared to the Santo Domingo
    Population, 1981   77

20. Last Home-Country Occupation of Dominican Urban
    Emigrants Compared to Resident Population   78

21. Last Home-Country Sector of Employment of Dominican
    Emigrants Compared to Resident Population   80

22. Duration of Stay Abroad of Return Migrants in Santiago   84

23. Education of Head of Household in Santiago, 1980, by
    Migratory Status   84

24. Occupation of Head of Household in Santiago, 1980, by
    Migratory Status   85

25. Social Class Distribution of Juan Pablo Emigrant
    Population, 1961–1981   109

26. Daily Average Expenditures of Selected Rural Households   119

27. Occupational Distribution of Dominicans by Sex, New
    York City, 1980   164

28. Occupational Distribution and Education of Hispanics by
    Sex, New York City, 1980   165

29. New York City Industries with Concentrations of New
    Immigrants, 1980   170

30. Occupational Distribution of Dominican Immigrants in
    Home Country and New York City, by Legal Status and
    Sex   172

31. Occupational Distribution of Dominican Immigrants in New York City, 1981, by Legal Status, Sex, and Educational Level 176

32. Industrial Sector of Employment of Dominican Immigrants in New York City, by Legal Status, Sex, and Educational Level 177

33. Size of Firm of Employment of Dominican Immigrants in New York City 179

34. Weekly Wages of Dominican Immigrants in New York City, 1981, by Legal Status and Sex 180

35. Ethnicity of Workplace of Dominican Immigrants in New York City, 1981 181

36. Level of Unionization of Dominican Immigrants in New York City, by Legal Status and Sex 191

37. Militancy at Workplace of Dominican Immigrants in New York City, by Legal Status and Sex 192

List of Charts and Maps

Chart 1. Research Sites and Data Gathered in the Dominican
Republic and the United States   52

Map 1. The Dominican Republic: The Research Sites of the
Project   53

PETER FELTEN

Acknowledgments

Collaboration is often more appealing in spirit than in practice. Happily, in both research and writing we have enjoyed the best that collaboration has to offer: confidence in the other's strengths, an openness to critical exchange, and a recognition that the other would always come through.

We collaborated on our research: although Grasmuck initially concentrated on surveys and Pessar on ethnographic fieldwork, we worked together on the analysis of these two types of data, as well as on other secondary materials presented in this book. The survey and ethnographic materials are not presented separately here, but, rather, are interlaced so that our discussions benefit from both the breadth of survey methods and the interpretive richness of ethnography.

This project would never have come to light if it had not been for Alejandro Portes. We were all at Duke University in 1979, and it was Alejandro who first recognized the need for in-depth research on Dominican migration. It was also Alejandro who introduced the two of us and suggested that we consider collaboration. Moreover, he assisted us in the Dominican Republic in the phase of survey design. We are especially thankful for his support throughout the project and his insistence that we not stop with articles but produce a book. Other colleagues then at Duke were particularly helpful during the proposal-writing stage. We owe particular thanks to Jan Brukman, Patricia Fernández-Kelly, Virginia Domínguez, and Carol Stack.

Our research in the Dominican Republic and New York was supported by grants from the National Institute of Child Health and Development (NICHD), the National Science Foundation, and New York University's New York Research Program in Inter-American Affairs. Earl Huyck, our program officer at NICHD, was consistently supportive of our research. Grasmuck would also like to acknowledge the study leave she received from Temple University during the writing of the manuscript.

Our research in the Dominican Republic was facilitated by many Dominican colleagues who gave generously of their time and taught us repeatedly the meaning of mutual aid in Dominican culture. The willingness of Noris Eusebio Pol to work as a field supervisor and adviser proved essential to the successful completion of the surveys. Her clear intelligence, wisdom, and friendship carried us through many difficult phases of the survey fieldwork. In the summer of 1979, when Pessar first traveled to the Dominican Republic to discuss our research plans, Julio Cross-Beras and Frank Moya Pons were both extremely encouraging and shared their thoughts about and materials on Dominican migration. Among the countless other Dominicans who enthusiastically assisted us in problem-solving, the following individuals stand out: Enmanuel Castillo, Rafael Yunén, José del Castillo, Carlos Dore y Cabral, and Isis Duarte. We are extremely grateful to Rafael Yunén and the Centro de Investigación of the Universidad Católica de Madre y Maestra for permitting us to establish a research base during the fieldwork in the Cibao, and to the Oficina Nacional Estadística in Santo Domingo for important institutional support in various stages of the project. Joshua Reichert assisted us in the early phase of selection of rural communities. Julia Tavárez conducted most of the ethnographic research in return migrant neighborhoods in Santiago. We are also indebted to Max Castro, who contributed in essential ways to the collection of ethnographic data in two rural communities. The survey research in the Dominican Republic could not have been completed without the careful work of the following interviewers: José Acosta, David Alba, Paul Almonte, Neuli Cordero, Elena García, Ziamara García, Claudio Jerez, Victor Martínez, Margarita Ramírez, Hugo Rodríguez, Osvaldo Ureña, Rosa Ureña, José Vargas, and Georgina Zacarias. We would also like to thank the people of Juan Pablo, who graciously accepted Pessar into their community and shared their hopes and thoughts about out-migration.

During the New York phase of our research, Christopher Mitchell at New York University generously provided us with a research base for both our survey and our ethnographic work. He also introduced us to a community of migration scholars and practitioners who assisted us in many ways. These include Muzaffar Chishti, Nancy Foner, Douglas Gurak, Adriana Marshall, Dawn Marshall, Glauco Pérez, Saskia Sassen-Koob, and Roger Waldinger. We were especially fortunate to have the support of a hard-working and careful group of Dominican interviewers, especially Helmer Duverge, María González, Ana Hernández, María Marcelo, Gil Santos, and Luis Manuel Tejeda. Pessar would like to acknowledge the skill and dedication of her fieldwork assistants, Catherine Benamou, Nancy Clarke, and Aneris Goris.

In conceptualizing and writing the book we have benefited greatly from the advice and critical reading of several friends and colleagues. David Bray, Rosario Espinal, Eugenia Georges, Eric Larson, and Magali Sarfetti Larson proved to be valuable critics and sounding boards over the years. Alejandro Portes and Ruben Rumbaut both reviewed the entire manuscript and indicated how we might strengthen arguments and more fully develop conclusions.

Owing to the collaborative nature of our project, many of our acknowledgments are mutual. There are, however, several people to whom we individually owe gratitude. Grasmuck especially thanks John Landreau for his constant love and advice during the most difficult phases of writing. She also owes profound gratitude to Deborah Luepnitz for her teachings and offerings of friendship and sisterhood during many meetings at the White Dog, where writing knots were untied. Grasmuck would like to thank her children, Tessa and Soren, not for gracefully accepting Mom's absences, but for always reminding her that life is short and academics long.

Pessar is deeply indebted to her husband, Gil Joseph, who proved to be an agile critic when she was most in need of advice and an enthusiastic supporter when it seemed as though the redrafting would never end. She commends her son, Matthew, who had the good sense and timing to be born when the research had been completed and the book was in the final editing phase. She would also like to thank Mary Ann Larkin and Gerardo Berthin of the Hemispheric Migration Project for their support and collegiality at various stages of the preparation of this book.

Finally, we are grateful to Anita Landreau for an early reading of the manuscript and especially to Jane-Ellen Long of the University of California Press, whose sensitive editing notably improved the manuscript. We also thank Gloria Basmajian for her expert word-processing and cheerful willingness to type endless revisions of the manuscript.

Introduction

The history of the Molinas, a three-generation Dominican family resident in New York City, illustrates a number of important features of the contemporary wave of Dominican immigration into the United States. Motivations behind Molina family members' decisions to leave Santo Domingo for New York between 1965 and 1981 included fear of political persecution, desire for marital reunification, greater economic opportunity, provision of child care for relatives, and opportunities for higher education. The history of the transplanting of three generations of Molinas demonstrates the difficulty of coming up with a definitive answer to the deceptively simple question of why Dominicans leave their island to live and work in the United States.

The Molinas' migration history begins with Rafael Molina. As a university student in Santo Domingo, Rafael studied education, because he felt deeply committed to improving the lives of the many impoverished Dominican children he saw all around him. However, events unfolded in such a way that he left his country and his political commitments in 1965. He was never to live there again. When Dominican president Juan Bosch was overthrown in a military coup in 1963, Rafael, as student leader at the Autonomous University in Santo Domingo, joined others in the street fighting which followed. During the evolving political crisis, which resulted in the defeat of Bosch supporters and U.S. occupation of the island, Rafael blamed the United States for thwarting his dream of transforming the political and economic landscape of his homeland. Yet, he also feared for his life and believed his political sympathies

would interfere with his aspirations to become a school administra-
tor. Despite his political hostility toward the United States, in the
summer of 1965 Rafael nonetheless applied for and easily obtained
a temporary resident visa for the United States.

In 1966 Rafael returned home briefly to marry Mercedes, his
high school sweetheart, who was working as an elementary school
teacher in a small rural town. The couple was reunited in New York
the following year. By 1970 they had two young children, and
Mercedes was anxious to begin work as a sewing machine operator
so that they might save for the children's education.

Back in the Dominican Republic, Rafael's father had died. With
only a third-grade education, his mother, Gertrudes, was obliged
to accept work as a janitor at a clinic to support her two younger
sons. All the children found this work demeaning for their mother,
who had previously been well supported by her husband, a police-
man. It was decided that Rafael would sponsor Gertrudes's emigration so that she might care for his two children and free Mercedes
to work outside the home. Rafael and Mercedes agreed to send
remittances to Gertrudes's sister, who was caring for Gertrudes's
two youngest sons.

When Rafael's two children entered elementary school, Gertrudes insisted on staying in the United States, so that she could
earn the money to send her two remaining sons to a university in
the Dominican Republic. By 1980, the middle son, Tomás, had
graduated from the university, only to find that jobs in communications were few and starting salaries low. Rafael convinced a Colombian clothing manufacturer to hire his brother as an accountant,
and Rafael, who was now a U.S. citizen, was able to sponsor
Tomás's emigration. Gertrudes's youngest son, Carlito, was sponsored by his mother the following year. Gertrudes had concluded
that if her youngest son was going to become a professional, he
should enroll in a U.S. high school and university.

The Molinas' story, drawn from our research on Dominican migration to the United States, illustrates the many facets of international labor migration, and, specifically, the range of influences
behind the massive displacement of Dominicans from their island.
First, the timing of the first migrant's departure, 1965, coincides
with a period of political turmoil after a thirty-year dictatorship in

the Dominican Republic and the appointment of a United States
consulate eager to facilitate out-migration in the face of rising political tensions. Second, from the time the first family member left
until the remaining brothers also entered the United States, the
Dominican Republic was governed by two radically different political parties. Despite the two governments' differences in ideology
and programs for economic development, out-migration steadily
grew in scale throughout this period. Third, none of the migrants
were poor, unskilled agricultural laborers. Indeed, Rafael and
Carlito were university trained, with ambitions that could not be
fulfilled in their home society. Fourth, it is possible to make sense
of the movement of these five individuals only by reference to the
meaning of family ties and the significance of the social networks
available to the family. These points illustrate one of the central
arguments of this book: international migration is a multifaceted
process involving economic, political, and sociocultural factors.
The migration process is dynamic and ever evolving.

This book presents the results of a two-stage interdisciplinary
study of rural and urban communities in the Dominican Republic
and related communities of Dominicans living and working in
greater New York. It focuses on the consequences of this population movement for the sending and receiving communities, the
immigrants and their families. In much recent theorizing, based on
specific instances of international labor migration, researchers have
tended to emphasize macroeconomic factors and to underestimate
the importance of political and sociocultural influences. This study
attempts to provide an integrated account of all these factors.

The central analytic concepts guiding our treatment of Dominican migration are: the international division of labor; state policy in
the receiving and sending societies; social class relations in the
sending and receiving societies; and immigrant households, social
networks, and gender and generational hierarchies.

The International Division of Labor:
Macro-Economic Influences

Dominican migration expresses a trend in U.S. immigration in the
post–World War II era away from traditional European nations

toward Third World countries of Latin America and the Caribbean, Asia, and Africa. The growing numbers of Third World immigrants and their concentration in a relatively limited number of urban locales in the United States have generated a wave of theorizing about the causes and consequences of these "new labor imports." Our understanding of the macroeconomic factors conditioning international labor migration is informed by analytical concepts associated with the historical-structuralist perspective. This perspective, associated with the dependency theorists of Latin America, has stressed the significance of a large pool of marginalized workers in developing societies as a prerequisite, and indeed stimulant, to large-scale out-migration from Third World countries. Historical structuralist accounts of population movements are offered as alternatives to traditional theories of migration (Bach 1978; Burawoy 1976; Castells 1975; Castles and Kosack 1973; History Task Force 1979; Maldonado-Dennis 1980; E. Petras 1981, 1988; Portes and Bach 1985; Sassen-Koob 1978; Zolberg 1978).

The critiques of traditional equilibrium or modernization theories of migration are by now well established. Such accounts depicted migrants as responding primarily to wage differentials between sending regions and receiving regions, conceptualized as relatively autonomous areas. Thus, conditions producing labor exports remained dissociated from conditions producing labor demand (Portes 1978a). Push-pull accounts of migration are associated with functionalist and ahistorical treatments that emphasize values and motivations based on rational calculations by *individuals*. According to such accounts, large population movements occur because large numbers of individuals make similar calculations regarding the advantages of moving. Moreover, as critics have pointed out, the consequences of migration are implicitly treated as benign, since labor flows act as correctives to imbalances in labor and capital distribution (Böhning 1984; Portes and Bach 1985; Wood 1982; Zolberg 1978).

In contrast, a historical structuralist understanding of population movements between receiving and sending countries depends fundamentally on the nature of the ties between such societies. From this perspective, the structural determinants of international labor migration relate both to domestic class relations of sending and receiving societies and to the international division among nation-states that specialize in the production of unequally rewarded commodities (Bonacich and Cheng 1984; Castells 1975; Castles and Kosack 1973; Sassen-Koob 1978; Portes and Bach 1985).

The historical structuralist approach links the contemporary movement of labor from low-wage to high-wage regions of the world to the hierarchically organized system of production which constitutes the modern world market. Most writers adopting this perspective now share a definition of the essential contours of the modern world system that derives from the flow of capital commodities and labor across international borders (Amin 1976; Bach 1978; Burawoy 1976; Castles and Kosack 1973; E. Petras 1981; Portes and Walton 1981; Sassen-Koob 1978; Wallerstein 1974). This world market is based essentially on a division of world labor into three geographically distinct zones: core, semi-periphery, and periphery. The nature of economic and political interdependence between these zones and the direction and nature of capital and commodity flows structure the pattern of labor movement that evolves between the zones. Emphasis has been placed in historical structuralist accounts on two phenomena: (1) labor scarcity—the demand for labor in core societies; and (2) labor "surplus"—the abundance of labor in peripheral societies.

The term *labor scarcity*, as applied to advanced capitalist societies, can mean either an absolute scarcity resulting from a depletion of the domestic labor supply or a relative scarcity of those prepared to work for low wages. That is, the nature of demand for migrant labor in advanced societies is non-uniform in three ways. First, this demand may merely reflect the need of sectors of the economy which, for example, if they are unable to rely on productivity increases, may seek to maintain profit levels by reliance on a continuous, cheap source of labor. This type of relative labor scarcity especially characterizes those agricultural and non-monopoly sectors of the economy in developed societies that are unable to rely on the costly methods for augmenting labor productivity that are available to the oligopolistic sectors (Bonacich and Cheng 1984; Castells 1975; Leahy and Castillo 1977; O'Connor 1973).

Second, as we shall see in the case of New York City, the overall shift to a service economy from one based predominantly on manufacturing generally results in a greater proportion of low-wage jobs (Singelman 1978). Coupled with this result, a downgrading of the manufacturing sector, especially the high-technology subsectors, has also expanded the proportion of low-wage jobs in production, as well as fostered growth in non-union firms, subcontracting, and industrial homework (Martella 1989; Sassen-Koob 1984). An alternative view of the economic role of immigrants in large cities such as New York holds that as the percentage of native whites declines, non-whites move up the hierarchy as replacements for "white flight" (Waldinger 1987).

Third, recent research has revealed that beyond supplementing the secondary labor market, immigrant labor can also facilitate a temporary downward transition in primary or core sectors of the economies of developed nations. Undocumented labor in automobile parts firms in Los Angeles has been important in keeping costs down under difficult economic conditions, while employers prepare for automation or the relocation of production overseas (Morales 1983). Nonetheless, an important debate exists over the question of whether the immigrant population, especially the undocumented immigrants, constitutes a super-exploited labor force relative to the native labor force in regard to wages and working conditions. We take this question up in Chapter 7, where we focus on Dominicans in the United States.

The notion of labor surplus is central to most accounts of population outflows. The historical structuralist perspective posits an association between labor exports and models of development that has characterized many peripheral countries. Despite variations in the development strategies of peripheral societies, a number of common structural features can be noted that have implications for labor migration. First, following the commercialization of rural areas, formerly isolated peasant and rural proletarians migrate to urban areas, creating a high need for mass employment that is typically unmet. The results are high rates of disguised unemployment and underemployment expressed in growing informal and service-sector occupations. Second, the marginalization of large numbers of people means increasingly unequal income distribution even in periods of sustained economic growth. Third, international advertising and communications bring modern consumer culture to both urban and rural areas, increasing awareness of and appetites for modern consumer goods; obtaining even a small fraction of these goods, however, remains beyond the reach of all but a small percentage of the population. The increased desire for "modern living" only aggravates the dissatisfaction already felt by those who have benefited little from growth in their country's economy.

The low wage conditions of Third World economies relate to what Alain de Janvry has called "disarticulated economies." Firms in many developing economies are not linked to each other in the same way as are firms in the economies of developed societies (de Janvry 1982). The lack of articulation between firms is typically linked to specialization in the export of a few primary products, making such economies extremely vulnerable to fluctuations in the international market. Due to this external orientation, employers tend to be interested primarily in keeping the costs of wages down in order to remain competitive on the international market. In contrast to developed societies, in these countries the internal market is extremely limited; thus, raising wages will not generate appreciable gains to capital in the form of increased demand for domestic commodities (de Janvry 1982). Moreover, trade dependency is often accompanied by a predominance or at least a large proportion of foreign ownership of the productive sectors of the dependent economy. The large-scale presence of foreign capital means that the multiplier effects of new investments are lost locally but instead are transferred back to the "center" economies (Evans 1979: 28).

Given the critical problem of underemployment and unemployment in the developing world, it is not surprising that in most discussions of the causes of out-migration the excess rural labor force is treated implicitly or explicitly as the most immediate and direct stimulant. However, in a number of empirical studies this assumption has actually proven to be unjustified. It is true that much of the available evidence on Mexican immigration, the largest component of the flow of labor into the United States, does point to a displaced rural peasant population (Portes and Bach 1985: 82). However, several studies challenge the idea that Mexican rural emigrants come from the most impoverished sectors or possess the lowest educational levels of the Mexican populace (Reichert 1981; Bustamante and Martínez 1979; Massey et al. 1987). Similarly, Puerto Rican emigrants to the United States in the 1950s were primarily urban dwellers with stable histories of employment. It was not until the 1960s that unskilled laborers came to constitute the bulk of Puerto Rican emigrants (Levine 1987: 97).

Increasingly, countries with more recent migration circuits to the United States, such as Colombia and Jamaica, have been shown to send migrants not predominantly from the rural, marginalized areas but from relatively skilled sectors of the urban economy (Gurak and Falcón-Rodríguez 1987; Urrea 1982; Anderson 1988).

We will document in Chapters 4 and 5 of this book that Dominican out-migration does not draw predominantly upon a labor surplus in the sense of unemployed, marginalized workers in either urban or rural areas. In contrast to much of the emphasis of the historical structuralist accounts of international migration, it seems clear that labor surplus must be considered as a necessary but not sufficient cause of population outflows. A large pool of unemployed people desperate for economic opportunities may serve as a stimulus to emigration only indirectly, by depressing the wages of the employed or putting pressure on the state for subsidies and resources that are denied to middle sectors of the society. These middle sectors, crowded, so to speak, by the misery of those around them, and blessed with the resources to leave, become the more likely candidates for emigration when transportation costs and knowledge of bureaucracies play a part in the logistics of border crossings, as is the case for Dominican international migration.

The movement of labor is not as straightforward or mechanical a process as is sometimes implied in discussions that stress the surplus of labor of sending countries and the relative labor scarcity of receiving countries. Beyond the macroeconomic features introduced above, a variety of political factors also operate as constraints and inducements to labor flows.

Political Dimensions
of International Migration

Fundamental to the structuring of labor flows is the interstate system. The international division of labor involves more than a geographical division between low-wage and high-wage regions: it reflects as well inequalities of power between nation-states. Since the nineteenth century, world economic forces have increasingly come to be managed by the interstate system. In contrast to the classical liberal policies of free trade, states have evolved progressively more restrictive policies for regulating population movements across state borders (Zolberg 1978). International migration is essentially a transfer of jurisdiction from one state to another. Yet, states differ widely in the degree of power they wield on a global scale. With infrequent exceptions, labor-exporting societies have not taken steps to limit the outflows of persons seeking jobs abroad. The policy of most Latin American and Caribbean countries has been either to ignore large-scale emigration or, more aggressively, to pressure receiving countries not to restrict inflow—sometimes in exchange for generous concessions to foreign capital in the sending countries. In some instances, however, developing societies have acted to restrict outflows that appear to be disadvantageous either politically or economically. As we shall see in the Dominican case, emigration was highly restricted locally during the period of the Trujillo dictatorship, owing to Trujillo's fear of emigrants causing political problems for him abroad. It was not until after his assassination that the contemporary outflow began. More recently, representatives of Third World emigration countries, speaking before the International Labour Organization, have questioned the equity of international labor and capital exchanges and called for international financial compensation to labor-exporting countries (Böhning 1984: 10). However, the doubts about the economic value of large-scale emigration expressed by spokespersons from the Sudan, Tunisia, and Egypt have not translated into policies aimed at controlling the exodus. And Caribbean governments, with the exception of Cuba, have, rather, sought discreetly to encourage out-migration or to keep silent about doubts, if they exist, of its economic utility (Levine 1987: 58).

The state policies of sending societies play a fundamental role in producing and reproducing the conditions that give rise to large population outflows. State policy establishes a structure of incentives which guide economic actors. For example, to the extent that state development policies sustain wage-repressive policies or subsidize investments that are inefficient or do not generate employment in a labor-abundant setting, the conditions are made ripe for emigration. Thus, the internal institutional factors of sending societies are as important for understanding international migration as are the external conditions of dependence or the unequal exchange implied by the world market. We shall see in Chapter 2 that Do-

minican state policy has been highly influenced by the mutual
interests of policymakers, a narrow range of politically powerful
industrialists, and foreign investors. An understanding of the social
class relations giving rise to particular political alliances that guide
state managers is fundamental to understanding movements of labor across international borders.

While a prerequisite for large-scale labor migration may be the
existence of a pool of unsatisfied workers seeking opportunities
abroad, actual population movements are predominantly "demand-
determined" (Piore 1979; Böhning 1981; E. Petras 1981; D. Marshall 1987). That is, the main controls on the inducement of labor
flows reside not merely in economic pressures or opportunities but
in the immigration policies imposed by the receiving societies.
These policies influence the magnitude of population flows as well
as the sources and characteristics of migrants. Since we are concerned ultimately with Dominican immigration to the United
States in the post–World War II period, we concentrate our argument on the legislation that affected Caribbean migration during
this time.

In the early 1960s, a collection of political interests in the United
States converged in opposition to the quota system, based on national origin, which had operated for forty years in a racist and
discriminatory manner. Agitation for immigration reform, supported by ethnic and religious groups and organized labor, comple-
mented the concerns of the civil rights movement with racial discrimination at home (Bach 1978). As a result the 1965 Immigration
Act was passed and, together with modifications in 1976, provided
the overall political and legislative framework for the flow of immigrants into the United States for the next twenty years. The new law
emphasized family reunification over labor needs and, by means of a
series of occupational preferences, sought to protect American labor. An annual numerical limit of 20,000 on all countries in the
Western hemisphere was established in 1976. As a result Western
hemispheric emigration to the United States shifted markedly away
from Canada and toward Caribbean countries (Keeley 1979: 58).

The 20,000 numerical limit on all countries placed formerly high
sending countries such as Mexico in a particularly difficult situation. The new law, coupled with the abolition of the old *bracero*
system (a labor-contract program between Mexico and the United

States), sharply reduced the number of aspiring Mexican immigrants who could expect to enter the United States legally (Stoddard 1976). Despite the tensions between the interests of receiving and sending societies, the disproportionate influence of advanced societies permits them to impose unilaterally such highly significant legislation.

Beyond the content of immigration laws is the question of how eagerly and effectively they are enforced. After the passage of the 1965 Immigration Law a contradiction emerged between the intentions of this legislation and the actual enforcement of the law in the United States (Bennett 1986). While the 1965 legislation imposed strict numerical limitations on immigrants from particular countries, the relatively lax border patrolling by immigration officials assured the presence of a vast pool of undocumented workers (Piore 1979; Portes and Walton 1981). Such workers are especially vulnerable and docile, since their fear of deportation often overrides their concern with and knowledge of labor laws.

In an attempt to stem this large flow of illegal immigration, the U.S. Congress passed the Immigration Reform and Control Act of 1986. This law makes it a crime knowingly to hire an undocumented worker. Although employers' sanctions are the backbone of the legislation, it also provided for two legalization programs under which certain undocumented immigrants could gain legal residency.[1] The inadequacy of the funding allotted to the Immigration and Naturalization Service to enforce employer sanctions makes it doubtful that this initiative to curb illegal immigration can and will be effectively enforced.[2]

1. The main legalization program was geared to immigrants who could prove that they had arrived in the United States prior to January 1, 1982, and had resided unlawfully since that time. A more liberal program was established for undocumented agricultural workers. These individuals had to prove that they had worked in U.S. agriculture for ninety days or more in 1985.
2. The response of Dominican policymakers to the passage of this new United States immigration legislation epitomizes the predicament of a country whose economy relies on a narrow export base. In a meeting in 1988 with a U.S. congressional commission on immigration and international economic development, which Pessar attended, Dominican congressmen argued that the United States must privilege either Dominican sugar quotas or immigration quotas. Neither concession has been made. Such a unilateral rejection underscores the weakness and vulnerability of a national policy that relies heavily on the export of sugar, workers, or both to secure needed foreign exchange.

Once the legal parameters of immigration have been established, foreign policy concerns affect the terms of entry of legal aliens. First, the definitions of *immigrant* and of *political refugee* in the United States largely reflect the foreign-policy considerations of the State Department. This point has been made recently in the cases of El Salvador, Nicaragua, and Haiti (Aguayo and Fagen 1988; Mitchell 1987; Stepick 1987). Second, whether or not an immigrant originates from a nation that is favored politically by the United States can streamline or impede the process of obtaining a visa. Prior to the passage of the 1965 law, the United States State Department had long opposed national quotas for the Western hemisphere, believing that such restrictions threatened pan-Americanism and the ability of the United States to establish special relationships with Latin American friends (Bach 1985b: 113). These concerns regarding the quotas for Latin American friendly nations were found to be justified in the case of the Dominican Republic, where, as we shall see in Chapter 2, the ability of the U.S. consulate to facilitate the awarding of Dominican visas helped cool a volatile political situation after 1965 (Mitchell 1987).

Thus we see that the macroeconomic forces operating to release labor from Third World societies and to create demand for that labor in advanced societies do not operate mechanistically to determine actual movements of labor. Political barriers to entry also shape the magnitude, the source, the characteristics, and even the legal definition of aliens seeking entry into the labor markets of developed societies.

Migrants' Social Networks, Households, and Gender Relations

The macroeconomic forces depicted by historical structuralists, as well as state policy in the receiving and sending societies, serve to explain the broad determinants of labor displacement from peripheral regions and the nature of economic demand for immigrant labor. A variety of questions, however, remain unanswered: Why do some "migrant-ripe" communities send large numbers of members abroad and others, nearby and with similar conditions, send few? Why do emigrants come disproportionately from specific social classes within given sending communities? Why do some classes within sending communities benefit from out-migration while others suffer disadvantages? How are migrant flows maintained even after the initial conditions which gave rise to migrant labor have eroded?

To answer such questions we must consider aspects of the social structures of sending and receiving societies. Social networks and households simultaneously mediate macrostructural changes, facilitate the migration response to these changes, and perpetuate migration as a self-sustaining social process (Dinerman 1978; Weist 1973; Massey et al. 1987; Kearney 1986). By including these social structures in our conceptualization and analysis of Dominican labor migration, we avoid the reductionism of arguments that overemphasize economic factors in accounting for international labor migration.

By *social networks* we mean the social relations that organize and direct the circulation of labor, capital, goods, services, information, and ideologies between migrant sending and migrant receiving communities. Migration itself has been described as "a process of network building, which depends on and, in turn, reinforces social relations across space" (Portes and Bach 1985: 10). Research in diverse parts of the world has confirmed the significance of migrants' social ties for neighborhood settlement patterns, psychological support, securing jobs, and maintaining links to the home communities (Lomnitz 1977; Arizpe 1978; B. Roberts 1978; Tilly 1978; Reichert 1979; Mines 1981; Massey et al. 1987).

In describing the role social networks play in migration, several authors have pointed to the fact that as social networks expand and increase, the range and magnitude of the "social capital" circulating within them broaden (e.g., access to loans, housing, and employment opportunities) and the social class composition of the migration stream diversifies (Böhning 1984; Massey et al. 1987). For example, Piore (1979) has argued that urban middle-class migration is transitional to more massive emigration of poorer migrants from rural areas. In light of the economic reversals in the Dominican Republic over the course of the 1980s, we speculate that its migration stream may also have diversified with increased numbers of migrants originating from both the upper and the lower classes. Nonetheless, Dominican emigration between the 1960s and early 1980s has been overwhelmingly an urban, middle-stratum phenomenon. Moreover, in the Dominican Republic, social class standing conditions which households have access to the local resources and the privileged social networks required to dispatch labor migrants. In Chapter 5 we discuss the ways social class mediates access to and accumulation of the material and social resources needed for out-migration.

Migration scholars have also noted that as the social networks of immigrants expand in the receiving society to include a wider range of people and exchanges, the immigrants tend to diminish their exchanges with persons in the home society and to enter into a new stage of settlement abroad (Piore 1979; Mines 1981). The Dominican immigrant community in New York has entered this stage. Relatively little attention, however, has been given to the role of gender in this movement to more permanent immigrant settlements. One issue we examine in Chapter 6 is the way gender influences the decision of immigrants to settle permanently in the United States.

We will also consider in Chapter 6 several ways that the migrant community in New York has created its own demand for additional migrants—a demand which may be in competition with or in contradiction to the interests of core capital. For social, cultural, and economic reasons migrant communities develop their own dynamism and patterns of recruitment. Recognizing this, we are in a better position to account for the persistence of migrant flows in times of economic downturns in receiving societies or of reduced recruitment by native employers.

Beyond social networks, the issue of how ideology circulates within transnational migrant networks and becomes a factor influencing the magnitude, characteristics, and direction of labor, capital, and commodity flows has been insufficiently explored. We take up such themes in several chapters. For example, we observe in Chapter 4 how the ideology of return influences the transfer of immigrants' savings back to the Dominican Republic (where homes are often purchased in middle-class neighborhoods). We also describe how consumption patterns attached to the notion of successful return migration often cannot be achieved within the confines of the Dominican economy. This failure commonly leads to a pattern of circular migration between the Dominican Republic and the United States for selected members of settled return migrant households.

The migrant household is the other social structure that medi-

ates the circulation of labor, capital, services, information, and ideology. Migrant households are in fact a primary constituent of social
networks. For some time the household has been recognized as
both empirically and analytically the appropriate unit to study
when tracing migration from the bottom up (Weist 1973; Dinerman
1978; Garrison and Weiss 1979; Selby and Murphy 1982; K. Roberts 1985). First, emigration is one strategy families in peripheral
societies may adopt to meet the challenges accompanying socioeconomic transformations (Wood 1982). As we show, the household is
the social unit that makes decisions about whether migration will
occur, who will migrate, and whether the migration will be temporary or permanent. These decisions, we argue, are guided by kinship and gender ideologies as well as by hierarchies of power within
households. Second, in any assessment of the impact of out-
migration for sending communities we must recognize that it is not
individuals but households that mobilize resources and support,
receive and allocate remittances, and make decisions about members' production, consumption, and distribution activities. As we
document in Chapter 5, an understanding of who remains behind
in migrant households and what these persons' relations are to
other migrant and nonmigrant households is essential to an assessment of the costs and benefits of out-migration for distinct social
classes within sending communities. Finally, our focus in Chapter 7
both on gender relations within the household and on family obligations and expectations helps us to appreciate differences among
migrants with regard to job satisfaction, labor militancy, and docility in the workplace.

Some of the best research employing the concepts of social networks and households has grappled explicitly or implicitly with
how migration brings together and helps to reinforce differing
modes of production (Meillassoux 1981; Kearney 1986). In most
cases, we are presented with a form of migration that links non-
capitalist modes of production in peripheral sending areas with
capitalist modes of production in advanced industrial areas. This
line of analysis has helped clarify why capitalist development in the
Third World has not obliterated all pre-capitalist modes of production, as modernization and traditional Marxist theories would lead
us to expect. Such analysis also helps to clarify an issue of some
concern to us in this study—the issue of class formation and class

consciousness. An example is Julian Laite's (1981) work on Peruvian peasant migrant workers in the mining industry. He argues that although these migrant workers are more proletarian than peasant, their partial participation in the peasant mode of existence hampers the development of a working-class consciousness and associated institutions.

Our work on Dominican migration adds several new twists to this useful modes-of-production framework. These variations, which we describe below, are apparent not only in Dominican migration but in much new migration from Latin America, the Caribbean, and Asia, as well. In these instances we are not, for the most part, dealing with workers who engaged in non-capitalist modes of production back home. Rather, we are confronted with members of the petty bourgeoisie and other middle sectors in their own countries, whose first experience of proletarianization has occurred in the United States. To add a further twist, a goodly number have helped revitalize antiquated forms of production, such as industrial homework and subcontracting, which until recently were associated with an earlier phase of capitalist development long passed from the American scene. Nonetheless, in regard to class formation and class consciousness parallels can be drawn between the peasant-proletarian migrant from Peru and recent Third World migrants in the United States. In Chapters 6 and 7 we describe how individual Dominican workers and their households maintain multiple class ideologies, relationships, and experiences. Like their Peruvian counterparts, Dominican immigrants are thus far less likely than fully proletarianized workers (e.g., Puerto Rican migrants) to develop working-class consciousness and organizations.

Between Two Islands

The name *Between Two Islands* is intended to evoke a central feature of the experiences of Dominican emigrants and their families resident on either Manhattan Island or the island of Hispaniola. As we have discussed above, these two islands are bridged by a binational market for labor and commodities, by social networks, and by transnational households. On the Dominican side of this divide, citizens commonly associate modernity and middle-class status with costly commodities exported from the United States.

Emigrants who return on visits bearing gifts and those who attempt to resettle permanently in newly purchased homes serve as constant reminders that *progreso* (progress) is a goal more easily attained in New York than in the Dominican Republic.

The psychic dependency this other-island orientation creates is so strong and pervasive that at least one church group in the Dominican Republic, dedicated to consciousness-raising and moderate struggle among rural proletarians and smallholders, will not accept into their training program individuals who are contemplating migration to the United States. As mentioned above, an ideology of return often makes Dominican settlement in New York seem "permanently temporary." This ideology encourages the maintenance of social networks and the transfer of people, money, and goods back to the home island. Yet the fact that many returnees must shuttle between the Dominican Republic and low-wage jobs in New York if they are to maintain their middle-class lifestyle at home once again illustrates that even resettlement does not ensure that Dominicans can escape a life between two islands. Moreover, Dominican cultural referents and social relations continue to inform the perceptions and actions of Dominican immigrants residing on Manhattan Island. These referents and relations condition how Dominican immigrants view work, social class standing, family life, and settlement in New York.

The fact that Dominican immigrants and their family members back home are poised between two islands became very clear to us when we received a photograph as a farewell gift from one of our Dominican friends (see front cover). The photo of our friend Lidia and her four sons had originally been taken to send to Lidia's husband, an immigrant who has lived in New York for many years. To show him that she and the boys were prospering with the remittance dollars he sent home monthly, Lidia had borrowed suits for the boys to wear while posing for the photograph. She chose not to have the photo taken in their rural home community. Instead, they journeyed to the Dominican city of Santiago and entered a photographer's studio. There Lidia and the boys, seeking to capture both their heightened status as a migrant family and their desire to be reunited, if only symbolically, with the absent husband and father, posed before a backdrop of the Brooklyn Bridge.

2

The Dominican State, Social Classes, and Emigration

The consequences of migration for a sending society depend on its social structure, the nature of the sending society's integration into the world economy, its state development policies, and the selectivity and type of migration. Many discussions of the causes of international labor migration from a world-systems or dependency perspective emphasize external constraints, especially the role of foreign capital, and unequal terms of trade between developed and developing societies.[1] Such factors have not been insignificant in the Dominican case; as a country oriented toward the external world market, the Dominican Republic has been subjected to influences that have resulted in disincentives to internal market expansion and have led to increased income inequality. Yet, external dependency has *conditioned*, not *determined*, emigration impulses. Institutional factors internal to the Dominican Republic, such as the influence on government policy of a select group of industrialists, development policies which have resulted from such class-state alliances, and the evolving class structure, account for the dynam-

1. Among the best-known statements of dependency that have stressed the external conditioning of underdeveloped societies are Myrdal (1957); Baran (1957); Frank (1970); Furtado (1971); Cardoso and Faletto (1979). In the case of the Dominican Republic, emphasis on external factors such as laws of unequal exchange are especially evident in the writings of Lucas Vicens, *Crisis Económica* (Santo Domingo: Alfa y Omega, 1982), and Roberto Cassá, *Capitalismo y dictadura* (Santo Domingo: Universidad Autónoma de Santo Domingo, 1982).

18

ics and selectivity of out-migration. This very interconnectedness
and complexity of the internal and external factors promoting outflows of workers make the Dominican Republic of interest to students of international migration.

In this chapter we shall consider several paradoxes: first, how it
came to pass that one of the richest of the Caribbean nations became one of the leading countries of the world in its per capita rate
of legal immigration to the United States, and, second, why the
flow of emigrants steadily increased despite the fact that two radically divergent political parties have ruled in the Dominican Republic since 1966. We begin by examining the historical patterns and
extent of Dominican emigration, and the history of the establishment of export agriculture and import substitution industrialization. We then turn to the impact of class relations on state development between 1961 and 1986 in the Dominican Republic.

Patterns of Dominican Emigration

Young Dominicans have emigrated from their country throughout
the twentieth century. The contemporary phase of emigration is
distinguished from earlier phases primarily by its intensity. Although the quality of early Dominican censuses is poor, the 1920 to
1981 censuses all show relatively high numbers of females to males
in the young adult age groups, which implies male out-migration
(Larson 1987b: 48). During the Trujillo dictatorship (1930–1961),
emigration was severely curtailed by a restrictive state policy that
limited even the issuance of passports to Dominican citizens
(Crassweller 1966; Frank Canelo 1982). The contemporary phase of
mass emigration began a few years after the assassination of Trujillo
in 1961. This out-migration did not begin gradually, but, rather,
rose sharply in the years following 1962. The total number of Dominicans legally admitted to the United States between 1961 and
1986 was 372,817. While fewer than 1,000 Dominican immigrants
entered the United States annually between 1951 and 1960, the
annual average for each decade climbed from over 9,000 in the
1960s to over 14,000 in the 1970s, and then to 20,000 in the first
half of the 1980s. Table 1 shows that the sharpest increases occurred in the mid-1960s and then rose only modestly throughout

TABLE 1
Dominican Immigrants Legally Admitted
to the United States

1961	3,045	1974	15,680
1962	4,603	1975	14,066
1963	10,683	1976	15,088[a]
1964	7,537	1977	11,655
1965	9,504	1978	19,458
1966	16,503	1979	17,519
1967	11,514	1980	17,245
1968	9,250	1981	18,220
1969	10,670	1982	17,451
1970	10,807	1983	22,058
1971	12,624	1984	23,147
1972	10,670	1985	23,787
1973	13,858	1986	26,175

Source. U.S. Department of Justice, Immigration and
Naturalization Service, Statistical Yearbook, 1961–1980, Immigration and Naturalization Service, 1984, 1986.
[a]Includes an additional three-month period (15 months),
because of change in the enumeration period that year.

the late 1960s and 1970s, with a dramatic increase beginning in
1978 and another large increase apparent in 1983. Indeed, since
1983 the number of immigrant visas granted exceeded the 20,000
ceiling mandated by U.S. immigration law.[2] The number of Dominican non-immigrants officially admitted to the United States also
climbed steadily in the 1960s and 1970s, from 18,227 in 1962 to a
high of 166,519 in 1978 and then leveled out to an annual average of
82,600 for the 1981–1986 period (Table 2).

Considering its small size, the Dominican Republic is one of the
countries in the world most dramatically affected by immigration.
It ranked third in the world, behind only Jamaica and Laos, in

2. The technical limit is set at 20,000 per country. In 1986, 19,071 Dominican
immigrants were admitted under these limitations; another 7,104 were granted
exceptional admission, most commonly on the grounds that they were immediate
relatives of U.S. citizens: Immigration and Naturalization Service, Statistical Yearbook of the Immigration and Naturalization Service, 1986, p. 13.

TABLE 2
Dominican Non-Immigrants Admitted
to the United States

1961	9,102	1974	143,512
1962	18,227	1975	149,386
1963	56,236	1976	207,505[a]
1964	64,476	1977	154,964
1965	52,638	1978	166,519
1966	68,870	1979	134,461
1967	78,791	1980	(not reported)
1968	81,073	1981	77,638
1969	101,454	1982	77,615
1970	105,191	1983[b]	111,912
1971	74,252	1984	82,049
1972	111,845	1985	79,994
1973	124,528	1986	66,700

Source. U.S. Department of Justice, Immigration and Naturalization Service, *Annual Reports* 1961–1977, and *Statistical Yearbook*, 1978, 1981–1986.
[a]Includes an additional transitional quarter, because of change in the fiscal year that year.
[b]Calendar year.

terms of per capita legal immigration to the United States in 1981, as measured by the number of immigrants per 10,000 population (Table 3).[3] The Dominican per capita figure was more than double that of Mexico in 1981.

It is problematic to rely on visa data as a source for estimating annual net emigration from the Dominican Republic, both because illegal entrants are not included and because substantial numbers of Dominicans return to their country after residence abroad (Bray 1984; Larson 1987b; Warren 1988). For these reasons, it is more reliable demographically to estimate net emigration rates by considering population growth and birth and death rates in the Dominican Republic. The total number of Domini-

3. The ranking of Laos as number two in the world in 1981 is misleading in that the Laotian rate reflected the large refugee movement at the turn of the decade rather than the sustained outflows which have characterized Jamaica and the Dominican Republic (Rubén Rumbaut, personal communication).

TABLE 3
Immigrants per 10,000 Population, 1981
(Countries with 10,000 or More Admissions)

	No. of Immigrants	Per 10,000
Jamaica	23,569	104.75
Laos	15,805	40.52
Dominican Republic	18,220	32.25
Kampuchea	12,749	21.26
China/Taiwan	25,803	14.34
Mexico	101,268	13.37
Cuba	10,858	11.02
Philippines	43,772	8.67
Korea	32,663	8.16
Canada	11,192	4.49
Colombia	10,335	3.62
Iran	11,105	2.68
United Kingdom	14,977	2.66
India	21,522	0.29

Source. U.S. Department of Justice, Immigration and Naturalization Service, 1981 Statistical Yearbook.

cans resident in the United States is probably much smaller than
the unsubstantiated range of 500,000 to 1,000,000, listed among
numerous sources in the 1980s that relied on visa data and other
arbitrary estimates (Larson and Sullivan 1987). Warren, using a
census-survival procedure, estimated the total number of Dominicans aged 15 to 44 residing outside the country during the 1981
census to be between 185,000 and 210,000 (Warren 1988: 11).
Larson and Opitz provide the most current analysis of the number
of Dominicans residing outside the Dominican Republic. Employing 1981 Dominican census data and estimated life tables, they
estimate that 342,605 Dominicans were living abroad (in all countries) in 1988 (including legal residents and the undocumented),
with 268,770 of them residing in the United States, 25,065 in
Puerto Rico, and another 48,770 in all other countries (Larson and

Opitz 1987: 18).[4] It should be noted that these figures exclude children born to Dominicans in the United States, because these children are U.S. citizens. If we define the "Dominican community" in the United States as including the second generation of Dominicans born in the United States, the estimates would considerably exceed these figures. The 1980 enumerated population in the United States included 170,698 persons who reported either single Dominican ancestry or reported Dominican as one of multiple ancestries (U.S. Bureau of the Census 1983: 14).[5]

Estimates differ regarding the extent to which the Dominican stream consists of undocumented workers. One study of undocumented Dominicans in New York concluded that although approximately 33 percent of Dominicans had been illegal at some point during their residence in the United States, only 17 percent were illegal at any given time, because a high proportion of illegals eventually succeeded in regularizing their status (Pérez 1981). Approximately 19,000 undocumented Dominicans were enumerated in the U.S. 1980 census, 14,000 of whom lived in New York (Warren 1988; Mahler 1988).

The impact of Dominican migration on the United States is even greater than is suggested by its volume, given the concentration of Dominicans in the New York/New Jersey area. In 1980 91 percent of the Dominicans in the continental United States resided in only three states: New York (77.6 percent of the total); New Jersey (8.4 percent); and Florida (4.2 percent) (U.S. Bureau of the Census 1984).

Early studies of Dominican migration concluded that most Dominican emigrants originated in rural communities (González 1970;

4. In an earlier analysis Larson and Sullivan cogently criticize the "numbers game" apparent in the literature on Dominican migration that has caused unjustifiably high estimates of the number of Dominicans living in the United States to be accepted as conventional wisdom. The estimates they present of the number of Dominicans living in the United States in 1980 are: 190,285 from the U.S. census of 1980; 149,536 from the Dominican census of 1981; and 128,507 from forward survival of the enumerated 1960 Dominican population to 1980 (Larson and Sullivan 1987: 1492).

5. It appears that few of these Dominican-Americans return to the Dominican Republic: the 1981 Dominican census reported only 2,915 enumerator-classified Dominican nationals who were born in the United States (Larson and Sullivan 1987: 1490).

Peña and Parache 1971; Hendricks 1974; Garrison and Weiss 1979). Sometimes this process was described as step-migration, with rural migrants spending a short time in larger urban areas before leaving the country (Kayal 1978: 13), and other times as migration from rural communities directly to the receiving societies (Sassen-Koob 1978: 317). This early research suggesting a rural-based emigration was based on small community studies whose methodologies did not permit generalizations beyond their circumscribed rural settings. Recent data from more representative studies, as well as our own, show that most Dominican immigration originates from urban areas (Ugalde et al. 1979; Pérez 1981; Ugalde and Langham 1980; Gurak and Kritz 1982). Similarly, the 1981 Dominican census contains information on the number of children living abroad, according to the declaration of their mothers in the Dominican Republic. The geographical distribution of migrant origins at the provincial level, as given in that census, are presented in Table 4. More than half of the mothers of Dominicans resident abroad lived in either the National District (Santo Domingo metropolitan area) (36 percent) or Santiago (20 percent), accounting for 72,978 migrants (Larson and Sullivan 1987: 17).[6] The total number of emigrants as reported by mothers resident in the Dominican Republic represented 2.3 percent of the 1981 Dominican population. The consequences of the urban selectivity of Dominican emigration documented here will be treated in Chapter 4.

At the beginning of this chapter we raised the question of the relationship between the external dependency of the Dominican economy, state development policy, and high rates of out-migration. Having established the historical patterns and the contemporary magnitude of Dominican emigration, we may now turn to an account of the historical origins and nature of Dominican export agriculture, especially as it was consolidated under the dictatorship of Trujillo. Many features of contemporary class structure in the Dominican Republic can be understood only by reference to the class alliances consolidated in the first half of the twentieth century and to the centralization of state power traceable to this earlier era.

6. These figures could be expected to reflect an underenumeration of entire migrant households and of children whose mothers were deceased. The figures are probably proportionally correct for migrants' origins, however.

TABLE 4
Emigrant Children, 1981
(by Mother's Province)

	No. of Emigrant Children	1981 Population	Emigrants as % of Total Population
National District	46,900	1,550,739	3.0
Azua	689	142,770	0.5
Baoruco	676	78,636	0.9
Barahona	1,370	137,160	1.0
Dajabón	1,044	57,709	1.8
Duarte	3,196	235,544	1.4
Elías Piña	329	65,384	0.5
El Seibo	1,461	157,866	0.9
Espaillat	3,535	164,017	2.2
Independencia	225	38,768	0.6
La Altagracia	2,942	100,112	2.9
La Romana	2,705	109,769	2.5
La Vega	7,975	385,043	2.1
María Trd. Sánchez	1,106	112,629	1.0
Monte Cristi	2,035	83,409	2.4
Pedernales	158	17,006	0.9
Peravia	3,887	168,123	2.3
Puerto Plata	3,681	206,757	1.8
Salcedo	3,362	99,181	3.4
Samaná	658	65,699	1.0
Sánchez Ramírez	1,130	126,567	0.9
San Cristóbal	6,492	446,132	1.5
San Juan	1,463	239,957	0.6
San Pedro de Macoris	3,093	152,890	2.0
Santiago	26,078	550,372	4.7
Santiago Rodríguez	556	55,411	1.0
Valverde	3,589	100,319	3.6
Total	130,335[a]	5,647,969	2.3

Source. *Dominican National Census,* 1981, quoted in Larson 1987.
[a]Includes 9,518 children declared by mothers who are not of Dominican nationality. Although some of these children may have Dominican fathers, it is probable that large numbers of them are children of foreigners resident in the Dominican Republic. The total number of Dominican nationals (as declared by mothers) is 120,817 (Eric Larson, personal communication).

Export Agriculture: 1880–1960

It is impossible to understand contemporary Dominican society without taking into account the development of the modern sugar plantations in the latter part of the nineteenth century. Beginning in the 1880s and 1890s, the Dominican Republic has been integrated into the world economy through the export of sugar and cacao and, to a lesser extent, coffee. With the technological advances at the turn of the century, a division of labor was established in the sugar economy between the industrial sectors, which processed and refined sugarcane, and the agricultural sectors, which produced it (Cortén et al. 1976: 59). This marked a vast expansion of sugar production in the Dominican Republic through the establishment of modern sugar *centrales* in the east of the country, largely stimulated by North American capital investments (del Castillo et al. 1974: 150; Acosta 1976: 123).

Many of the essential characteristics of the contemporary Dominican sugar industry originated between 1900 and 1920. The sugar industry, which remains one of the pillars of the Dominican economy, was consolidated under foreign interests (principally North American) between 1916 and 1924, after the first U.S. military occupation of the island. This occupation facilitated, among other things, the forced appropriation of land to the benefit of foreign interests (M. Knight 1928; Báez Evertsz 1978; Calder 1982) and followed an explosive growth in sugar production directed almost exclusively toward export. Total production grew from 4,000 tons in 1880 to 50,000 tons in 1905 and by 1919 had reached 204,018 tons (del Castillo et al. 1974: 150).

The characteristics associated with plantation enclaves (Cardoso and Faletto 1979: 71) manifested themselves during this epoch: a high degree of concentration of land ownership; a relatively high labor/capital ratio, especially in the agricultural sectors; the erosion of local forms of subsistence agriculture through the confiscation of land; and the production of a primary product which serves as the raw material for the dominant export trade. Sugar expansion destroyed the local subsistence economy in the eastern regions of the Dominican Republic (del Castillo et al. 1974: 151) and produced an uprooted mobile labor force there, in this case dependent on the sugar *centrales* for employment and income on a seasonal basis

(Hoetink 1971). However, exclusive reliance on a native labor force for the agricultural sector of this industry was undesirable from the point of view of sugar industrialists. For one thing, the bulk of the native population was located in the northern regions known as the Cibao, and not in the east, where the large sugar *centrales* were established (Hoetink 1965: 8). For a second, the Dominican population at the turn of the century was relatively small, about 600,000 (Moya Pons, 1974: 21), which meant a relative abundance of agricultural land (del Castillo 1978: 28). Communal land tenure patterns characterized a majority of landholdings in 1907 (López 1973: 129), and subsistence agriculture was viable. The relatively low wages offered by the emerging sugar industry and the seasonal nature of the work thus meant that an abundant local, cheap labor force was not available to the emerging sugar enclaves.

These factors encouraged sugar industrialists to opt, at a strategic time, for the importation of proletarian labor in the form of freed slaves from the Antilles, particularly the English, Danish, Dutch, and French possessions in the Caribbean. The drop in world sugar prices in 1920 and the subsequent 1929 depression encouraged a progressively greater reliance on the cheaper laborers from Haiti, to the exclusion of the other national groups formerly imported. This pattern became especially marked with the growth of American influence in the sugar industry. Until very recently Haitian labor has played a central role in the harvesting of sugarcane in the Dominican Republic. The ramifications are beyond the scope of the current discussion, but it is worth noting that Haitian immigration to the Dominican Republic during the past twenty-five years, combined with the continued outflow of Dominican labor to the United States, illustrates the complexity of labor flows and of the term *labor surplus* in a peripheral society (Grasmuck 1983).

The weakness of the Dominican internal market compared to the weight of international demand meant that the export trade associated with the sugar industry continued to serve as the backbone of the economy. The most advanced capitalist techniques were introduced in the export trade, which remains among the more modern sectors of the economy. These advances, however, have scarcely compensated for the low levels of productivity and the undercapitalization in agriculture as a whole, including the agricultural sectors of the sugar industry (Vilas 1979: 181; Casasnovas 1981: 39; Lozano 1985a).

The predominance of the state in the contemporary sugar sector is a carry-over from the Trujillo period. Trujillo used his political power unscrupulously to secure private economic control of enormous sectors of Dominican society. Having acquired the sugar plantations of the West Indies Sugar Company in 1953, he expanded his engagement with sugar such that, by the time of his assassination in 1961, he controlled two-thirds of the total Dominican sugar production. The overlap between the personal interests of Trujillo and the state during this period is crucial for understanding certain features of the development of sugar production that continue to distort the contemporary Dominican economy. First, Trujillo invested in sugar, not primarily for profit, but, rather, to gain access to the primary source of foreign exchange in the country and to increase his personal power. Second, as a president willing to use whatever means necessary, he could expand sugar holdings without significant personal cost (Vedovato 1986: 63–66). By using state power and funds, Trujillo could: evict peasants from their land to acquire additional acreage; construct the needed infrastructure for his sugar industry at no cost to himself; grant his industry tax exemptions; and in general remain impervious to the falling sugar prices and deteriorating terms of trade of 1948–1960. Trujillo was so unconscionable, in fact, that the acreage allocated to sugarcane doubled in this period (Vedovato 1986: 68).

The legacy the distortions introduced by Trujillo's style of business left to the contemporary Dominican state and the state-owned sugar industry, the Consejo Estatal de Azucar (CEA), are made clear by Vedovato:

Neither Trujillo nor the present CEA management (or the government for that matter) would incur personal losses if sugar prices turned out to be low. On the other hand, if prices turned out to be high, they would profit. Trujillo would profit directly, through his owning of the sugar industry, the CEA management through increased opportunities to spend on larger desks, larger offices, etc. . . . many CEA officials have also been able to make personal profits from the running of sugar industry.

(Vedovato 1986: 108)

The other principal exports of the post–World War II period, coffee, cacao, and tobacco, were developed through small-scale agriculture, not plantation production. Trujillo had established a monopoly on the commercialization and semi-processing of cacao and coffee. In the twenty years following Trujillo's death, competitive conditions in the marketing of these crops evolved from complete monopoly, through open and fierce competition, to a tightly controlled oligopoly (Cordero et al. 1974; Bray 1983a: 108). In the 1950s and early 1960s, prices for these traditional exports reached relatively high levels. Export earnings in cacao rose from an average of D.R. $3 million in 1941–1946 to an average of D.R. $22 million in 1950–1955. Similarly, coffee exports, at D.R. $4 million in 1947, rose steadily in the 1950s to a high of D.R. $32 million in 1956 (Gómez 1979: 116–17). Because of the nature of organization of coffee and cacao production, the increase in earnings of these crops benefited an expanding agroexport sector and a rural petty bourgeoisie (Sharpe 1977; Cordero et al. 1975; Bray 1983a). As a result of rising export prices, landholdings devoted to these export crops also expanded.

The high proportion of rural land devoted to sugar and other export crops negatively affected the organization of other agricultural resources. One percent of the farm owners controlled over half the total farm land in 1960 (Clausner 1973: 239). Scarcity of land and minimal credit to small producers meant that production of important food products decreased during the decade of the 1950s. The Dominican price index of food in 1960 was the highest of twenty recorded Latin American countries (Clausner 1973: 241). The fact that the labor requirements of the export crops were less than those of the formerly dominant food crops meant that more farming families had less need for household rural labor and, consequently, the agrarian labor surplus grew.

State Development, 1930–1986

The Dominican Republic evolved from a predominantly agricultural society to one of low-level industrialization while the economy was for all intents and purposes still the property of Trujillo. This one person–state promoted industrial development under conditions of monopoly, political control, an extremely small internal market, and unabashed personal whim (Bosch 1979; Gutiérrez 1972; Vilas 1979).

Capitalist industrialization under Trujillo took a decidedly different character than it had taken in Western Europe. For one thing, competitive conditions—which in Europe maximized revolutionary industrial techniques, rationality in production, and high levels of productivity—never existed in the Dominican Republic. Thus, the economic enterprises controlled by Trujillo and his friends tended to be monopolistic and backward, with relatively low levels of productivity (Franco 1966: 82; Vilas 1976: 175).

The Trujillo economic model meant that limited industrialization was accomplished without the consolidation of a national bourgeoisie, nor did such a class benefit from it. Trujillo's control of the economy was almost absolute: almost 35 percent of all cultivated land was his, more than 25 percent of cattle livestock, most of the production and exportation of rice, and 12 of 17 sugar refineries, as well as partial or complete control of the remaining sectors of the economy (Crassweller 1966; Vilas 1979: 171; Bosch 1979: 263).[7] The legal provisions that permitted the confiscation of the Trujillo empire after his death provoked a de facto nationalization of major sectors of the economy, a step Gutiérrez has described as an artificial advance in the face of an atrophied bourgeoisie (Gutiérrez 1972: 133). In fact, the relatively high degree of economic centralization and the extensive role played by the state in contemporary Dominican economic development are features of the Dominican economy inherited from the military epoch of Trujillo. The strength of the state is evident in the fact that in 1962, one year after the fall of Trujillo, total capital investment in the Dominican Republic, in order of size, was as follows: state investment, 51 percent; foreign investments, 42 percent; and private national investments, 7 percent (Bosch 1979: 269).

The Trujillo-period industrialization policies of tariffs, tax exemptions, and government subsidies were designed to protect the industries controlled by the dictator and his friends and relatives from foreign and internal competition. The highly selective application of these governmental supports prevented competition and made substantial profits possible (Vedovato 1986: 115).

Import-substitution industrialization has continued in the post-Trujillo period. As we shall see, Trujillo's system of state policy guided by the narrow interests of a small group of industrialists and self-interested state bureaucrats is reflected in the Dominican state

7. See Clausner (1973) for a list of the enterprises confiscated by Trujillo.

today. These political and economic alliances shape the effects of emigration on Dominican society.

State development in the Dominican Republic in the post-Trujillo period passed through three distinct phases. The first period, 1961–1966, was one of great political instability, beginning with the assassination of Trujillo and including the civil war and the military occupation by United States Marines. The second period represents the twelve-year reign of the Reformist Party (PR) under the leadership of Joaquín Balaguer from 1966 to 1978. Finally, the election of the Dominican Revolutionary Party's (PRD) candidate to the presidency in 1978 marks the beginning of the third period, which lasted until that party's defeat in 1986 and the return of Dr. Balaguer to power.

These three periods may be contrasted in terms of the class alliances which brought the respective parties to power, overall economic climates, levels of political mobilization, labor force development, and average annual emigration rates. Establishing the character of state policy during these periods is important to an understanding of the multiple influences behind the tremendous growth of Dominican out-migration over the last three decades.

Our overall argument is that migration was politically induced after the 1963 revolution by an extremely unrestrictive immigration policy favored by the United States. Both sides of the border perceived the receptive approach taken by U.S. immigration authorities to Dominican out-migration as a safety valve for political discontent, but for different reasons. Once stimulated, however, the outflows were sustained economically by two subsequent phases of development which, despite differences in political regimes, failed to modernize agriculture, excluded labor from the benefits of increasing industrialization, and produced an expanding and increasingly frustrated middle class. Over time a critical mass of Dominicans came to live in the New York City area, and since then the city has served as an autonomous pole of attraction for new Dominican immigrants.

Political Crisis, Foreign Occupation, and Emigration Take-Off

Following Trujillo's assassination in 1961, a five-year period of explosive political upheaval ensued that revolved around the issue of who would control the state and the inherited resources of the Trujillo family. Although alliances shifted during this period, the basic contenders were a conservative anti-Trujillo oligarchy, populist middle- and working-class sectors, and the revolutionary left (Bell 1981: 77–98; Gleijeses 1978; Espinal 1987b: 87). Between 1962 and 1965 three different regimes controlled the state. Following the interim Council of State (January 1962–February 1963), the elected constitutionalist government of Juan Bosch survived for seven months before it was overthrown by a coup which established the military-backed triumvirate headed by Donald Reid Cabral. In April of 1965 the pro-Bosch, constitutionalist forces initiated what came to be called the April Revolution, which culminated in the military occupation of the Dominican Republic by the United States Marines. The constitutionalist forces were overcome and agreed to an Organization of American States (OAS) surrender with U.S.-sponsored elections in 1966. Following the revolutionary upheaval, bloodshed, and economic stagnation of the preceding five years, veteran Joaquín Balaguer of the newly established Reformist Party, promising order, sovereignty, and economic prosperity, was elected president of the Dominican Republic, and remained head of state for the next twelve years.

United States influence in the Dominican Republic, direct and indirect, increased dramatically after the assassination of Trujillo. The United States had already weakened the Trujillo dictatorship through its support of economic blockades and various assassination plots, including the successful one of 1961. Then after the fall of Trujillo and during the ensuing political turmoil, steps were taken to assist the emergence of a stable pro-U.S. government. Since then, the foreign policy interests of Washington have centered on the desire to avoid another Castro-style regime in the Caribbean. The Dominican Republic, after all, shares with Cuba a history of poverty, dictatorship, and close proximity to the United States. In the most dramatic intervention, the island was militarily occupied in 1965 to prevent the nearly victorious pro-Bosch constitutionalists from regaining power. Fears revolved around the fact that the recent post-Trujillo years had been a time of rapid social and political mobilization of popular sectors—and memories of the Cuban missile crisis of 1962 remained fresh. Finally, it was in this period of political and economic turmoil that the stimulus to out-migration was politically induced (Báez Evertsz and D'Oleo Ramírez 1985: 19; Mitchell 1987).

The United States ambassador, John Bartlow Martin, took the initiative in granting wider access to visas for Dominicans to enter the United States. This step was perceived as a safety valve against further radical political mobilization and as a way of improving bilateral relations (Mitchell 1987). Martin established a new consulate building in 1962, far removed from downtown Santo Domingo, where lines of visa applicants would be less visible. Moreover, in the same year three extra vice consuls and a new consul were appointed (Martin 1966: 120). The immediate consequence of these actions was that the number of immigrant visas issued by the U.S. consulate in the Dominican Republic doubled between 1961 and 1962 and then almost tripled between 1962 and 1963, jumping from 1,789 to 9,857 in three years (Mitchell 1987). The political barriers to emigration during the Trujillo period would inevitably have resulted, even without encouragement from the United States, in an increase in the numbers of Dominicans seeking to leave after 1961. It is doubtful, however, that the accumulated demand could have been met without these politically motivated simplifications of the procedure.

At the time that this migration flow to the United States was released it was not possible to foresee the longer-term consequences of a growing community of Dominicans living abroad. Nonetheless, as will be shown, once it had been stimulated, sustained out-migration came to complement the model of economic development adopted by Balaguer during the period from 1966 to 1978.

Authoritarian Politics and Migration-Dependent Development, 1966–1978

Balaguer promoted an economic development policy that paralleled the import-substitution models common in other Latin American countries. Having inherited a relatively strong state, Balaguer allied himself politically with the military, the civil bureaucracy, and a small group of emerging industrialists. Balaguer's policies supported the expansion and diversification of a new urban business class which was somewhat independent of the traditional oligarchy linked to the traditional export economy (Vilas 1979; Moreno Ceballos 1984;

Lozano 1985b; Espinal 1986). Indeed, the logic of the industrialization policies promoted by the Balaguer government can most effectively be understood in terms of the influence that a small group of major industrialists, especially import-competing producers, had with the government (Wiarda and Kryzanek 1982: 65; Vedovato 1986: 116).

The industrialization strategy introduced by Balaguer was based on protectionist measures, tariffs and tax exemptions, a legal dual-exchange market, and cheap financing for the promotion of industrial activities (Vedovato 1986: 116–19). Industrial expansion was largely financed by massive import of foreign capital and by the liberal tax provisions of the industrial laws passed in 1966 and 1968. In addition, owing to the improved prices of traditional exports, the expansion of industrialization was subsidized locally by the export sector and, in the case of sugar, was largely directly controlled by the state. Direct foreign investment grew from $108 million in 1962 to $120 million in 1968, accelerated to $172 million in 1971, and reached $233 million in 1974 (Gómez 1979: 185). Economic modernization was also stimulated during this period by heavy investments in such aspects of the infrastructure as roads, public housing, and hydroelectrics (Alemán 1975: 15; Lozano 1985b: 134).

This early industrialization accompanied growth in the gross domestic product (GDP) at an annual real rate of 10 percent between 1970 and 1974, one of the highest growth rates in the world during that period, second only to Brazil and Ecuador. Thus Balaguer's industrialization policies have been widely viewed as favorable to growth. However, it is unclear whether the growth should be attributed to the industrialization strategies or to other confounding variables, such as the coincidental dramatic increase in the price of the country's main export products, especially sugar and cocoa, and to Balaguer's heavy investment in public construction projects. In any case, after 1974, with the overall worsening of commodity export prices, the national economy seriously declined—averaging approximately 4 percent annual GDP growth in the late 1970s (Iglesias 1983: 11).

Beyond the question of growth, however, a number of serious economic distortions resulted from these policies. First, overall efficiency, as measured by output produced per unit of capital, declined between 1970 and 1977 (Vedovato 1986). Second, the industrialization which was stimulated by the incentive laws favored capital-intensive production (World Bank 1978: 56), a rather irrational plan, given the scarcity of capital and the abundance of labor in the Dominican Republic. Third, the exchange rate system operated to cheapen imports artificially at the expense of domestic inputs. Fourth, the classification system that exempted certain firms from duties on imported capital and intermediate goods was politically biased, giving classified firms considerable influence on the decision of how to classify other firms (Vedovato 1986). Finally, the incentive system favored firms that processed foreign inputs and thus did not tend to aid the severe balance-of-payments problem (Vega and Castillo 1980: 4–5).

Import-substitution policies almost inevitably discriminate against rural sectors. In the Dominican case, this was expressed most dramatically in the restrictive food policies of the Institute for Price Stabilization (INESPRE). Artificially keeping the prices of food low subsidizes urban sectors at the expense of rural producers. Agricultural workers experienced this squeeze especially dramatically between 1973 and 1979, when the prices for agricultural inputs increased more than the prices of agricultural outputs (Vedovato 1986: 129). The internal terms of trade between agriculture and industry fell from an index of 100 in 1969 to one of 663 in 1979 (World Bank 1981: 12). This adverse relation between the costs of inputs and the selling price of agricultural products, one of the most dramatic manifestations of a weakening in the position of Dominican small producers, is reflected in a sharp increase in the annual importation of food between 1976 and 1981 (Vega 1981).

As a result, small farmers and rural labor suffered most from the Balaguer-era economic policies, whereas the industrial bourgeoisie and the urban middle class were among those who profited. The declining opportunities for rural farmers and workers were expressed in persistently high rates of rural-to-urban migration throughout this period. The economically active population in urban areas grew from 472,450 in 1970 to 998,590 in 1981, an increase of 111.4 percent (526,140), compared to a growth of only 6.3 percent (46,369) in rural areas (Larson 1984: 18).

While the rural sector contracted, a middle class sprang up as a result of the increased professionalism and the growth of certain service-sector jobs in the high-growth years of the 1970s. The presence of this growing class was especially visible in Santo Domingo and Santiago in new housing developments, modern supermarkets with an abundance of imported goods, specialty shops, and exclusive restaurants catering to modern consumption tastes and wallets.

Table 5 presents the relative occupational changes which occurred in the Dominican Republic between the censuses of 1970 and 1981. The three fastest-growing occupational groups were the "managers and administrators," with a 436.3 percent increase, "personal service occupations," with 228.7 percent, and "professionals and technicians," with a 127.7 percent increase. The last column of Table 5 presents for each occupation an "absorption ratio" calculated by Larson (1987b: 69). The absorption ratios show which occupational groups are absorbing workers at rates exceeding those of demographic increase. A ratio of more than 1.00 indicates a redistribution of workers to that occupation, both in relation to their number in 1970 and to the increase in the labor force in 1981. Once again, we see that those categories representing middle-class occupations, namely, managers and administrators, and professionals and technicians, with absorption ratios of 3.64 and 1.55, respectively, accounted for relatively large proportions of labor absorption in relation to the numbers of workers employed in these occupations in 1970.

Beyond relative occupational growth, middle-class expansion is expressed in the dramatic gains made in education in the 1960–1980 period. The rates of enrollment increased dramatically for all age groups during this period, but it is the expansion in advanced education that most directly signals an expanding middle stratum. The rate of enrollment of young people between 18 and 23 years of age grew from less than 4 percent in 1960 to 21 percent in 1980 (Table 6). This increase of almost 17 percent slightly exceeded the comparable increase in education among the youngest group, the 6- to 11-year-olds. Or, in other terms, post-secondary enrollment increased from 3,400 in 1960 to 23,500 in 1970, and to 139,300 in 1982 (IDB 1987: 108). These striking figures indicate a climate of overall rising expectation of social mobility for those gaining these educational benefits. Yet, as we shall see, there are numerous indications that these expectations were not met for significant numbers of the newly educated. Their disappointments relate to the

TABLE 5
Economically Active Population, Dominican Republic, 1970–1981

	1970	1981	1970–1981 Change (%)	Absorption Ratio
Professional and technical	34,060	77,573	127.7	1.55
Managers and administrators	3,797	20,364	436.3	3.64
Clerical	81,193	96,592	18.9	0.81
Sales	61,705	133,168	115.8	1.47
Farmers and ranchers	551,617	428,045	−22.4	0.53
Transportation equipment operators	38,662	53,375	38.1	0.94
Artisans and operatives[a]	84,296	175,229	107.9	1.41
Other artisans and operatives	51,717	51,922	0.4	0.68
Laborers and workers	66,825	65,017	−2.7	0.66
Personal service	63,171	207,662	228.7	2.23
Occupation not specified	174,661	475,266	172.1	1.85
Total	1,211,704	1,784,213	47.2	

Source. Censo de Población, 1970, adapted from Larson 1984: 47–48; Larson 1987: 69.
[a]In occupations related to textiles, construction, and graphic and mechanical arts.

TABLE 6
Rates of School Enrollment by Age, Dominican Republic, 1960 and 1980

Age	1960 (%)	1980 (%)	% Change 1960–1980
6–11	66.8	82.2	15.4
12–17	39.4	64.4	25.0
18–23	3.7	20.6	16.9

Source. Iglesias 1981: 13.

overall shortcomings of the development policies pursued by the state.

High rates of unemployment and income inequality are other markedly negative consequences of import-substitution policies. The capital-intensive nature of industrialization meant that the waves of rural migrants arriving in urban areas could not be absorbed. In social terms, this has translated into soaring urban unemployment and underemployment. Open unemployment in Santo Domingo was estimated at 20 percent of the labor force in 1973. Indeed, one source estimated that in 1970, 73 percent of the economically active in the Dominican Republic belonged to the informal proletariat, the sector of labor that does not receive regular money wages or social security coverage and that works informally on a non-contractual basis (Portes 1985: 23). Underemployment in rural areas was estimated by the World Bank to be as high as 60 percent in 1978 (World Bank 1978: iii).

Unemployment in the Dominican Republic is not, however, simply a problem of the unskilled or rural migrants who arrive in urban areas without the necessary job training for urban employment. Indeed, additional years of education have not necessarily improved students' rates of employment. Table 7 presents the rates of unemployment of the economically active population in Santo Domingo in 1979. The rates of unemployment are relatively similar for all educational levels. Thus, the 1970s witnessed an educational-level mismatch between employment supply and demand. This phenomenon has been noted in other Latin American and Caribbean countries, where it appears to reflect an oversupply of people with certain types of higher education in these economies (IDB 1987: 131; Anderson 1988).

Even among those educated workers who did manage to obtain appropriate-level employment as a result of growth in the number of middle-class jobs during the 1970s, many were paid salaries which scarcely distinguished them from manual workers. Table 8 presents the growth between 1966 and 1977, by category of monthly salary, in the number of state employees. Whereas the number of state employees grew from 64,389 in 1966 to 90,805 in 1977, the bulk of this expansion remained at the lowest wage levels. Although a large percentage of workers did move from the lowest to the second lowest category between 1966 and 1977, in 1977 over one-third earned less

TABLE 7

Rates of Unemployment of Economically Active Population
of Santo Domingo, by Level of Education, 1979

Years of Education Completed	Rate of Unemployment		
	Men (%)	Women (%)	Total (%)
0	21.1	18.5	20.0
1–3	14.8	20.9	17.4
4–6	18.3	18.2	18.2
7–9	18.2	26.5	20.7
10–12	15.5	23.6	19.1
13 or more	18.9	8.3	15.2

Source. ONAPLAN 1981: 35.

than 100 pesos and only approximately a tenth earned more than 200 pesos. These are not salaries that permit a level of consumption commensurate with Dominican standards of middle-class life.

The profile of the labor force was also changing over this same period. The decade of the 1970s witnessed slower growth in the number of persons employed in most of the occupations associated with labor than in the overall labor force: the overall labor force grew by 47.2 percent, "transportation equipment operators," "other artisans and operatives," and "laborers and workers" all grew at rates below this (see Table 5). As was noted above, opportunities for rural labor decreased sharply. Those occupations associated with agriculture, "farmers and ranchers," decreased somewhat or at best remained constant during this decade.[8] The International Labour Organization estimated that in 1980 the informal sector in Santo Domingo made up 50 percent of the work force—the third highest percentage of all Latin American urban areas studied (IDB 1987: 126).

Not only was there a contraction in the job opportunities for labor, but also the real wages of those employed as laborers simi-

8. It is probable that many of the occupations not specified in the 1981 census are in agriculture and hence that agricultural occupations actually remained more or less stable rather than declining at the stated rate of −22.4 percent (Eric Larson, personal communication).

TABLE 8
Number of Dominican Republic State Employees by Category of Monthly Salary, 1966–1977
(D.R.$)

	$0– 100	$101– 200	$201– 300	$301– 400	$401– 500	More than $500	Total Employees
1966	51,235	7,800	3,248	1,154	489	463	64,389
1967	49,150	10,965	3,800	1,166	420	166	65,667
1968	49,453	12,599	4,184	1,184	303	172	67,895
1969	48,615	13,165	4,258	1,221	217	286	67,762
1970	49,466	13,245	4,200	1,289	200	290	68,690
1971	50,009	13,612	4,149	1,397	292	311	69,770
1972	56,638	13,963	4,388	1,454	345	341	77,129
1973	50,481	15,205	4,101	1,586	648	449	72,470
1974	50,934	17,223	4,124	1,839	707	465	75,292
1975	53,597	20,733	4,358	1,990	728	530	81,936
1976	33,691	44,701	5,108	2,296	748	580	87,124
1977	33,941	47,493	5,573	2,419	768	611	90,805

Percentage Distribution

1966	79.6	12.1	5.0	1.8	0.8	0.7
1967	74.8	16.7	5.8	1.8	0.6	0.2
1968	72.8	18.6	6.2	1.7	0.4	0.2
1969	71.7	19.4	6.3	1.8	0.3	0.4
1970	72.0	19.3	6.1	1.9	0.3	0.4
1971	71.7	19.5	5.9	2.0	0.4	0.4
1972	73.4	18.1	5.7	1.9	0.4	0.4
1973	69.6	21.0	5.6	2.2	0.9	0.6
1974	67.6	22.9	5.5	2.4	0.9	0.6
1975	65.4	25.3	5.3	2.4	0.9	0.6
1976	38.7	51.3	5.9	2.6	0.9	0.7
1977	37.4	52.3	6.1	2.7	0.8	0.7

Source. Oficina Nacional de Presupuesto, quoted in Lozano 1985b: 152.

larly deteriorated. Nor were these negative outcomes for labor only indirect consequences of market mechanisms. The Balaguer regime enacted economic and politically repressive policies concerning the working class. First, Austerity Law No. 1, introduced in 1966, established a wage freeze which lasted for nine years. Although the minimum wage was permitted to rise in 1975, the high rate of inflation during this period meant that real salaries were actually lower in 1978, at the close of Balaguer's twelve-year term, than they had been in 1966, when he assumed office (Table 9).

The Austerity Law also meant that if the working class were to fight for better working conditions, they would come into conflict, not directly with employers, but with the politically repressive state (Espinal 1987a: 120). The intensity of political repression during the authoritarian regime of Balaguer is well established. The repressive measures to silence political and economic opposition included the murder of union leadership by para-police squads, the deportation and jailing of political opponents, and the creation of parallel, pro-management unions to counteract radical ones. In the peak years of repression, 1966 to 1970, the estimated number of political assassinations and disappearances reached 650 (Vilas 1979: 35). Moreover, the large percentage of the population which was marginalized, in the sense of being outside the bounds of formal employment, similarly meant that the state, and not the employing class, increasingly came to be recognized as the logical target for political protest.

The high GDP growth experienced in the 1960s and 1970s did little to correct the persistent inequality in income distribution. Data from a study on income distribution in the capital city give an indication of the relative change during the years of maximum GDP growth (Table 10). The bottom fifth of the population earned relatively less in 1973 (1.4 percent of the total) than it had in 1969 (2.9 percent). In contrast, that fifth of the population earning the highest income in 1969 maintained its position in 1973 (54.8 percent of the total income in 1969 versus 54.4 percent in 1973). To the extent that the middle 30 percent succeeded in capturing a larger share of total income during this period (27.6 percent in 1969 and 30.2 percent in 1973), it did so at the expense of the poorest stratum of the population, not the wealthiest.

Throughout the 1970s the high rate of out-migration established

TABLE 9
Minimum and Real Wages in the Dominican Republic,
1966–1984
(Base 1980=100)

	Minimum Monthly Salary (D.R.$)	Consumer Price Index	Real Salary[a]
1966	60	35.0	171
1967	60	35.4	169
1968	60	35.4	169
1969	60	35.8	168
1970	60	37.1	162
1971	60	38.7	155
1972	60	41.8	144
1973	60	48.1	125
1974	60	54.4	110
1975	95	62.3	152
1976	95	67.1	142
1977	95	75.8	125
1978	95	78.5	121
1979	125	85.7	146[b]
1980	125	100.0	125
1981	125	107.5	116
1982	125	115.8	108
1983	125	121.3	103
1984	175	154.0	114

Source. International Monetary Fund, International Financial Statistics
(Washington, D.C.: International Monetary Fund), consumer price index, 1985,
p. 267.
[a]Data prior to 1978 refer only to consumer prices in Santo Domingo.
[b]The minimum wage was raised in May; therefore estimate refers to May–
December period.

in the late 1960s continued, with an annual average of over 12,000
for the Balaguer period (see Table 1). In the early 1960s the U.S.
consulate had initiated relatively lenient visa policies, and these
were continued as administrative routine, with no evidence of gov-
ernment-to-government discussions of the issues (Mitchell 1987).

TABLE 10
Changes in the Distribution of
Family Income in Santo Domingo,
1969 to 1973

	1969	1973
Lowest 20%	2.9%	1.4%
Lowest 50%	17.6	15.4
Middle 30%	27.6	30.2
Top 20%	54.8%	54.4%

Source. ONAPLAN, *Bases para Formu-
lar una Política de Empleo en la República
Dominicana*, quoted in Cabral 1975: 2.

The sustained exodus of Dominicans throughout this period com-
plemented the development policy described above, with its relatively low utilization of labor, especially in urban areas. Moreover,
out-migration reduced political opposition to the Balaguer regime.
Since much of his electoral support was rural, the rapid urbanization of the Dominican Republic threatened to undermine his political base (Lozano 1985b: 253). The urban portion of the economically active population grew from 39 percent of the whole in 1970 to
60 percent in 1981 (Larson 1984: 18). By permitting relatively high
rates of out-migration, especially urban-based, Balaguer's administration could actually export potential sources of political opposition and sustain itself in power for the subsequent twelve years
(Mitchell 1987: 25).

The mention of political repression raises the important issue of
the complexity and diversity of migrant motives. It is difficult to pin
down the extent to which migrants during this period had political
motives for leaving their country. However, undoubtedly many
Dominicans sought refuge abroad because they had witnessed the
murder of compatriots with whom they shared political sympathies. We may recall the history of the Molina family. Rafael Molina
feared direct or indirect political repression owing to his involvement in radical politics. It was also during this period that the PRD
established its opposition headquarters in New York. During the
early years of the Balaguer regime, therefore, Dominican emigration should not be characterized as purely an economically moti-

vated, labor migration; although they did not have formal refugee status, some migrants shared some of the characteristics of political exiles. While we certainly would not argue that political concerns motivated the majority of Dominicans who settled in New York City at this time, the presence of such exiles within the Dominican colony which established itself abroad underscores the diversity of motivations and social forces behind Dominican emigration.

Democratic Politics, Economic Crisis, and Sustained Migration, 1978–1986

The electoral defeat of Balaguer and the Reformist Party and the rise to power of the PRD in 1978 represented a dramatic change in the political leadership of the Dominican Republic. The PRD successfully mobilized a multiclass alliance to defeat the Reformists in a campaign emphasizing human rights and political and economic democracy. However, the PRD victory also represented a repudiation of allegiance to Balaguer on the part of important sectors of the dominant industrial class. Increasingly, the modern bourgeoisie perceived Balaguer as an obstacle to their political participation. The PRD's campaign to end political repression and its promises of economic justice appealed to labor and to the formerly excluded groups in urban areas, but the relative weakness of labor also meant that strategic sectors of industry, finance, and commerce had little fear of supporting the PRD, a social democratic party (Espinal 1987b: 141).

During the PRD's first two years in power, the new president, Antonio Guzmán, took significant steps to implement the PRD's program of expanded economic democracy. First, Guzmán liberalized the overall political climate. The period 1978–1980 saw a surge in the number of new labor organizations and unions, leading many to prophesy a general mobilization of labor. In 1979, the minimum salary was raised for the first time in five years. And, second, Guzmán introduced a program of induced demand in the form of expanded state employment to address the problem of unemployment and to stimulate consumption. The extent of this expanded state employment stands in contrast to the earlier decade. Whereas the Balaguer administration had added approximately 30,000 public employees to the state sector between 1970 and 1978, the administration of Antonio Guzmán increased these employees by 72,000 in the four years between 1979 and 1982 (Espinal 1987b: 163).

Yet, in spite of the early optimism about the PRD's proposals for political and economic democratization, the party's term in office actually coincided with the worst economic crisis of the postwar Dominican Republic. Balaguer's model of economic development had been largely financed by an expanded external sector dependent on high prices for traditional exports. This strategy entered into crisis when those prices, especially sugar, fell and the price of petroleum and interest rates rose. Under such conditions, the state had fewer resources to distribute either to the expanding bourgeois sectors or to the visibly expanding middle class, which was also demanding greater political participation (Lozano 1985b: 89). International inflation, the rising price of petroleum, and the consequent severe deterioration in the balance of payments had by early 1983 forced the second PRD president, Jorge Blanco, to negotiate austerity policies with the International Money Fund, in exchange for loans amounting to several hundred million dollars (Black 1986: 138–46). The social impact of these policies was extremely severe. The policies attempted to curtail imports and stimulate exports; they in fact resulted in drastic increases in the costs of basic consumer goods, while wages were frozen until the end of 1984.

Indeed, over the course of the administration of President Blanco, a 98 percent increase in consumer goods caused real salaries to decline by 22 percent (IDB 1987: 278). The per capita GDP, which in the 1970s had risen from $998 to $1433, an increase of 44 percent, dropped by 8 percent, to $1319, between 1980 and 1986 (IDB 1987: 2). Not even the middle class could escape the hardships inflicted by inflation of this magnitude in conjunction with declining real salaries. The Dominican popular sectors' extreme frustration with these policies expressed itself in the apparently spontaneous food riots of April, 1984, when demonstrations in Santo Domingo turned into riots and spread to more than twenty towns and cities (Black 1986: 140).

Moreover, despite the social-democratic agenda of the PRD, labor remained largely excluded from political influence throughout most of the party's tenure. Labor organizations remained highly fragmented, and the party failed to develop institutionalized channels for the incorporation of labor into party or administrative decisions. Nor was legislation introduced that would have corrected the traditional labor codes, which were highly restrictive to labor (Espinal 1987b: 175). Despite the critical worsening of international export prices and repeated official reports on the need to diversify exports to lessen dependence on sugar, no such steps were taken under Blanco's regime. An important source of foreign exchange, the state sugar bureaucracy has provided many persons with great personal benefits. Employment with CEA has also been an important expression of political patronage (Vedovato 1986: 72). Thus, rather than supporting diversified agricultural production, under the leadership of the PRD the state continued its high reliance on sugar exports, with the consequent substantial importation of foodstuffs.

Finally, beyond worsening the economic climate, the monetary policies introduced during this period served indirectly as an additional powerful incentive for out-migration. That is, exchange policies were revised; exports would continue to be officially priced on a par with the dollar, while imports (with the exception of petroleum) would be priced according to the "parallel market," with its fluctuating and invariably higher rate. The rate of exchange of the dollar for the peso rose dramatically: from 1.25 in 1978 it climbed to 2.76 in 1984, and it reached a high of 4.00 in 1987 (Table 11).

The steady decline in Dominican real wages throughout this period made a grim contrast to the rising relative value of the dollar. To appreciate the significance of these monetary changes from the perspective of the average Dominican, consider the difference in the minimum monthly salaries of the two countries over time. The salary differential between the two countries, based on the annual average exchange rate and the minimum monthly salary, rose steadily from 287 pesos in 1974 to 1,794 in 1987 (see Table 11). Thus, by 1987 the minimum monthly salary for full-time work in the United States was six times higher than that of the Dominican Republic. Any Dominican contemplating a move to the United States could only be encouraged by these calculations—and encouraged they were, as the sustained high rates of out-migration throughout this period reveal.

TABLE 11
Dominican and United States Minimum Monthly Salaries
Compared, 1974–1987

	Dominican Minimum Monthly Salary (D.R.$)	Rate	U.S. Monthly Minimum Salary[a] (U.S.$)	U.S. Monthly Minimum Salary[b] (D.R.$)	Minimum Salary Differential[c] (D.R.$)
1974	60	1.14	304	347	287
1975	95	1.18	320	377	282
1976	95	1.20	352	422	327
1977	95	1.22	368	449	354
1978	95	1.25	424	530	435
1979	125	1.23	464	571	446
1980	125	1.26	496	625	500
1981	125	1.28	536	686	561
1982	125	1.46	536	783	658
1983	125	1.59	536	852	727
1984	175	2.76	536	1,479	1,304
1985	250	3.09	536	1,656	1,406
1986	250	2.87	536	1,538	1,288
1987	350	4.00	536	2,144	1,794

Source. Banco Central de la República Dominicana, Boletín Mensual 41, no. 2 (February 1987), and various volumes for earlier years.

[a]This figure represents the salary received for working a forty-hour week, four weeks a month, with no overtime, based on the federal minimum wage rate for 1974 to 1987: U.S. Bureau of the Census, Statistical Abstracts of the United States (Washington, D.C.: U.S. Bureau of the Census, 1986), table 684.

[b]Calculated according to the exchange rate for the relevant year.

[c]Unofficial end-of-year estimate.

Conclusion

The history of Dominican Republic involvement with the international market led it, like many other Latin American societies, to specialize in the export of a few primary products. One lasting legacy of the Trujillo period has been the economic predominance of the state. Despite a desperate need for export diversification and despite two radically different political regimes since the 1960s, the Dominican state has not taken the necessary measures to diversify. Instead, rural producers have been discriminated against and terms of trade between agriculture and industry have deteriorated over time, with a consequent steady increase in the quantity of primary foodstuffs that must be imported. Moreover, the decline of agriculture has provoked high rates of rural-to-urban migration and the resulting rapid urbanization that has marked the Dominican Republic since the 1950s.

The legacy established by Trujillo, whereby state policy is guided by the narrow interests of a small group of industrialists and state managers, has been visible in more recent industrial strategies pursued by the Dominican state. Import-substitution policies have favored the interests of large-scale business by means of tariff policies that tax agriculture; exchange rate policy; and price and credit policies. Such policies have been instituted at the expense, not only of the agricultural sector, but of small-scale and traditional industries as well. Capital-intensive industrialization and dependency on imported inputs have favored wage-repressive policies with limited internal-multiplier effects. Once the world price of export commodities fell, the economy retracted severely, revealing its extreme vulnerability. And yet, this vulnerability, or the high dependence on traditional exports, is continually reproduced by state policymakers who stand to benefit personally and politically by bolstering inefficient state enterprises and by favoring the interests of a politically powerful group of industrialists.

Emigration from the Dominican Republic began in earnest in the early 1960s, following a thirty-one-year period of political dictatorship that had placed severe constraints on the movement of Dominicans abroad. Once Trujillo died, a period of political crisis ensued as competing social groups vied for control of the state. The United States, interested in avoiding the radicalization of its Dominican neighbor, engaged in the politics of conservative preemption and simultaneously introduced administrative procedures that would facilitate the exit of relatively large numbers of Dominicans who were believed to be potential recruits to radical causes. With the coming to power of the Reformist Party and the pro-U.S. candidate Joaquín Balaguer in the early 1970s, authoritarian politics,

Sloppy
w/ history

heavy foreign capital investment, and an emphasis on traditional exports combined to produce high rates of economic growth. The economic model of development introduced by Balaguer stimulated an expanding urban middle class and simultaneously excluded labor from the significant economic benefits of the high growth. The subsequent phase of state development did little to ameliorate the poverty and marginalization of large sectors of Dominican society. The democratic opening of the state to the opposition party, the PRD, which achieved victory with campaign promises of human rights and economic justice, accompanied the international debt crisis. Austerity policies resulted and further provoked declining consumption standards for the working class.

Throughout both phases of state development, education, especially at the higher levels, grew at an unprecedented rate. These trends, which were experienced as well in many other parts of Latin America, produced a more highly educated stratum with high expectations for social mobility and the life-styles of modern consumption. The growth of a relatively more educated labor force did accompany an expansion in the number of jobs which could be considered middle-class: employment among such groups as professionals, technicians, state managers, and public employees rose in the 1970s, and this trend continued in the early 1980s, with the dramatic boost to public-sector employment stimulated by the PRD administration. However, much of the middle-class growth occurred in low-paid occupations. Moreover, the unemployment rates of the relatively educated indicate that the relatively large growth of occupations associated with advanced education did not suffice to meet the demand for such employment. These internal structural factors have made the Dominican Republic ripe for emigration.

In addition to the expansion of education, the integration of the Dominican Republic into the world economy through the presence of multinational firms also greatly increased local awareness of and aspirations for life-styles characteristic of the United States. This awareness, combined with the unlikelihood of securing many modern goods in the low-wage economy, increased the attractiveness of emigration.

Despite the radical divergence between the two political administrations that governed between 1966 and 1986, large numbers of Dominicans throughout this period sought employment abroad. The consequences of this persistent out-migration for development in the Dominican Republic must be analyzed in terms of the selectivity of migration and the impact migration had on the class structure both of the sending communities and of the nation as a whole.

3

Research Design

Our study, conducted jointly by a sociologist and an anthropologist, pairs survey and ethnographic data from both the Dominican Republic and the United States. This interdisciplinary approach, a principal methodological feature of our project, served to minimize several problems associated with unidisciplinary studies, such as the low generalizability of community-based, ethnographic findings and the interpretive shallowness of surveys. Our research was completed in two stages, one in the Dominican Republic and one in the United States. Chart 1 provides an overview of the research stages, the locations of the research communities, and the nature of the data collected at each phase of the investigation.

We selected the northern region of the Dominican Republic, known as the Cibao, and the New York Metropolitan Area as the field sites of our project. Past research had identified the Cibao as a major source of migration to the United States (González 1970; Hendricks 1974; Ugalde et al. 1979). Moreover, this region was characterized by socioeconomic and ecological diversity, and it was the home of many return migrants. New York was chosen because, as was mentioned above, past research had shown that Dominican migration was largely an East Coast, urban-centered phenomenon, with the majority of migrants settling in the New York Metropolitan Area.

Phase I: The Dominican Republic

In 1980, when we began our research in the Dominican Republic, it was unclear whether migration to the United States originated pri-

CHART 1
Research Sites and Data Gathered
in the Dominican Republic and the United States

Phase I: The Dominican Republic

Rural Community:	Juan Pablo Census, 1980
	Juan Pablo Ethnography
	Juan Pablo Census, 1981
Rural Town:	Licey Survey
	Licey Ethnography
Urban Area:	Santiago Survey
	Santiago Return Migrant Ethnography

Phase II: New York Metropolitan Area

New York Survey
New York Ethnography

marily from rural or from urban areas, let alone whether a "typical migratory community" existed or what it looked like. The few ethnographic accounts that existed had been conducted in rural communities but were not generalizable to the broader society (Peña and Parache 1971; Hendricks 1974). A study by Ugalde et al. (1979) had indicated that a sizable percentage of out-migration originated from urban areas, but no in-depth studies of urban communities had confirmed that finding. Therefore it was important that we not limit our selection of migratory communities to one type. Instead we selected for study three communities in the Cibao region: the city of Santiago de los Caballeros; a small, rural community in the Sierra zone of Santiago province that we will call Juan Pablo; and Licey al Medio, a medium-sized agricultural town also in the province of Santiago (see Map 1). The communities differ in ecology; urbanization and commerce; employment opportunities in the informal, primary, and secondary sectors; incorporation of the agricultural population into the marketing system, as measured by production of cash crops for national and international consumption; and socioeconomic diversification based on property, employment, income, and education. We felt that such diverse settings would allow both a broad characterization of the migrant and non-migrant populations and a determination of the range of ecological, demographic, economic, social, and cultural forces that contributed to external migration.

Juan Pablo, the smaller of the two agricultural communities, is

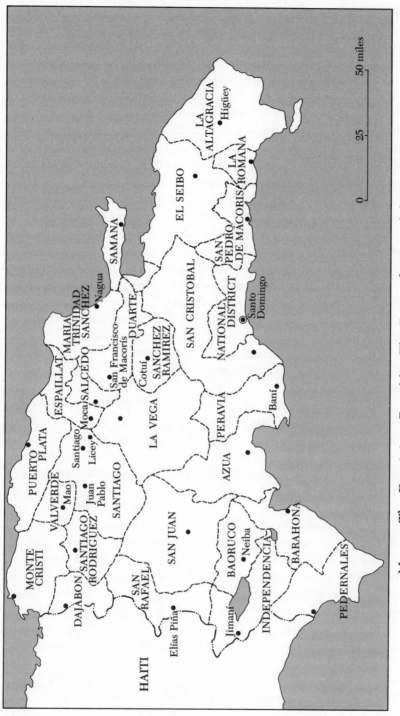

Map 1. The Dominican Republic: The Research Sites of the Project

located in the Sierra, a highly mountainous region plagued with
severe soil erosion and declining fertility.[1] The region's unpaved
roads and lack of electricity make transportation and communication within and out of the Sierra extremely difficult. Classified as a
sección (the smallest administrative and political unit in the Dominican Republic), Juan Pablo had a population of 4,121, according to
the 1981 Dominican census (ONE 1983). Approximately one-fourth
of this population resided in the town of Juan Pablo, the *sección's*
commercial and administrative center.

Juan Pablo is a typical impoverished agricultural community in
the Sierra. It is characterized by harsh ecological conditions, tech-
nologically simple forms of production, and a high incidence of
semi-proletarian farming households which rely on income from
family farms and irregular wage employment. Most farmers who
engage in commercial agriculture specialize in coffee and cattle.
Few employment alternatives exist beyond agricultural wage employment, save self-employment in commerce and government
jobs in education, administration, and public works.

The second agricultural community, Licey al Medio, contrasts
sharply with the depressed setting of Juan Pablo. Licey lies in the
northern zone of the Dominican Republic, in the rich flatlands of the
Cibao. The community supported some 15,700 persons in 1981.
Minifundios, or small landholdings, characterize Licey; nearly half
of the population is either completely landless or owns less than 3.1
hectares of land. Nonetheless, in contrast to Juan Pablo, agricultural
production is fairly intensive by Dominican standards, with tobacco
as the major export cash crop.

In addition to agriculture, Licey has a relatively important agro-
industrial sector. There are three tobacco-processing warehouses,
which in 1981 were affiliates of large international exporting firms,
as well as a peanut processing firm. The majority of workers in
these firms were women. Thirty-seven active egg-producing operations and six chicken-raising firms were in business. These operations, along with an assortment of small family groceries and shops,
constituted the industrial and commercial sector of Licey (Castro
1985). The diversity of employment possibilities and infrastructural

1. Juan Pablo is the pseudonym that we have chosen to protect the anonymity
of the residents and emigrants of this small rural community.

facilities in Licey stands in sharp contrast to conditions in Juan Pablo.

Santiago de los Caballeros, the urban site, is the second largest city in the Dominican Republic and, with a population of approximately 280,000 in 1981, is in effect the capital of the northern region of the country (Yunén 1985: 83). Much of the rapid growth experienced by Santiago during the past two decades resulted from migration from the eastern and western rural zones, where the majority of the people are sharecroppers or rural day laborers (ONAPLAN 1983: 13). The tobacco industry has historically been an important sector in Santiago and in the region as a whole, and it remains so today (Yunén 1985: 107). However, during the expansion of the early 1970s, construction was one of the fastest-growing industrial sectors (Veras 1976: 35). Santiago was also the base of one of the three free-trade zones operating in the Dominican Republic in the early 1980s. The city's limited industrial growth has absorbed only a fraction of the expanding urban population. A survey conducted by the National Statistics Office in 1979 estimated that almost half of the economically active population of Santiago was openly unemployed or underemployed (ONAPLAN 1981: 129).

Comparable survey data were gathered in these three Dominican communities during October and November of 1980. The survey data consist of three samples: (1) a complete census of the agricultural community of Juan Pablo and its immediate environs, totaling 138 households; (2) a multi-stage probability sample of 247 households in the second agricultural community, Licey, where the much larger population base made a complete census unfeasible; and (3) a multi-stage probability sample of the urban area of Santiago. The Santiago data were based on a sampling frame provided by the Dominican National Office of Statistics. The sample objective was twofold: first, for the urban universe of Santiago, to estimate the proportion of households with members who, either at the time of the survey or in the past, had lived abroad; and, second, to generate a sufficient number of cases of migrant households to be able to compare migrant and non-migrant households using a variety of dimensions. Known migrant neighborhoods were oversampled in order to maximize the number of migrant households, and these cases were subsequently weighted accordingly, resulting in a working sample of 535 households. These survey data collected for the three communities provide representative information concerning the migrant population. The findings are presented in Chapters 4 and 5.

An interview team consisting of fourteen Dominican students, largely from the National Catholic University of Santiago (UCMM), received a one-week training session and subsequently conducted the interviews for the three surveys under the supervision of Grasmuck, the sociologist of our team, with the assistance of Noris Eusebio Pol, a Dominican sociologist. The survey instrument included information on household size and composition, primary and secondary occupations of all household members, employment history of the household head and spouse, household dependence on and use of remittances from abroad, and employment information for all members currently residing outside the country. The duration of the interviews ranged from half an hour to two hours and took place in the homes of the respondents. In 98 percent of the cases the interview was conducted with the head of the house or with the spouse of the head of the house (50 percent and 48 percent, respectively). In 72.5 percent of the cases the respondent was female. Female-headed households constituted 25.8 percent of the sample. The response rate was high: 91.9 percent.

In addition to the survey, extensive ethnographic research was conducted in Juan Pablo and, to a much lesser extent, in Licey and the city of Santiago. Pessar, an anthropologist, spent nine months in the *sección* of Juan Pablo gathering ethnographic material on the causes and consequences of out-migration. This ethnographic research included the gathering of detailed demographic, genealogical, social, and economic data for all the households residing at any point over a twenty-year period in the town of Juan Pablo and several neighboring hamlets. Pessar conducted a second census of Juan Pablo in 1981, at the conclusion of the ethnographic fieldwork. This ethnographic material contributed greatly to our analysis of how social class, household composition, and social networks influence who emigrates and who stays behind. The household histories also examined issues such as fragmentation or consolidation of family holdings, as well as changes in land use, in levels of investment, in tenure patterns, and in demand for wage labor. These ethnographic data enabled us to document, via historical cases, the time sequence of certain variables which were found to be correlated in the census data previously gathered, especially regarding the question of the impact of out-migration on agricultural production and employment in Juan Pablo. Daily household budgets, collected over a six-month period for three migrant and three non-migrant households, provided insights into the ways that remittance income affected consumption patterns and the ways that poor, non-migrant households survived on irregular, subsistence incomes. The results of the Juan Pablo ethnography and surveys are presented in Chapter 5.

Some ethnographic research was conducted in Licey and Santiago by Max Castro and Julia Tavárez, both graduate students at the time, from the University of North Carolina and Yale University, respectively. Both of these researchers contributed to the project's overall success by gathering information on the economic strategies of return migrants. The ethnographic research of Castro in Licey offered a historical background to our survey findings.[2] The focus of Chapter 5 will be on the ethnography and survey results from Juan Pablo, but some of the survey data from Licey are also presented there. In the urban areas of Santiago, Tavárez, by means of a snowball sample, collected income and employment data on thirty-five return-migrant households. In addition, Tavárez asked open-ended questions to explore how return migrants' experiences in the Dominican Republic were influenced by gender ideology and the sexual division of labor in the household and labor market. These findings are analyzed in Chapter 4.

Phase II: The United States

The usual destination of Dominicans bound for the United States is the New York Metropolitan Area. It is here that we embarked on the second phase of the project. As in the Dominican Republic, in New York we conducted both survey and ethnographic research. Whereas we employed representative sampling techniques in the Dominican Republic, in New York we drew a snowball or nonprobability sample of Dominicans living and working in New York City, because part of our intention was to compare roughly equal

2. For a complete treatment of the ethnographic research and secondary data analysis completed by Castro in Licey al Medio, see Castro (1985).

numbers of documented and undocumented Dominicans.[3] We
originally planned to base our New York sample on the list of
referrals we had received from our contacts in the Dominican Republic. This method proved unworkable because of the high costs
of locating families in different boroughs of New York, the high
residential mobility of Dominicans in New York, and the state of
apprehension in which most undocumented Dominicans lived at
that time. Indeed, in one case when we were pretesting our instrument, we approached a Dominican woman with what we considered to be the impeccable reference of our close friendship with
her cousin, an undocumented Dominican. The Dominican woman,
a female head of house, responded patiently throughout our pretest
questionnaire, thanked us, and immediately upon our departure
called her cousin to inform him that immigration officers had just
been questioning her about him! As an alternative strategy, we
selected a group of seven Dominican interviewers who came from
different neighborhoods and social circles in New York and generated a chain of interviews originating from the familial and social
contacts of the interviewers themselves.

The New York survey consists of 301 interviews with persons
born in the Dominican Republic and employed at the time of the
survey in New York City. It was permissible for an interviewer to
select more than one employed person per household. Of the total
sample of 301, 232 interviews (77.1 percent) represent separate
households, with the remaining 22.9 percent coming from households with more than one case. The interviews typically took place
in the respondent's home and generally lasted about one hour.
Interviewers tried to secure equal numbers of documented and
undocumented Dominicans, but often the legal status of a migrant

3. The term *snowball* refers to a nonprobability sampling procedure, in that
cases are initially deliberately selected on the basis of certain variables (in this
case, work experience in the United States) and expanded by means of referrals or
contacts established by the early interviews. Thus, for example, ten interviews
may be given with subjects of interest, who then each recommend two or three
others, and so on. This kind of procedure is often employed when the population
of interest is not likely to appear in adequate numbers in a representative sampling. The snowball sample, being unrepresentative, involves the risk of unrecog-
nized biases in regard to other variables. It is possible, however, to evaluate the
overall representativeness of a snowball sample by comparing it on key variables
with other representative samples of the subject population.

was not clear until the actual interview was conducted. The result was that 57.6 percent of the sample are legal and 42.4 percent are undocumented immigrants. We wanted a high representation of undocumented Dominicans in order to be sure to have enough cases for a reliable comparison with documented Dominicans. Consequently, our sample can clearly be seen to overrepresent the undocumented Dominicans in the population, when it is compared with official estimates of the percentage of the Dominican population residing illegally in the United States—almost 12 percent, according to the 1980 U.S. census.[4]

Statistical comparisons with representative surveys of Dominican immigrants living in New York City indicate that the sample on which our survey is based is unbiased with respect to such characteristics as average age, education, and occupation. Approximately 58 percent of our sample is male, which is comparable to one of the more reliable recent sex-ratio estimates of Dominicans residing in the United States (Larson and Opitz 1988: 14).[5] A large majority of our respondents (79.7 percent) reported their last residence in the Dominican Republic as having been urban. A series of studies

4. It is well established that official census data underrepresent the number of undocumented aliens residing in the United States. In order to provide a more accurate estimate of Dominican illegals, Warren has employed census survival techniques based on the 1981 Dominican census. He has estimated that the total number of Dominicans aged 15 to 44 residing outside the country during the 1981 census was about 185,000 to 210,000. About 160,000 were estimated to be living legally in the United States and other countries in December, 1981. By this count about 25,000 to 50,000 or between 15.6 percent and 31.2 percent of the Dominicans aged 15 to 44, would have been residing illegally in the United States and other countries (Warren 1988: 11).

5. The 1980 U.S. census, which counted 169,147 Dominican-born persons, shows an apparently female-dominant population, or about 46.6 percent males aged 15 to 39. However, Larson and Opitz have argued convincingly that the 1980 census probably undercounted male Dominican nationals given the deficit of males in the age-specific sex ratios. Larson and Opitz conclude that a population range of 60 to 70 percent male is more credible (Larson and Opitz 1988: 13). Báez Evertsz and D'Oleo Ramírez (1985: 28) also found that 60 percent of the Dominicans applying for immigrant visas at the U.S. consulate in the Dominican Republic in 1985 were male; Acosta (1986: 348), relying on data from the U.S. consul general in Santo Domingo, concluded that of the 220,000 persons who received immigrant visas between 1960 and 1980, 52 percent were male. Our sample is comparable to the adjusted estimate of the Dominican male population made by Larson and Opitz (1988). If, however, the U.S. 1980 census has not significantly undercounted Dominican males, then our sample overrepresents the proportion of men in the Dominican population by about 11 percent.

(Ugalde et al. 1979; Pérez 1981; Gurak 1981) have also concluded that the Dominican population in New York is indeed predominantly of urban origin.

Our ethnographic data for New York come from structured interviews with informants, as well as casual conversations and participant observation in households, workplaces, and social gatherings over a two-year period (1981–1983). Two principal groups form the basis for much of the ethnographic material we present on Dominicans in New York: members of fifty-five immigrant households who were periodically contacted through visits and phone conversations over a two-year period, and twenty-five Dominican apparel workers.

We sought diversity among our informants, in order to explore how the immigrant experience was affected by such variables as gender, class background, time of arrival, legal status, age, marital status, household composition, and work history. We used various strategies to identify and contact informants. These strategies included reactivating ties with Dominican immigrants we had met in the Dominican Republic, using referrals provided by our Dominican-based informants, and relying on introductions extended by New York-based informants and community leaders.

Methodological Notes on Interdisciplinary, Cross-National Immigration Research

The combination of ethnographic and survey research methodologies proved essential to many of our final interpretations concerning the causes and consequences of emigration from the Dominican Republic. A survey that is formulated without an initial phase of participant-observation and in-depth interviews with key informants runs the risk of repeating pat questions drawn from previous studies and minimizing the importance of the social categories migrants themselves employ. Lost are opportunities to raise new questions and explore missed connections—opportunities that may emerge when informants are invited to join the ethnographer in puzzling about and commenting on the subject matter the survey will eventually probe. Moreover, participant-observation allows the conceptual categories of social actors to emerge and to play an active role in the research goal of investigation and interpretation of findings. While time did not allow us to conduct as extensive ethnographic research as would have been desirable prior to constructing our survey instruments for the Dominican Republic and New York City, we were nonetheless able to include certain topics in our surveys that would very likely have received minor, if any, attention had we not engaged in preliminary fieldwork. For example, our early ethnography in one of the rural communities sensitized us to a common local perception that linked emigration directly to reduced agricultural production and employment. Through both survey research and additional ethnographic study, we were able to gather generalizable evidence on the accuracy of these impressionistic data for the two rural communities we studied. Through conversations with New York–based informants, we learned that they associated migration with socioeconomic advancement, or *progreso*. In our survey and ethnographic research, we sought to determine whether such social mobility had occurred and how it was measured by Dominican migrants.

Conducting survey research is difficult under the best of circumstances. Our task was further complicated by several factors. Many of our informants had lived through the dark years of the Trujillo dictatorship. Many people have emerged from that experience with the conviction that strangers asking questions represent threats—to be managed through polite avoidance or claims of ignorance. Moreover, many of our questions dealt with such topics as emigration, employment abroad, and sources of income. These are highly charged issues for many, and are especially so for illegal immigrants and for households that have illegal immigrant members. We sought to minimize problems of access and reliability of the findings by placing an ethnographer in Juan Pablo, the smallest rural community, several months before conducting the surveys. Pessar spoke to community leaders and others in order to gain their endorsements for the survey research and their assistance in urging their families and friends to cooperate with the interviewers. We believe this strategy was generally successful in easing the distrust Dominicans experience when faced with unknown survey researchers. As was described above, problems of access and trust were eased in New York by drawing our respondents from a snowball sample generated by our trained Dominican interviewers.

In some cases, our initial ethnographic research led us to exclude highly sensitive questions from the surveys. In these few cases, we both doubted the validity of the responses we were likely to receive and feared the potential repercussions of such community-wide probing of sensitive issues on the success of our ethnographic work. The following episode illustrates these points. Pretests of the survey instrument were administered in Juan Pablo, the community in which Pessar conducted ethnographic research. When Pessar explained the purpose of the survey to one of her neighbors, Señora Rodríguez, a return migrant, she eagerly agreed to be included in one of the pretests. At the appointed time, Pessar introduced her neighbor to Grasmuck and the Dominican university student who was administering the pretests. All seemed to be going well. Señora Rodríguez responded to the survey questions with rapt interest and goodwill—until the interviewer posed a question about the amount of land the household possessed. At this point Señora Rodríguez turned to Pessar with a conspiratorial wink and reported less than one-third of her household's actual landholdings. As the wink attested, it had become somehow obscured or irrelevant that moments before Pessar had introduced her neighbor to the interviewers and had made clear that they were collaborating on the study. What was important to Señora Rodríguez was that she was confronting an outsider who had asked a sensitive question that required "ignorance" as well as collusion on Pessar's part. Such reactions persuaded us that the size of the family plot was among the sensitive subjects best omitted from the census questionnaire and reserved for a later phase of the ethnographic study.

In addition to the issue of validity, the question of causality or the time ordering of variables is often problematic in narrowly conceived survey research. The integration of ethnographic and survey techniques proved helpful in several ways. First, our community ethnohistories and household histories allowed us to uncover in some cases, and to refine in others, the causal links between variables which were merely correlated in our surveys. For example, in one of the rural communities we found that migrant households were more likely to report reduced levels of agricultural production in the five-year period prior to the survey than were non-migrant households. The survey permitted generalizable statistics on the extent of this problem. However, the survey questionnaires could not provide a narrative account of how production decisions were made by migrant households or the range of considerations involved in making such decisions, such as the number of non-migrant adult sons or fears of losing land to agrarian reform. Our ethnographic research documented that productivity decreases were directly related to the loss of household labor due to out-migration.

Second, for their part, ethnographers must confront the common charge that their fine-textured analysis may not be generalizable beyond the community actually studied. To gauge the generalizability of our ethnographic study accurately, it would have been necessary to compare our community studies with national survey data on migration issues in the Dominican Republic and the United States. Short of this ideal situation, however, our claims that certain of our ethnographic findings probably hold for the larger Dominican migrant population are more authoritative when these findings are independently verified by our surveys of households in all three Dominican migratory communities and in New York. We will illustrate the complementarity of ethnographic and survey findings in our later treatment of the impact of migration on agricultural production and in our discussion of the role of gender in Dominican migrants' work experience.

Moreover, because the two methodological strategies were employed in both place of origin and place of destination, we were able to cross-check information given by respondents in one context with responses given in the other. For example, our ethnography in New York, in contrast to earlier literature, revealed important gender divisions within households over the decision to return to the Dominican Republic. Yet the unrepresentative nature of the ethnographic sample did not assure the generalizability of these findings. However, these same gender conflicts were uncovered in our ethnography of return migrants in the Dominican Republic. Hence, the consistency of ethnographic findings in two different contexts built our confidence that such anthropological observations had some general applicability.

Finally, because the Dominican community in New York has attracted migrants from all over the Dominican Republic, the New York community must be studied in its own right and not strictly from the partial view of a few sending communities. For example, migrant communities, be they rural towns or urban neighborhoods, begin sending members to the United States at different times. Some communities have been sending members for twenty years: others have only recently dispatched members abroad. Adjustment to life in New York is very much conditioned by the availability of a wide range of kin and former community members that a new immigrant can draw upon for support but also by the size of the Dominican immigrant colony itself. Yet, a researcher talking to members of three different sending communities in the Dominican Republic could easily get three different descriptions of the settlement process, if the communities were consolidated at different moments in the history of the Dominican colony in New York. In contrast, by putting together the history of migrants from a wider range of sending communities found at the point of destination, it was possible to trace the overall consolidation of the immigrant colony and not only as it relates to a few sending communities.

It might be argued that the social-science equivalent to Marshall McLuhan's insight is that "methodology is the message": particular methodological strategies predispose researchers to particular types of substantive generalizations (Sjoberg and Nett 1968). In our research project, the combination of an anthropologist and a sociologist attempting to pair ethnographic and survey research on international labor migration may have predisposed us to conclude that migration is a sociocultural and economic process not reducible to macroeconomic forces or to individual migrants' decisions alone. In that respect we consider that our initial methodological strategy of an interdisciplinary approach was wise, in that it permitted us to uncover much of the complexity and dynamics behind the process of international labor migration.

4

Urban Emigration and Return Migration

Consequences for National Development

Given the critical problem of underemployment and unemployment in the developing world, it is not surprising that in many discussions of the causes of out-migration from these areas the excess labor force is treated, implicitly or explicitly, as the most immediate stimulant. Statements concerning out-migration typically portray the local upper class and the dominant classes of developed societies as mutually benefiting from the labor transfer. The upper class of peripheral countries is seen to benefit because migration minimizes the political threat of a large mobilized and unemployed population. Emigration of people who are younger and more ambitious on the average minimizes the threat that they might be mobilized politically to resist the strategies of development adopted by the dominant class (Marshall 1973; Castells 1975; Alba 1978; Sassen-Koob 1978; Portes and Walton 1981).

To the extent that labor migrants come disproportionately from the unemployed population, it can be argued that out-migration results in an increased demand for the remaining labor force, which, if significant enough, will mean a rise in local wage rates. Similarly, if migrants come from the unemployed, their exit becomes a safety valve protecting dominant groups against potential social disruption, since the physical reminders of economic failures are removed from sight.[1]

1. The interests of dominant classes in peripheral areas are typically depicted in the dependency literature as being served because out-migration reduces the

If, on the contrary, the already employed migrate, then the question of the skill level of emigrants and the general availability of other workers at similar levels, that is, their replaceability, becomes an important factor in evaluating the cost of their loss. The models of development adopted by developing societies can, in some cases, be associated with the out-migration of professional workers. For example, the so-called "brain drain" from poor nations can be seen as a consequence of educational institutions in developing societies training their students in ways that are appropriate only for advanced societies. Thus, Third World societies such as Argentina, Jamaica, South Korea, and Egypt can successfully import technological innovations and train a highly skilled labor force, but the economic and political conditions for employing those trained workers are often absent (Portes and Walton 1981; Anderson 1988).

A precise determination of the value of labor exports for sending countries is difficult because the nature of the labor supply of exporting countries varies and because the nature of labor exports can change over time. Sassen-Koob has argued that within the labor surplus of developing societies an "apparent surplus" must be distinguished from a "hard-core surplus" (1978: 53). Authors who speak of labor surplus usually mean in fact the hard-core sectors of labor, which could not be absorbed even with significantly expanded industrialization. However, a share of labor surplus may be necessary should significantly expanded industrialization occur. If labor exports deplete this "apparent labor surplus," the consequences could be detrimental to subsequent development.

Most of the evidence we have on this question comes from studies that have focused on out-migration from rural sending communities in societies such as Yugoslavia, Greece, Portugal, Mexico, and the Dominican Republic (Baučić 1972; Dinerman 1978; Poinard and Roux 1977; Cornelius 1976, 1990; Weist 1970; Reichert 1981;

---

political threat of a large mobilized but unemployed population (A. Marshall 1973: 119–28; Castells 1975; Alba 1978; Portes 1983; Sassen-Koob 1978). Although there are clearly local economic advantages, in the form of downward pressure on wages in the periphery, to be derived from a large supply of cheap labor, the capital-intensive nature of many development models has meant that the absolute size of the unemployed sector often becomes much larger than is necessary for extracting such advantages. It is, in fact, a situation of overkill.

Mitchell and del Castillo 1987; King 1986; Massey et al. 1987). Caribbean migration to the United States differs from other Latin American streams, and principally from the Mexican, in that larger numbers of Caribbeans leave from urban, as opposed to rural, areas (Gurak and Kritz 1982; Chaney 1985; Larson 1987; Anderson 1988). For these reasons we included the urban setting of Santiago in our inquiry. The central questions of our analysis are: Who are the Dominican emigrants? May the migrant population be considered a hard-core labor surplus, or does it represent instead a skill drain and significant loss to the Dominican Republic? What have been the experiences of return migrants and what has been their impact on the urban economy?

Urban Migrant Households

The data presented here document the pervasiveness of urban out-migration in the Dominican Republic and challenge the frequent assumption that labor exports draw predominantly from the marginalized surplus population.

According to our survey in 1981, almost one out of four Santiago households has been directly involved in out-migration. Fully 16.7 percent of Santiago households include at least one member living outside the Dominican Republic (present migrant households), and 11.0 percent of the households contain at least one member who has returned to live in Santiago after having lived in the United States (return migrant households). Some households include both migrant and return migrant members. Combining present with return migrant households, we find that 23.0 percent of Santiago residences have been directly touched by migration. Moreover, once a family decides to send one of its members abroad, it often chooses to send a second member as well; the median number of migrants per migrant household is 1.4.

It is important to underscore the magnitude of this phenomenon and the sheer quantitative impact that migration has had on this urban community. Basing our calculations on the sampling frame of unemployed and the total economically active population, we may conservatively determine the approximate number of adult Santiagüeros living abroad in 1981 to be 9,940, or 10.9 percent of the urban labor force of Santiago.[2] Likewise, the adult return migrant population is estimated at 6,626, or 7.3 percent of the economically active population of Santiago.[3]

These figures actually underestimate the extent to which migration has affected this urban community; the survey deliberately excluded those families that moved as intact households and thereby left no remaining household members in the community of origin. Indeed, when we employ the term *migrant household* we are effectively describing the true international household, with its members residing on different sides of national borders.

Most of the migrants are male (65.9 percent). The consequence of this predominantly male exodus has been to increase the relative number of female-headed households in the community. However, although the percentage of female-headed migrant households is almost double that of non-migrant households (45.1 percent compared to 22.5 percent), they do not constitute the majority of the migrant families. The reason for this is the high proportion of cases in which the outside migrant is not the husband or wife of the remaining head but is instead the son or daughter (see Table 12). In 16.6 percent of the migrant households, the first migrant is the husband of the remaining female head; in 58.3 percent the migrant is the son or daughter of the head; and in 22.7 percent the outside member is some other relation, most often a sibling or parent of the head of house. Therefore, in our discussion, when we refer to the head of a Santiago migrant household, in the majority of the cases we are saying something about the parent who has witnessed the out-migration of his or her child. The predominance of adult children among the emigrants rather than heads of households expresses the economic difficulty of establishing separate residences

2. These figures were arrived at in the following manner: $a = 16.7$ percent, the percentage of sampled households containing at least one migrant; $b = 43,449$, the N of the total sampled population of households; $c = 1.37$, the median number of outside migrants per household in the sample; $d = 91,250$, the total economically active population of Santiago. Then $(a \times b \times c)/d = 10.9$ percent. The values a, b, and c are based on our project survey, and d is the figure given by the National Statistics Office.

3. Return migrants as a percentage of the economically active was calculated as follows: $a = 11.0$ percent, the percentage of sampled households containing at least one return migrant; $b = 43,449$, the N of the total sampled population of households; $c = 1.39$, the median number of return migrants per household; $d = 91,250$, the total economically active population of Santiago. Then $(a \times b \times c)/d = 7.3$ percent.

TABLE 12
*Relation of Outside Migrant to Remaining Head
of Household in Santiago*

	First Migrant (%)	All Migrants (%)
Husband	16.6	8.4
Wife	2.4	1.2
Son	32.1	30.5
Daughter	26.2	15.6
Parent or parent-in-law	10.7	15.6
Other	12.0	28.7
Weighted migrant N	(84)	(167)
Weighted household N	(84)	(84)

Source. Project data, Santiago Survey.

for young adults in Dominican urban areas and should be included among a series of social motivations leading to emigration.

An important consideration in urban out-migration is whether migrants who left their country from urban areas had been longtime dwellers in those urban areas or had only recently arrived from the countryside prior to their departure. This point is crucial for an assessment of the extent to which labor exports may be tapping a displaced rural labor force or may be drawing on the established urban working population. With this in mind, respondents were asked about their last and penultimate places of residence prior to Santiago. As Table 13 shows, present migrant households are no more likely to have come recently from the countryside than are non-migrant households. Migrant and non-migrant households have about an equal likelihood of having always been located in the urban areas of Santiago (43.9 percent and 45.0 percent, respectively). Among those families who had moved to Santiago from another area, the migrant households were slightly less likely to have come directly from a rural area than were the non-migrant families. Among those who had emigrated from outside Santiago, the migrants were more likely to have come most immediately from smaller urban towns.

TABLE 13
Previous Residence of Head of Household in Santiago,
by Migratory Status

Last Residence	Non-migrant (%)	Present Migrant (%)	Return Migrant (%)	Total (%)
Rural	10.1	6.1	6.4[a]	9.2
Semi-urban (4,900 or less)	21.6	27.3	32.3	23.2
Urban (5,000 or more)	23.3	22.7	19.4	23.0
Native resident	45.0	43.9	41.9	44.6
Weighted N	(338)	(66)	(31)[b]	(435)

Source. Project data, Santiago Survey.
[a]Fewer than 5 cases.
[b]Excludes cases whose prior residence was New York.

It may be concluded, therefore, that urban out-migration is not predominantly an expression of step-migration, with real senders being the rural communities and Santiago being only a stopover place. Households that sent migrants abroad were just as likely to be native to Santiago as were the non-migrant households. Although it is true that a majority of the present migrant households have not always resided in Santiago, this appears to be a reflection of the generally high rate of internal migration characterizing the population as a whole (Ramírez, Tactuk, and Breton 1977) and not a salient feature of the migrant population only.

Remittances

Migrant households often receive remittances from absent members. Policymakers from developing societies often point to the positive contributions that such remittance payments from abroad make to the balance of payments. Other sources have pointed out that remittances could also have the detrimental effect of turning significant numbers of agricultural producers into consumers; this could decrease the domestic food supply or contribute to demand-pull inflation (ILO 1975: 65). The difficulty of the issue is compounded by the lack of systematic information regarding the regularity or quantity of remittance payments, especially for areas larger than small towns and villages.

The Santiago survey reveals that one-third (33.8 percent) of the urban families have at some time in the past received some form of aid from relatives living abroad. At the time of the survey, 67.9 percent of the surveyed households received no remittances, 12.0 percent received aid, but irregularly or only on special occasions, and fully 18.3 percent reported sustained, consistent support from abroad. With few exceptions, these recipients received monthly payments. Table 14 shows the regular monthly amounts received by Santiago migrant households. Although the majority of families (71.2 percent) received payments of less than 200 pesos (U.S. $156) a month, close to a quarter of them received more than 300 pesos (U.S. $234) a month. The mean amount received per household was 130 pesos (U.S. $102) for regular recipients. These payments are substantial contributions to household income: the median monthly wage for heads of house in 1979 in Santiago was 173 pesos (ONAPLAN 1981). Furthermore, extrapolating from the surveyed households to the city as a whole, we can conservatively estimate that approximately 16 million pesos (U.S. $13 million) were entering Santiago in 1981 in the form of regular remittances.[4] This figure does not include the value of appliances, gifts, or savings brought back by migrants during vacations.

Households were asked about all sources of income in addition to remittances. Migrant households are somewhat more likely than non-migrant households to be represented in the highest income group (see Table 15). The differences are statistically significant, although the strength of the association is weak. The difference in household income of migrant and non-migrant households is not large, but it seems clear that remittance income augments the advantages of migrant households.

One immediate result of increased income for migrant house-

4. This calculation is admittedly a rough estimate. It is based on the following assumptions: (1) that 18.3 percent of 43,449 households received a mean of D.R. $149.56 a month, 12 months a year = D.R. $14,270,118.00; and (2) that 12.0 percent of 43,449 households receive a mean of $66.44 a month but on an irregular basis, which we translate to mean on the average of six times a year = D.R. $2,078,461.00. Therefore, the regular and irregular recipients receive D.R. $16,348,579.00 annually. At an exchange rate of 1.28 in 1981, this translates as U.S. $12,772,327.

TABLE 14
Regular Payments from Abroad Received
by Households in Santiago, 1980

Received Monthly (D.R.$)	% of Regular Recipients
Less than $50	23.0
$50–99	21.8
$100–199	26.4
$200–299	5.7
$300 or more	23.0
Weighted N	(87)
Mean = $130.17	

Source. Project data, Santiago Survey.

TABLE 15
Household Income in Santiago, 1980, by Migratory Status

Household Income (D.R.$)	Non-Migrant (%)	All Migrant[a] (%)	Total (%)
Less than $100	15.8	3.2	12.8
$100–300	44.1	48.0	45.1
$300 or more	40.1	48.8	42.1
Weighted N	(392)	(125)	(517)
Chi^2 = 13.727; p < .01			
Goodman & Kruskal's tau$_r$ = .03			

Source. Project data, Santiago Survey.
[a]Includes present migrant households and return migrant households.

holds is access to modern consumer goods. Indeed, larger incomes and remittances, combined with the possibility of gifts from relatives living abroad, create a dramatic contrast in living standards between migrant and non-migrant families (see Table 16; only those households that earn more than 100 pesos monthly are included, since few migrant households earn less). Combining present migrant households with return migrant households, and comparing these with

TABLE 16
Possession of Household Consumer Items in Santiago,
1980, by Migratory Status

Household Consumer Items by Income Level (D.R.$)	Non-Migrant (%)	All Migrant[a] (%)	Total (N)	Significance Level Chi²	θ²
$100–300					
Television	64.8	89.6	(166)	p < .01	.06
Any other appliance	71.9	89.3	(178)	p < .01	.03
Refrigerator	68.9	76.4	(136)	not signif.	—
Stereo	26.8	42.9	(60)	p < .05	.03
$300 or more					
Color television	5.2	23.4	(23)	p < .01	.07
Stereo	57.0	66.4	(130)	not signif.	—
Automobile	43.0	56.9	(102)	p < .10	.02

Source. Project data, Santiago Survey.
[a]Includes present migrant households and return migrant households.

non-migrant families at the same general income level, we see that the former were more likely to possess consumer goods associated with the middle class. Among those households receiving incomes between 100 and 300 pesos a month, migrant households were more likely than their non-migrant counterparts to possess television sets, refrigerators, and stereos. These differences are also evident among those earning more than 300 pesos monthly. Within the highest income group, migrant households are more likely than non-migrants to possess color television sets, stereos, and automobiles. As with income, however, although most of these differences are statistically significant, the strength of the association between migratory status and the possession of consumer items is weak.

Most of the modern consumer goods that distinguish migrant households are, of course, imported. This inflow of purchasing power for goods that in the domestic economy are in short supply and expensive could produce negative effects on the balance of payments. That is, if the consequence of substantial sums of money entering the city or the society as a whole is increased demand for imported goods with inflationary pressure, then the net contribution to the balance of payments may be minimal, if not negative.

In one important aspect the migrant household fares less well than the non-migrant population, that is, the ability of the remaining head to sustain local employment. Table 17 presents employment levels for non-migrant, present migrant, and return migrant households. A much higher percentage of the heads of migrant households were unemployed than were heads of non-migrant families. Nor was this relatively high unemployment for migrant heads merely a reflection of the greater concentration of female heads among these households. Both male and female heads of migrant households reported dramatically higher rates of unemployment than did the heads of non-migrant households.

Return migrant heads are also more likely to be unemployed than are the heads of non-migrant families: almost 30 percent of male return migrant heads were out of work, compared to 20.3 percent of the non-migrant heads. This pattern of relatively higher unemployment rates for return migrant households is especially marked among female-headed households, with almost four-fifths of the return migrant heads being unemployed, compared to 47 percent of the non-migrant female heads. As is shown in Table 17, the relationship between employment and migratory status is statistically significant with a modest degree of association (Tr = .14). Furthermore, the pattern of relatively high rates of unemployment for migrant heads and the return migrant heads is reproduced over the five-year period prior to the survey, although the differences are not statistically significant (see Table 18). Only about 42 percent of the migrant and return migrant heads reported full employment during the five years, compared to 53.6 percent for the non-migrant heads. Whereas 19.4 percent of the non-migrants had been out of work for two or more years, this was true of approximately 29 percent of both the migrant and return migrant heads.

The fact that many of the heads of migrant households are parents of a migrant may mean that the inability of the parent to secure viable employment was a factor that induced the son or daughter to seek work outside the country (or the family to sponsor the trip). This possibility is significant because it indicates the complexity of

TABLE 17
*Employment of Head of Household in Santiago, 1980,
by Sex and Migratory Status*

	Male-Headed			Female-Headed		
	Non-migrant (%)	Present Migrant (%)	Return Migrant (%)	Non-migrant (%)	Present Migrant (%)	Return Migrant (%)
Unemployed	20.3	36.5	29.8	47.0	76.7	78.0	68.2
Employed	79.7	63.4	70.2	53.0	23.3	22.0[a]	31.8
Weighted N	(311)	(37)	(39)	(90)	(31)	(16)	(524)

Chi^2 = 18.661; p < .001

Goodman & Kruskal's tau$_r$ = .14

Source. Project data, Santiago Survey.
[a]Fewer than 5 cases.

social factors motivating emigrants. Emigrants themselves, that is, need not be unemployed but may be members of extended families where unemployment looms large. Alternatively, the very fact of having a son or daughter working abroad may have tended to produce a dependence on remittance payments rather than on local sources of employment. It is probable that both of these motivating factors are at work.

Relative Labor Surplus and Emigration

The New York data reveal that Dominican labor exports draw from a disproportionately young and educated population.[5] The median age of the New York sampled population is 32.9. The educational levels of New York respondents were significantly higher than na-

5. Since we are interested in analyzing the impact of labor exports on the urban economy, only migrants who reported their last residence in the Dominican Republic to be urban (n = 239) are included here. The Santiago survey included the employment history of all household members present at the time of the survey but did not include the employment history of migrant members prior to departure. For this reason, our survey of Dominican migrants living in New York is utilized here. The fact that this is a snowball sample (see Chapter 3) means that generalizations from this sample to the broader migrant population must be made with caution.

TABLE 18

Employment, over a Five-Year Period, of Head of Household
in Santiago, 1980, by Migratory Status

	Non-migrant (%)	Present Migrant (%)	Return Migrant (%)	Total (%)
Fully employed	53.6	42.2	42.8	51.3
Unemployed for 1 year or less	15.0	7.8[a]	12.1	13.9
Unemployed for 1–2 years	12.0	20.8	15.3	13.3
Unemployed for 2 or more years	19.4	29.0	29.8	21.5
Weighted N	(365)	(47)	(53)	(465)

Chi² = 8.357, not significant

Source. Project data, Santiago Survey.
[a]Fewer than 5 cases.

tional Dominican averages. As can be seen from Table 19, even when we compare the New York migrant population with the population of the capital of the Dominican Republic, which is known for educational levels higher than the national average, we see a disproportionate concentration of migrants in the higher educational levels. Whereas only 7.6 percent of the population of Santo Domingo in 1981 had completed thirteen or more years of school, 17.2 percent of our sample of urban migrants living in New York had done so. Moreover, while only 13.0 percent of the sampled Dominican New Yorkers had completed less than three years of school, this was true of 28.0 percent of those living in Santo Domingo. The median number of school years completed by the New York migrants is 8.2.

To address the issue of labor surplus or the extent to which labor exports draw from the working labor force, we asked migrants about the nature of their last employment immediately prior to departure from urban areas in the Dominican Republic. The overwhelming majority (69.8 percent) of the migrants reported that they had in fact been working prior to departure. This means that only 30.2 percent of them were without some kind of employment, and this pattern holds for males and females alike. It is true, how-

TABLE 19

Educational Levels of New York–Based Migrants
from Urban Communities Compared to the
Santo Domingo Population, 1981

Years of Education Completed	Urban Migrants (%)	Santo Domingo Population (10 years+) (%)
0–3	13.0	28.0
4–6	22.4	26.1
7–9	23.9	23.1
10–12	23.5	15.2
13 or more	17.2	7.6
N	(238)	—

Source. For urban migrants, project data, New York Survey. For
Santo Domingo population, ONAPLAN 1981: 32, table 27.

ever, that this figure is higher than the unemployment levels of
Santo Domingo (19.3 percent) and Santiago (18.5 percent) in 1977,
the two largest urban zones (ONAPLAN 1981: 6). Thus, migrants
come disproportionately from the unemployed. Yet, one must keep
in mind the fact that most of the migrants are younger than the
average economically active person in the Dominican Republic,
and the unemployment levels of younger workers tend to be much
higher than that of the population as a whole (ONAPLAN 1981: 6).
What is notable here is that the migrant population sampled in this
survey does not come predominantly from an unemployed or displaced labor force.

It is nonetheless possible that although migrants held jobs prior
to departure, they were significantly underemployed or occupied
insecure and unstable jobs, perhaps in the low-skilled or informal
sectors of the economy. In this case, their decision to look for
foreign employment would not be likely to cause significant imbalances in the home economy, since they would readily be replaced
from the abundant pool of unskilled, unemployed workers concentrated in Dominican urban communities. Figures in Table 20 compare the occupational attainments of emigrants prior to departure

TABLE 20

Last Home-Country Occupation of Dominican Urban Emigrants
Compared to Resident Population

	Dominican Urban Immigrants, 1981 (%)	Santo Domingo Population, 1979 (%)	Dominican Urban Zones, 1981 (%)
Professional and technical	19.9	8.6	8.9
Managers and proprietors	4.5	3.9	2.5
Clerical	11.5	9.8	11.4
Sales	15.4	14.3	14.3
Drivers	5.7	5.3	2.0
Artisans, operatives, laborers (except farm)	24.4	28.5	30.1
Personal service (including private household)	12.8	26.3	21.6
Other (including agriculture)	5.8	3.3	9.2
N	(156)	(2,673)	(736,069)

Source. For Dominican urban immigrants, project data, New York Survey. For Santo Domingo population, ONAPLAN 1981: 17, table 9. For urban zones in the Dominican Republic, *1981 Dominican Census,* quoted in Larson 1984: 48, table 20.

with those of Dominicans living in Santo Domingo and also with Dominicans in all urban zones.[6] As is shown in Table 20, emigrants do not come disproportionately from the lower strata of the occupational pyramid. On the contrary, they are more heavily represented in professional, technical, and kindred jobs than are adult Dominicans in the capital city or all urban zones in the Dominican Republic. Almost one-fifth of the emigrants reported such jobs, compared

6. It is important to note that the Dominican 1981 census includes a high percentage (23.9) of urban occupations not identified, which makes precise comparisons with our sample difficult. For this reason the ONAPLAN data based on the Santo Domingo population (column 2) are important for comparative purposes.

to only 8.6 percent of the population of the capital city, which is known to have a high concentration of professional employment, and to 8.9 percent for all urban zones. Most of the other occupational categories are fairly closely matched for the emigrants and the broader urban Dominican population, with the exception of service workers, where the emigrants are substantially underrepresented (12.8 percent, compared to 26.3 percent for the capital city and 21.6 percent for all urban Dominicans). However, we are not dealing here with a drain of the most highly trained Dominican professionals. A disaggregated look at the jobs held by migrants *within* the professional and technical trades reveals a high concentration in the lower-skilled professions, with an especially large proportion of elementary school teachers.

In order to assess further the loss to the Dominican Republic of these workers, it is important to specify the industrial sector in which migrants were employed prior to departure and to assess the general employment levels of these sectors. These data are presented in Table 21. The last jobs held by migrants were generally in sectors of the economy with relatively low levels of unemployment, at least as measured in the capital city of Santo Domingo. Migrants worked with less frequency than the Santo Domingo population as a whole in two of the three sectors with the highest rates of unemployment (construction and personal and social service), whereas almost 30 percent of the migrants worked in a sector with one of the lowest rates of unemployment (commerce, restaurants, and hotels), compared with only 20.6 percent of the resident population of Santo Domingo. It is unlikely that these persons felt threatened with redundancy. More plausibly, migrants employed in such sectors were likely to have been regularly exposed to foreigners and tourists, who continually exhibit a life-style and consumption level not attainable by service workers or low-level professionals in the Dominican Republic.

Given the unrepresentative nature of our New York survey, these results must be interpreted cautiously. Taking into account the limitations of the sample, however, the overall results bring into serious question the notion that Dominican emigrants, especially illegal ones, are predominantly unskilled, unemployed workers. It is not objective unemployment that most immediately motivates Dominican migrants to leave their island. Thus, the central question in evaluating the impact of this population loss becomes

TABLE 21

*Last Home-Country Sector of Employment of Dominican Emigrants
Compared to Resident Population*

	Dominican Immigrants, 1981 (%)	Santo Domingo Population, 1979 (%)	Rate of Unemployment, Santo Domingo[a] (%)
Manufacturing	20.8	17.1	13.0
Construction	3.1	5.5	32.6
Transport	8.1	5.1	18.2
Commerce, restaurants, hotels	29.5	20.6	6.5
Personal and social services	28.9	47.3	10.8
Other (including agriculture)	9.4	4.4	6.1
N	(149)	(1,051)	(145)

Source. For immigrant's last occupation, project data, New York Survey. For Santo Domingo population and rates of unemployment, ONAPLAN 1981: 10, table 4.

[a]Calculated by dividing the number of unemployed in each sector by the total economically active in that sector.

that of the degree of ease with which such workers could be replaced in the Dominican labor market and the relative scarcity of educated workers and lower-level professionals. This issue is one to which we return in the conclusion to this chapter.

Return Migration

An important consideration in assessing the impact of emigration on national development is the extent of return migration, with its possibilities for infusions of capital, productive investments, and skills and ideologies learned abroad. Larson (1987) provides an overview of the return migrant population as identified by the 1981 census. It must be noted, however, that return migrants are defined by the 1981 census as those persons who resided abroad in 1976. This accounting omits all episodes of migration before and after 1976, although it includes persons who were born abroad (Larson 1987: 175). The portrait of return migrants that emerges from these data is the following. First, return migrants constitute a very small proportion (0.5 percent) of the Dominican national labor force. Almost 88 percent of the total reside in urban areas. The majority (66.7 percent) lived in the National District (Santo Domingo) area, followed by 13.9 percent in the Santiago region and 11.6 percent in the Cibao region. Second, return migrants were more highly educated than either members of other migrant households or the non-migrant population. Third, return migrants were members of occupations more prestigious than those of the general population: for example, 12.2 percent were professionals, compared to 4.2 percent, and 12.5 percent were office workers, compared to 5.3 percent.

Most notable were the vastly superior incomes of the return migrant population: the median monthly income for return migrants was 400 pesos, compared to 213 pesos for other members of migrant households and 124 pesos for members of domestic or non-migrant households (Larson 1987: 187–91). It is not apparent from the analysis, however, whether the return migrants have higher rates of unemployment than the non-migrant population. Larson concludes that, in spite of the apparently advantageous position of the return migrants, their overall impact on the local labor force is negligible: they are "not present in sufficient numbers to make a significant difference" (Larson 1987: 199).

Our representative sample of Santiago households allows us to compare the subsample of households containing return migrants with the rest of the Santiago population in order to characterize further the experience of those who return and to judge their probable impact on the home economy. Although not as significant as Santo Domingo, Santiago is nonetheless a major site for the resettlement of return migrants (11.0 percent of all households of Santiago include at least one return migrant).

It has sometimes been argued that international migration exacerbates internal migration, with many rural dwellers using foreign employment to finance resettlement to an urban area in the sending country. If this were true, one would expect the number of return migrants reporting former residence in rural areas to be disproportionate to the number in the non-migrant population. The survey data, however, do not confirm this interpretation. It will be recalled that the heads of the three household types (non-migrant, present migrant, and return migrant) have about an equal likelihood of having always resided in the urban area of Santiago: 45.0 percent of the non-migrant households, 43.9 percent of the migrant, and 41.9 percent of the return migrant households (see Table 13). Among those families who had moved to Santiago from other parts of the Dominican Republic, the present migrant and return migrant families were less likely to have come directly to Santiago from a rural area—6.1 and 6.4 percent, respectively— than the non-migrant households (10.1 percent).

Actually, more return migrants are native residents of Santiago than Table 13 indicates. Those cases where the head of a return migrant household reported his or her place of last residence to be outside the country were excluded from the above analysis, but in fact 65 percent of the return migrants reported that their penultimate residence had been the urban area of Santiago. It is consistent with these data that a slightly higher proportion of the heads of return migrant households were born in the urban area of Santiago: 50.1 percent, compared to 44.8 percent for the migrant households and 43.0 percent for the non-migrant households.

Former rural dwellers do not, then, form a majority of the returnees. They do, nonetheless, constitute a sizable group. Perhaps for this reason, they have made an indelible impression on the consciousness of many native dwellers of Santiago, who are fond of the stereotype of the rural dweller, the *campesino*, returning from New York with a lot of cash and little capacity for "proper" urban consumption. Indeed, it is our impression that in the early 1980s, members of the Santiago upper middle class were especially fond of the idea that return migrants were "upstart" *campesinos* disguised in dollars and gold chains. This attitude reflects the classic hostility held by the "traditional" middle class toward the rapidly upwardly mobile among its ranks. The Dominican with a rural accent who buys a new house in Santiago with cash may be dominant in popular imagery but, as our survey data indicate, is not in fact the most typical return migrant.

The amount of time spent abroad by an adult member may affect the degree of familial and community disruption experienced. It is also true that the longer the time spent in the foreign society, the less likely the migrant is to return (Böhning 1984). In this regard, the Caribbean migrant stream differs significantly from the Mexican pattern of labor migration to the United States. Mexican migrants can easily return to their communities of origin at various times during the year; some return as often as several times a month (Cornelius 1976; Portes 1979; Reichert 1981; Massey et al. 1987). This is true, moreover, even of undocumented workers, because of a loosely enforced border policy and the relatively low cost of travel home.

For Dominicans, the journey from the home community to the protection of the Hispanic community, especially in the New York area, is expensive; hence Dominican migrants tend to stay for relatively long periods. Table 22 presents the distribution of the duration of stay abroad for those Dominicans who had returned by 1981 to Santiago to live after employment experience overseas. The duration refers to periods of time (excluding vacations) in which the source of employment was foreign work. Fewer than one-third of the returnees stayed abroad for less than one year, and fully one-half of all Dominicans who left their country and returned home to live by 1981 had resided outside for more than three years. Some stay for considerable stints; almost one-quarter reported having lived abroad for ten or more years.

The 1981 census data showing higher than average educational attainments of return migrants are confirmed by our Santiago data. The data summarized in Table 23 show that return migrants are relatively more educated than the general population, although the differences reported are not statistically significant. Return migrants are underrepresented among those with no formal education and in all the lower ranks of educational attainment. By contrast, almost 45 percent of return migrants report having completed at least one year of high school, compared to only 28 percent of the non-migrants. And slightly more return migrants than heads of non-migrant households report having completed one or more years of university education. Also notable is the extent to which the heads of present migrant families are overrepresented in the lower educational levels and underrepresented in the higher ranks, particularly university education. Many of these family heads are parents of adult migrants; they are thus likely to be older than the non-migrant population and hence to have fewer years of schooling.

We have already seen that the higher educational levels of re-

TABLE 22
*Duration of Stay Abroad of Return Migrants
in Santiago*

Duration of Stay (years)	Return Migrants (%)
1 or less	29.6
1–2	18.5
3–5	21.0
6–10	6.2
11–15	13.6
16–20	11.1
Weighted N	(81)
Median stay = 3.0 years	

Source. Project data, Santiago Survey.

TABLE 23
Education of Head of Household in Santiago, 1980, by Migratory Status

Years of Education Completed	Non-migrant (%)	Present Migrant (%)	Return Migrant (%)	Total (%)
0	18.4	24.1	8.9[a]	18.1
1–3	9.2	14.4	8.3[a]	9.8
4–6	13.3	13.7	12.3	13.2
7–9	22.0	14.9	13.9	20.0
10–12	28.0	30.6	44.6	30.2
13 or more	9.1	2.3[a]	12.0	8.5
Weighted N	(390)	(68)	(57)	(514)
Chi^2 = .0763, not statistically significant				

Source. Project data, Santiago Survey.
[a]Fewer than 5 cases.

turn migrant families do not ensure greater labor-force participation rates for the returnees (see Tables 17 and 18, above). Equally
important, however, is the type of job the return migrant secures
when he or she does find employment (see Table 24). Return migrants who do work are proportionally better represented in the

TABLE 24
Occupation of Head of Household in Santiago, 1980,
by Migratory Status

	Non-migrant (%)	Present Migrant (%)	Return Migrant (%)	Total (%)
Professional, technical, managers, proprietors	14.2	13.7	33.0	16.2
Clerical	3.8	0.4[a]	8.8	4.1
Sales	19.7	18.4	19.3	19.5
Farmers, farm managers, agricultural laborers	9.0	0.4[a]	9.1[a]	8.1
Operatives	35.0	32.1	25.4	33.5
Personal service (including private household)	12.6	28.5	1.4[a]	13.0
Laborers (except farm)	5.7	6.5[a]	2.9[a]	5.6
Weighted N	(366)	(49)	(54)	(469)

Chi^2 = 37.094, p < .001

Goodman & Kruskal's tau$_r$ = .01

Source. Project data, Santiago Survey.
[a]Fewer than 5 cases.

higher-skilled occupations than are non-migrants. Fully one-third of all employed returnees who are household heads hold professional, technical, or managerial jobs, compared to only 14 percent of the sampled non-migrant population. Return heads are also more likely to hold clerical jobs (8.8 percent) than are non-migrant heads (3.8 percent). Similarly, the return migrant heads are underrepresented as operatives, compared to non-migrant heads (25.4 and 35.0 percent, respectively). Only 1.4 percent of the return heads held jobs in personal or domestic service, compared to 12.3 percent of the non-migrant heads. While the reported differences are statistically significant, the degree of association is weak.

How may we explain the higher occupational status of return migrants? While it could be the case that return migrants achieve higher occupations because they acquired greater human capital abroad, we do not believe this is the proper explanation. Instead, we would argue that, first, migrants had relatively greater human capital to begin with and, second, the relatively more skilled of the emigrants were the more likely to return.[7] Upon their return, fortified with savings to sustain a more extended search for desirable employment, some succeeded in landing relatively attractive employment, and the others (especially those with less human capital) remained unemployed for longer periods or, as we shall see in our discussion of our ethnography of returnees, returned to the United States.

The Fragile Conditions of Return

It has sometimes been observed that whatever skills return migrants have often do not match the labor demand in their home countries. Frustrated job searches and unemployment are common experiences which result in disillusioned workers seeking to re-emigrate (Böhning 1984: 185). In contrast to this more pessimistic view, Báez and D'Oleo have argued that return migration in the Dominican Republic has helped to stabilize the middle class (Báez Evertsz and D'Oleo Ramírez 1985). There is much circumstantial evidence to lend credence to this optimistic view. In particular, the very visible housing developments that are associated in the minds of most with New York money support the premise that returnees have established solid middle-class life-styles in the Dominican Republic. Indeed, interviews with several Dominican bankers confirmed the fact that the great bulk of home mortgages in the Dominican Republic since the early 1980s have been granted to return migrants or "absent Dominicans" (*dominicanos ausentes*). Thus, the dependence of this banking sector on Dominican foreign employment is extraordinary.

Our ethnographic research in return migrant neighborhoods in Santiago in the early 1980s reveals the fragile basis of the middle-class life-style of many return migrants. If judged strictly by Dominican standards of income, the return migrants clearly rank as middle class. We found, however, that the bulk of these households are not able to meet their consumption needs through *locally* generated income and instead remain dependent on income acquired

7. The skill selectivity of return migrants has also been noted in the Jamaican case (Nutter 1986).

outside the Dominican Republic.[8] Nearly two-thirds of the thirty-five households included in our sample obtained all or the majority of their income from U.S. sources. These sources included savings, child support, alimony, and salaries acquired by temporary U.S. employment. The latter source reflects the existence of a pattern of circulating migration which characterized almost one-fourth of the returnees. While circulating migration has not been typically associated with the Dominican Republic in the past, it may be that as the economic crisis described in Chapter 2 intensified, the income gain from short-term employment became more attractive. Only 22.8 percent of the households relied totally on local sources of income, with 14.3 percent existing on income from both the United States and the Dominican Republic.

The question arises as to whether the economic dependency we have described is temporary, an outcome of the fact that the majority of the return households are in an initial reconsolidation phase. In this case, the return households would either be missing primary providers who still resided in the United States or would have recently resettled and be exploring investments or new employment. Closer scrutiny of the family situations of the households dependent on U.S. sources of income, however, does not confirm this idea of a temporary dependence soon to be overcome. We found six households that are missing primary providers and subsisting largely on remittances from these absent members. Three of these return migrants were separated or divorced from the spouse, who was providing alimony and/or child support in U.S. dollars. These are instances of economically dependent, divided households that are unlikely to become socially and materially reunited in the Dominican Republic. One of the remaining three was a woman, aged thirty-five, who was planning after a five-year separation to rejoin her husband in the United States; another, a twenty-seven-year-old woman who had been resident in the Dominican Republic for less than one year spent in a prolonged, unsuccessful job search, planned to return to her family in the United States. The last woman, with a resident spouse in the United States, had already lived apart from him for four years and intended to wait

8. The ethnographic findings reported below should be interpreted with caution, since the number of cases was small.

another four years until her husband retired and returned home. There is little reason to believe that these divided return-migrant households will evolve into households that are no longer dependent on U.S.-acquired income.

A further indication that a few years of social and economic reconsolidation do not generally lead to a solution for the pattern of U.S. economic dependence was found among those domestic units which have resided in the Dominican Republic for one to two years and were living solely on U.S. earned savings. These households uniformly expressed an intention to return shortly to the United States. Moreover, the already noted high incidence of circulating migration among the returnees appears to be a relatively permanent solution to the lack of employment opportunities in the home country and not a temporary readjustment strategy. The following two ethnographic cases further exemplify this pattern:

Matilde, fifty years old at the time of our interview, emigrated to New York in 1962. A year earlier she had left an abusive husband and had moved back to her parents' home with her small child. Matilde did not want to strain the limited resources of her parents, who had eleven other children, so she left her daughter behind and joined a sister in New York. Nine years later Matilde was able to bring her daughter to New York, and shortly afterward Matilde remarried. In 1977 Matilde, her husband, and her daughter returned to the Dominican Republic. Matilde was tired of working so hard and wanted to return to her country of origin. Since the return, Carlos, Matilde's husband, has worked in the United States for half of every year. Carlos works in a country club which is only in operation six months of the year. So, according to Matilde, "It is perfect. Carlos is home half of the year and then goes to New York where he lives and works in the country club." Matilde has not been employed since her return and claims that "A woman should not work if the husband provides for her and their children."

Carmen is forty and her husband, Simon, is thirty-five. They emigrated in 1965 and returned to the Dominican Republic the last time in 1979, with their two children. Two previous attempts at return—lasting one and one-half and two years, respectively—had proved abortive. In both cases the small businesses Simon invested in had failed to provide the income the family required. Since the household's return to the Dominican Republic three years ago, Carmen has worked in New York for five months each year. Simon, who has established himself as a moneylender in Santiago, also works approximately one month per year in New York, in a cousin's store.

Both these cases show creative solutions to the difficulty of surviving on local sources of income. As such, they illustrate the broader pattern uncovered of a return migrant population hoping to reintegrate into the local labor force but doing so only with considerable difficulty.

The introduction of skills and ideas acquired abroad, and the new investments leading to increased employment and capital circulation, are often pointed to as positive contributions by return migrants. Our ethnographic data, however, indicate scant evidence that the exposure to new ideas and opportunities, assuming this occurs at all, translates into usable skills or widens the range of entrepreneurial activities in which returnees engage. First, there is a redundancy in the types of businesses returnees establish. The majority of our entrepreneurial informants had established themselves as moneylenders and owners of groceries, restaurants, and gasoline stations. Several key informants attributed what they perceived as high rates of business failure and reemigration by returnees to such redundant activities. Second, many of the "new businesses" established by return migrants represented skills or interests they had had prior to emigration. For example, of the eleven male returnees who were currently merchants, seven had been either shop owners or salespeople prior to emigration. Third, the experiences of Dominican women in the United States, in particular in the garment industry, typically translated into unemployment upon their return to Santiago. While approximately one-half of the thirty-five female return migrants had worked in the United States, all but one of these women were unemployed in the Dominican Republic after their return. The following case illustrates a perception among some return migrants that they are often taken advantage of in the Dominican Republic.

Rosario, who had been a floor lady in a U.S. garment shop, said that she had learned "how to run a factory." When she returned to the Dominican Republic, she brought five sewing machines with her, intending to start her own shop in Santiago. She soon abandoned the plan because, in her own words, "Electricity and rent are high and arbitrary. The company is hard up and charges exorbitant rates to those people it thinks can afford it. Consequently, the company takes special advantage of returnees. . . . I wasn't going to subsidize the electric company with my hard-earned income."

Finally, we uncovered minimal evidence of educational attainment in the United States among returnees. Only two of thirty male return migrants in our ethnographic sample had completed some formal education in the United States, and the formal training of women was almost exclusively restricted to beautician classes.

Our urban ethnography did reveal some slight employment generation among the return migrant enterprises. That is, a total of thirty-five workers were employed in the fifteen enterprises established by the return migrants. In a country of high unemployment, even modest increases in jobs are important. However, it should be recalled that more than half of the entrepreneurs were reestablishing the same type of business they had owned prior to emigration. Thus, it is very likely that many of these jobs were not actually new, but reestablished. The expectation that returnees would be entrepreneurs who would be able to multiply their U.S. savings through diversified investments at home also proved false. Of the twelve return migrant households that had businesses in Santiago at the time of the research, only two had been able to expand and diversify by reinvesting profits obtained in the Dominican Republic.[9]

9. Since the completion of our investigation, a study of the linkage between remittances, returnees' savings, and the development of small enterprises in Santo Domingo and Santiago has been conducted by Alejandro Portes and Luis Guarnizo. They also conclude in this 1989 study that the bulk of remittances were destined for household consumption. Nonetheless, their survey of 113 small businesses owned and/or operated by returnees and immigrant entrepreneurs does provide a more dynamic and successful picture of migrant entrepreneurial activity than does our study. For example, they found evidence of modest job creation and income generation: an average of seven workers per surveyed firm, and average monthly wages of U.S. $138 (Portes and Guarnizo 1990: 13).

The fact that they obtained more positive findings than we did is influenced by at least two factors. First, very different research methodologies were employed. They chose to study entrepreneurial activity and thus sought out migrant enterprises. By contrast, we sought a broader characterization of the migrant and returnee population and thus utilized household survey and ethnographic research methods. Second, the New York immigrant community has matured over the decade of the 1980s, and with this have come greater financial investment and commercial involvement back home. For example, Portes and Guarnizo found that 42 percent of the sampled businesses continued to receive capital from abroad and that owners reported periodic trips to stimulate new investment among immigrants (Ibid.: 16).

Beyond its economic impact, return migration has affected the Dominican Republic in important cultural and ideological ways. Most dramatically, the visible signs of the success of returning migrants have intensified aspirations for styles of consumption associated with life in developed societies. Modern consumption values are created and catered to by advertisements from foreign and local firms seeking to expand the internal market for their products. The situation is fueled by migration itself. Return migrants bring with them the consumption orientations characteristic of New York. Indeed, many of the consumption patterns common abroad are exaggerated among return migrants intent, perhaps, on compensating for years' of status deprivation in New York, or used as protection against the perceived contempt of the traditional middle class, which tends to view return migrants condescendingly as *nouveaux riches*. It should be recalled that Dominicans have been migrating to New York in significant numbers since 1964. Over twenty-five years of exposure to waves of returning "absent Dominicans," to use the local term, be it for visits or for temporary or permanent residence, have contributed to the craving for foreign consumer goods and for inaccessible life-styles. The examples abound. One has only to stand at the international airport in Santo Domingo during the Christmas season to witness this inflow of modern consumption symbols—the ubiquitous electrical appliances, the conspicuous New York swagger and East Coast fashions of Dominican migrants. Moreover, the almost exclusive dominance by Dominicans in New York of the new housing construction on the island reinforces the idea that the most prominent forms of growth are fueled abroad.

Migrants experience a great deal of social pressure to prove themselves, perhaps to compensate for the sacrifices their families have made in order to send them abroad. A popular refrain in the Dominican Republic, spoken to someone about to depart for work in the United States, is, "If things go well for you over there, write."[10] The clear implication is that if things go poorly, the migrant should not add the failure to the historical record and per-

10. "Si te lleva bien allá, escribe." This is the refrain of the popular song "Elena" by the Dominican group Quatro Quarenta. The song describes the misfortunes of Elena, a Dominican who leaves in a boat and encounters the drug-filled underworld of New York City.

haps, more to the point, should think twice before returning. In this way, the successes of emigrants become mythologized while their misfortunes are minimized.

Since the time we began our research in 1980 in the Dominican Republic, we have noticed a change in the way the upper middle class tends to view "absent Dominicans." In the early 1980s, we heard many instances of ridicule of those who went abroad because they needed to improve their social position at home. Jokes about *campesinos* arriving in Manhattan laced many urban conversations. However, since then, the economic crisis of the 1980s has stung even the most affluent and reinforced the perception, even within the upper middle class, of a paucity of local sources of dynamism. By the late 1980s, expressions of contempt for returnees appear to have diminished among the traditional middle class. Perhaps this is because more from their inner circles have opted to leave. One upper-class woman from Santiago even suggested to us, in 1988, that a national monument ought to be erected in honor of the sacrifices of the *dominicanos ausentes.* "If it weren't for them, nothing would be happening on this island," she commented.[11] The idea of a statue representing the absent heroes and heroines illustrates the almost mythic standards by which the accomplishments of migrants have come to be measured against a backdrop of high inflation, economic recession, and soaring unemployment in the home economy.

Participant-observation and interviews revealed that returnees have invested their savings and income in commodities and memberships that symbolize a middle-class standard of living, including an American car, private-school enrollment for their children, and membership in prestigious social clubs. Unfortunately, for many return households the acquisition of these markers of social mobility carries with it the risk of undermining the economic foundation needed to sustain so extravagant a life-style. In other words, the pursuit of upper-middle-class consumption patterns in the Dominican Republic threatens the economic stability of the aspirants.

11. It is only fair to point out that this same woman, when reminded of her comments a year later, had a more ambivalent attitude toward the returning Dominicans because of the recent spread of illicit drugs in the Dominican Republic and the association in the minds of many between illegal drugs and migrants from New York.

Many returnees attributed their previous unsuccessful attempts to reestablish themselves at home to an inability to limit their consumption to a level that matched their income.

This growing external orientation undermines a positive sense of national identity. It would be difficult to exaggerate the extent to which New York life-styles are esteemed by certain sectors of the aspiring middle class. In 1979, even the Dominican state conceded the relative attractiveness of foreign symbols over national ones. The official state tobacco corporation, La Tabacalera, launched a national campaign to promote a new cigarette that was designed to challenge the recent market advances made by Marlboro. The name selected, after extensive market research, for the indigenous attack against the cowboy symbol of Marlboro was Hilton!

Another ideological factor that emerged in our ethnographic research was the dissatisfaction expressed by many return migrant women with the traditional gender roles in the Dominican Republic. As has already been noted, employment among returnee women in the households studied was extremely low. Some of the women shared Matilde's traditional belief, as described above, that a woman should not work when her husband is a good provider. But the majority of the women missed working for wages and bridled under their renewed dependency on their husbands. In the case of Carmen and Simon we see the tensions dramatized:

> While Simon was satisfied with the arrangement of return trips to New York to sustain the money-lending business in Santiago, Carmen was unhappy that she had to give all her wages to Simon for his business and for the maintenance of the household. Her desire for the household to return to the United States was based in large part on her desire once again to have greater control over how her own and the household income were administered. Carmen resented the fact that now, back in the Dominican Republic, Simon had assumed control over the household budget, even though the bulk of the income was furnished through Carmen's labor.

Men commonly asserted control over household decision-making and expenditures even when the family income came from savings from money both husband and wife had earned in the United States. Nor was this a "business as usual" situation. As we describe in detail in Chapter 6, these patriarchal patterns reverse more egalitarian patterns of household decision-making that prevailed in the United States, where both husband and wife were wage earners. Several of the "circulating" migrant women indicated that they were motivated in part by the desire to achieve greater financial independence than was possible as unemployed women in the Dominican Republic. Moreover, all the women in the nine households that indicated an intention to return to the United States stated that their desire to work and become less dependent on their husbands was a primary motive for reemigration. These gender-role dissatisfactions uncovered among return migrant women are not likely to translate directly into collective feminist demands of equal pay for equal work by the non-migrant population in the Dominican Republic, but they have nonetheless been a factor in the negative experiences and adjustment problems of some return migrant households, and they must be included in any general account of the impact of return migration on the home society.

The 1981 Dominican census, in defining return migrants as those living abroad in 1976, excluded short-term migrants who may have been the relatively unsuccessful return migrants. In contrast, our survey and ethnography of return migrants in Santiago in 1981–1982 included recent arrivals and return migrants of many years. Our approach revealed the high failure rates and external dependency which probably characterizes the return migrant population at any point in time. Undoubtedly, some portion of the return migrant population does successfully integrate itself locally. As we saw from the results of the 1981 census, the incomes and occupational attainments of these returnees are impressive and clearly superior to the non-migrant population. The point, however, is that the return migrant pool at any given time also includes a substantial segment whose unemployment level is higher than that of the non-migrant population and whose investments, such as they are, are often redundant and uncoordinated with any national development strategy.

Conclusion

If we look at migration from the perspective of the migrants' stated intention of social mobility, then we must conclude that the migrants and their household members in the Dominican Republic have by and large been successful. That is, regardless of high levels of external income dependence, members of migrant households have attained the markers of a middle-class standard of living. Income from abroad is used to buy goods and services in the home community which otherwise might not be purchased.

From the perspective of the state bureaucracy and the dominant class, migration has permitted thousands to acquire the sociocultural trappings of upward mobility without the wrenching transformations that such mobility would have required if it had been generated locally. Furthermore, the state has been absolved of some of the responsibility of helping this new middle class maintain its comfortable standard of living, since in many cases this life-style is subsidized by transfer payments from abroad and by the circulation of household members between the Dominican Republic and the United States. Finally, this exchange eases the political pressures of widespread underemployment and low wage levels.

The early emphasis on capital-intensive industrialization in the Dominican Republic meant that the mobilized, unskilled work force could not be adequately absorbed; yet it is *not* for the most part these workers who migrate. A growing percentage of the relatively educated, lower-level professional workers have also been unable to find secure employment. Dominican urban labor exports from the early 1960s through the early 1980s fall somewhere between the categories of unskilled labor and professional workers. It is true that migrants come from sectors of the economy with relatively low levels of unemployment. But this is compared to the overall high levels of redundancy characterizing all sectors of the economy. In none of the sectors from which migrants predominate do conditions appear to approximate labor scarcity.

Contrary to popular belief, labor exports have not drawn heavily from the large pool of marginalized workers. It is not the unemployed themselves, but the relatively skilled and educated, whose wages and security are threatened indirectly by the existence of a large reserve of labor, who choose to migrate. The migrants are workers who, precisely because of their relatively advantageous positions, were able to finance the expensive move to the United States. They are persons motivated by a sense of insecurity, by a desire to improve their wages and general comfort, and by a conviction that although they themselves have jobs, overall conditions are insecure and have begun to operate against them as well. They aspire to a different kind of consumption pattern: one available to the wage worker in the United States, not to the lower ranks of the middle class in the developing world. One migrant in New York explained that when he left Santo Domingo in 1965 he had had a good job as a printer but all around him he could see smart, talented people without work. Fear of becoming like them coupled with the desire to give a better life to his new wife meant that he made use of his "dreamy" spirit and packed up.

The steady erosion in real salaries in the Dominican Republic since the mid-1960s, combined with the dramatically increasing salary differential between the Dominican Republic and the United States over the same period, has made even the most reluctant Dominican evaluate the costs of staying put. Under such conditions those with the resources and "social capital" to get out have often opted to do so.

Any evaluation of the costs of out-migration to a sending society must be provisional, since both the nature of labor exports and the manpower needs of the sending society can change over time. For example, it is only possible to argue that the loss of trained and relatively educated workers signals a shortage of trained manpower or a "brain drain" if it is apparent that such workers are irreplaceable in the short run and that their exit results in other factors of production lying idle (Reubens 1980: 435; Anderson 1988). In the Dominican Republic, the problem has been, not a shortage of educated workers per se, but rather a shortage of effective demand for such workers. The dramatic increase among the unemployed of those with secondary education was noted in Chapter 2. Under such conditions, it is not accurate to argue that emigrants represent irreplaceable societal investments; on the contrary, they have been in oversupply. The larger question, in terms of national development, centers on the rationality of high investments in advanced education, to the detriment of primary education or agriculture, for example, when effective demand for high-skilled labor is not on the horizon. Higher education, despite its intrinsic value, has created expectations for social mobility that have not been met. The emigration outlet has thus far proved an effective escape valve, reconciling the contradictions between high societal investments in educated workers and society's inability to employ such workers at levels of remuneration that make their training worthwhile.

Most Dominican migrants leave home with the desire to return to their country. But their permanent return is problematic. Many have important, albeit limited, investments to make in their communities and could presumably be encouraged to do so with modest incentives or policy initiatives designed to provide credit and pricing breaks for small-scale productive investors. Currently, however, the Dominican state prefers to continue to finance the relatively costly education and training of a labor force which continues to opt for employment, legal or otherwise, at higher wages in the United States.

5

Dominican Rural Emigration

A holistic treatment of the topic of Dominican emigration requires a consideration of rural out-migration. As we have already discussed, we now recognize the urban origin of the majority of Dominican immigrants to the United States. We also know, however, that numerous agricultural communities have sponsored large numbers of emigrants and that emigration has had a significant impact on the sending communities (Hendricks 1974; Pessar 1982; Bray 1983b; Grasmuck 1984a; Castro 1985; Georges 1987; Ravelo and del Rosario 1986). Although fewer than one-third of all Dominican emigrants come from rural areas, concentrated, selective emigration can be extremely important to the sending communities and to the agricultural economy as a whole.

Research on out-migration from agricultural communities commonly focuses on the reciprocal relationship between migration and development. On the one hand, researchers seek to determine how different modes of agricultural production (e.g., subsistence versus capital-intensive farming) affect rates of migration (Bach 1985a). On the other hand, they debate migration's impact on agricultural production and on well-being in rural migrant communities (Böhning 1975; Griffin 1976; Rubenstein 1983). The central issue is whether out-migration ameliorates or exacerbates social and economic inequality in rural sending communities. Many early researchers assumed that migration would ultimately result in less population pressure on shrinking land bases, increased production and productivity in sending communities, and greater economic opportunities in agriculture for non-migrants (Griffin 1976). Unfortunately, much current research on the impact of migration on agricultural sending communities does not support these optimistic expectations (Rubenstein 1983; Reichert 1981; Rhoades 1978).

Before conclusions can be drawn about the negative consequences of out-migration for development, however, important questions of causation must be addressed. The literature that documents the deleterious effects of migration on rural development is plagued by the chicken-or-egg dilemma. Do the deteriorating social and economic conditions which provoke emigration persist whether or not out-migration occurs, or does emigration exacerbate those conditions? Moreover, how do we determine what a negative impact on "the community" is, when community members and classes may be affected differently by migration patterns? In their assessments of the impact of emigration, both equilibrium and dependency theorists have paid little attention to the class structures of migrant sending communities. This is highly inadequate treatment, since the impact of emigration depends on the social class from which the migrants originate and the economic relations these migrants and their remaining family members maintain with non-migrant community members.

As an alternative to these approaches, in this chapter we rely on an analytical framework that includes the following elements: social class composition; relations of production within rural migrant communities; and flows of people, money, goods, and information out of and into labor-exporting communities. It is only within such an expanded analytical framework that we can account for the fact that migration affects different segments of the rural population in different ways.

Juan Pablo: A Case Study of a Rural Migrant Community

Juan Pablo, it will be recalled, is located in the eastern half of the Cordillera Central (Central Mountains) in a region known as the Sierra. Were we to use a map to locate the *sección* we have named Juan Pablo, we might be fooled into thinking that transportation, commerce, and communication between this agricultural community and Santiago are relatively simple and frequent. In fact, poor roads and the lack of electricity and phone service militate against such easy access and interchange. Juan Pablo is a relatively isolated and backward community. It is characterized by poor ecological conditions (e.g., thin topsoil, eroded hillsides), backward farming techniques (predominantly slash-and-burn), and relatively few opportunities for employment outside of agriculture. Coffee and cattle are the community's major agricultural commodities. According to the 1981 Dominican census, the town and hamlets that comprise the *sección* of Juan Pablo had a combined population in 1980 of approximately 4,121 (ONE 1983).[1] Our own two surveys of the town of Juan Pablo and four neighboring hamlets revealed that approximately one-fourth of all households had one or more emigrant members.

Juan Pablo, 1880–1961

Juan Pablo was founded in the 1880s by a *hatero* (livestock breeder), who, according to informants, possessed a vast herd of cattle. Señor Rodríguez had discovered the deserted countryside when he was searching for a way to escape the overpopulated range around San José de las Matas in the Western Sierra. As was the case with all land in the Republic at that time, the countryside had the status of *terreno comunero* (communal land). Only usufruct rights over this communal land could be transferred, in the form of purchased shares. Señor Rodríguez purchased rights to 770 shares (*pesos*) of land (approximately 962 hectares).

Families from overpopulated or drought-stricken communities of the Western and Eastern Sierra soon converged on Juan Pablo, seeking land to farm or on which to raise livestock. In a few cases, newcomers were freely granted the right to work the land; most settlers, however, paid the Rodríguez family. These new arrivals staked out land that was not already claimed, generally following natural boundaries such as streams or outcroppings.

The year 1920 marked a watershed for the community. With the establishment of the national cadastral survey in that year, land passed from being a factor of production with use-value to being

1. We believe this census figure includes many emigrants who were residing in the United States at the time of the census.

defined as a privately owned commodity. The survey introduced the first shadowy traces of what were later to become permanent class divisions within Juan Pablo.

On the national level, the survey was motivated by American commercial interests wishing to protect and extend their investments in sugar plantations (M. Knight 1928: 104). Although the survey failed to reach many of the most mountainous areas of the country (Georges 1990), surveyors did arrive in Juan Pablo. Or, to be more precise, they were contracted by a few of the most prosperous agricultural families, who wished to have their property rights formalized and legalized. In the words of an elderly informant who witnessed the survey:

[These families] were not afraid of land grabs by outsiders. What they feared was their neighbors, because we all had the same rights. There were no property boundaries based on law. If there are laws, then indeed they must be respected, but if there is just consensual understanding, then one can honor it or not. In the survey, they sought a legal right to defend their property.

As was demonstrated by a feud in 1918 over property boundaries which left two men dead, consensual agreement between neighbors did not necessarily accord with the expansionist aspirations of certain farming families.

The man who championed the local survey had been the first in the community to plant coffee. He was also one of the earliest muleteers to transport food crops from Juan Pablo for sale in Santiago. In fact, what appears to have been the specific motivation for the survey was an attempt by the small merchant-capitalist class of muleteers/agriculturalists to protect and expand agricultural production at the expense of herding families. The latter favored livestock breeding on unenclosed, communal grazing land. This interpretation would account for the "curious" fact that the cattle-raising descendants of Señor Rodríguez did not pay to have their property surveyed, whereas the muleteer/farming families did. Several other herding and farming families also did not have their land surveyed for lack of funds.

Rancor among the descendants of pioneering families still exists more than sixty years after the survey. Those families whose land was not surveyed were confined to the property that they were actively exploiting at the time of the survey. As a consequence, the descendants of these families who live in Juan Pablo today often find themselves landless or living on less-than-subsistence plots. Paradoxically, this is the condition faced by many of the direct descendants of the founding Rodríguez family. By contrast, those who contracted for the surveyors' services apparently claimed far larger tracts than they had originally purchased and staked out. One resident of Juan Pablo quoted an epigram to characterize this controversial appropriation of vast stretches of communal land: "He who has more saliva can gulp down more pastries." In sum, the 1920 survey both stratified the population with respect to property ownership and, according to informants, raised land values so that most later settlers could not afford to purchase as expansive tracts of land as the earliest arrivals had obtained.

Until the mid-fifties, most economic activity in Juan Pablo revolved around subsistence agriculture. Only the principal beneficiaries of the survey, the muleteer/farming families, engaged in commercial activities such as growing cash crops, buying local surplus and selling it in Santiago, and running local stores and warehouses. Carlos Ureña, an octogenarian in 1981 who had been part of this elite group, encapsulated the basic peasant economy of those decades in the following anecdote:

Let me tell you what it was like back then. People ate well, better than they do today, because they raised all that they ate. Most had full bellies, but not a penny in their pockets. Now, I always had my little reserve. So back in '34 a neighbor comes to me and he is desperate. He is finally marrying a nice girl from a good family and he doesn't have a penny for a wedding suit. So this poor fellow straight out offers to sell me two hectares of land if I will give him the money for the suit. That's what it was like in those days.

On the one hand, as this anecdote shows, Juan Pablo's peasant economy afforded the merchant-capitalist class the opportunity to purchase land cheaply. Carlos Ureña, for example, did purchase the humble groom's two hectares, as well as some ninety additional hectares from other proprietors over the years. On the other hand, the basically subsistence economy furnished little local surplus for this merchant class to market in Santiago. Moreover, these merchants, who were also large landholders, could not increase production greatly on their own land, because there were few local field hands for hire. Consequently, those farmers who regularly cultivated crops for sale in Santiago relied on a system of labor exchange (*juntas*) during periods of high labor demand.

Faced with the problem of accumulating capital to invest in commerce and farming, a few of the merchant elite of Juan Pablo looked to more distant markets. In 1941, the first Juan Pablo native emigrated to the United States. He was followed by a handful of other young men who departed in the forties and fifties. A few of these men worked in New York for three or four years and returned with several thousand dollars to invest in businesses, land, and real estate in Santiago and in Juan Pablo. In these early years, however, the majority of the population did not have the social and political contacts,[2] funds, or, in many cases, sufficient motive to emigrate.

The 1950s marked another watershed in the history of Juan Pablo. At this time, changes internal and external to the community challenged its basically precapitalist economy and social structure. The internal changes involved land shortages and soil erosion. The external changes were prompted by the community's incorporation into national and international coffee markets.

The shortage of land evolved as a result of the survey of 1920, in combination with local population growth. The survey limited the possibility of land acquisitions for most of the Juan Pablo farming families. For three decades these people had reared large families and divided their land equally among all heirs,[3] but after the survey many of the younger generation faced the prospect of working below-subsistence plots of land. For example, the two daughters of the founder of Juan Pablo produced a total of twenty-five children. Their offspring in turn produced one hundred and forty-four children, many of whom laid claim in the 1940s and 1950s to the much

---

2. According to Christopher Mitchell (1987), no more than a few hundred Dominican citizens held passports at the end of the 1950s, under the security-obsessed regime of General Trujillo. Mitchell observes that travel to the United States was a privilege reserved for the Dominican social and political elite.

3. This practice did not subdivide the land as much as might be expected, since women generally resided on their husbands' land, and sisters commonly sold their shares of inherited land to one or more of their brothers.

reduced and fragmented family estate. A case history illustrates the problem:

In the 1930s and early 1940s, Casimiro Rodríguez, a grandson of the founder, lived comfortably with his family of six boys and seven girls on the twelve hectares Casimiro had inherited. In the mid-1940s, when the sons began to marry and ask for family land to work, the landholdings no longer sufficed. In fact, two sons tried to ease the pressure on the family land by migrating temporarily in the fifties to the southeast coast of the Republic. There they worked for an American-owned banana exporting company. Other sons supplemented farming on their own land with occasional stints of working on the farms of larger landholders.

This fourth generation was the first in which all members could no longer continue the peasant mode of production that had characterized the community for so many decades.

Furthermore, beginning in the 1950s, agriculturalists faced declining ecological conditions. Throughout the Sierra, decades of deforestation led to run-off that eroded the land and depleted the rich topsoil (cf. Secretaría de Estado de Agricultura 1978).[4] As soil fertility diminished in Juan Pablo, so did the average yield per hectare planted. This situation posed special problems for small-holding households, who routinely had to supplement subsistence agriculture on their own land with sharecropping and wage work to meet their families' basic consumption needs.

Thus, by the 1950s, several Juan Pablo households faced the threat of downward mobility. For some the threat signified a transition from occasionally profiting from agriculture to merely subsisting upon it. For other households subsistence itself was in danger. Like the two young men in the Casimiro Rodríguez family, about fifty others responded to the shortage of family land and of money to buy additional property by migrating temporarily in pursuit of work in the banana industry. Another thirty or so families sold their small plots in Juan Pablo and headed for cheaper, more abundant farmland near the southern city of Bonao.

The second challenge to Juan Pablo's economy and social struc-

4. This deforestation occurred as increasing numbers of farming households relocated from the overpopulated valleys to mountainous wooded areas. There they cleared the land, cutting trees and removing the underbrush using slash-and-burn techniques. Forests also declined when the lumber industry was introduced in the teens and twenties in selected Sierra communities.

ture had its origins in a growing market demand for the type of coffee grown in the community. Whereas population growth, and soil erosion threatened to lower class standings throughout the community, the favorable market for coffee held the promise of raising the class position of a select few and rescuing other families from downward mobility.

Members of the merchant-capitalist class were the prime benefi-ciaries of the new ties to national and international markets. Since the 1910s, when mule-train owners carried potatoes and beans from Juan Pablo to Santiago, members of these families had culti-vated business and social relations with members of Santiago's com-mercial elite. These contacts proved invaluable to the next genera-tion as it negotiated purchase prices and arranged advances with large coffee-exporting houses in Santiago and Puerto Plata. These advances were used to buy provisions for the merchants' stores and to extend interest-bearing loans to local coffee producers. In most cases, members of the merchant-capitalist class also expanded cof-fee production on their own lands. The increased labor that coffee planting, conditioning, harvesting, and processing required was met by a newly formed, permanent pool of local laborers who needed to work for wages. By the late 1950s, merchant capital extended beyond mere circulation in the Juan Pablo economy. It now entered into the production process itself as merchants estab-lished relations with local farmers based on interest and with local laborers based on wages.

Local coffee producers had sufficient landholdings to grow food crops for household consumption while at the same time investing additional land, household labor, and capital in coffee, but in the early years of increased production these households commonly found themselves short on funds to invest in improved strains of coffee, in wage labor, and in technology—factors of production that would increase their profits over time. A number, however, were able to secure comparatively low-interest loans from members of the merchant-capitalist class. In this transaction, members of these large and mid-sized landholding families received preferential treat-ment because of their kinship and marriage ties to members of the merchant-capitalist class. This group of coffee producers also im-proved their class position. In the past, they had relied largely on household labor and had occasionally produced surpluses that were sold to the muleteers. Now these households began to use wage labor periodically and were able to reinvest their profits in increased coffee production. This group emerged as a new petty-capitalist class.

Expanded coffee production did not benefit all households, however. Coffee crops required greater cash outlays than traditional food crops, and tracts dedicated to coffee plants could not be intercalated with any food crops other than bananas. Many small-scale coffee-producing households could neither dedicate several hectares to coffee nor afford the added expense of processing and storing the beans. They found themselves in debt to merchant-moneylenders during most of the year, having contracted both for high-interest loans (some 3 to 5 percent per month, a much higher rate than the 2 percent or so paid by the petty capitalists) and for store credit. For these households, coffee production did not bring economic improvement or stability. In fact, for some families it brought a decline in class position. In years of low market prices, bad weather, or personal hardship, these households slipped deeply into debt. This caused some to supplement farming on their own property with wage work. For others, such temporary wage work was insufficient; the debtor was forced to sell his coffee, at a loss, when it was still on the vine or, worse still, to forfeit parcels of his land to the creditor. Many such households eventually were forced into permanent wage labor.[5]

Juan Pablo's Social Class Composition in 1961

In 1961, at the start of large-scale emigration to the United States, the Juan Pablo economy was basically agrarian.[6] The vast majority of the households were engaged in one or more facets of agricul-

5. For an excellent analysis of class formation in a Venezuelan coffee-producing region, see Roseberry 1983.

6. Information was gathered on the eighty-six households that had resided in 1961 in the town of Juan Pablo and in four neighboring hamlets. That is, household histories were collected for all households that had resided at that earlier date in the communities included in our 1981 census. Our attempts at historical reconstruction were aided, in our opinion, by the fact that 1961 was the year of Trujillo's assassination and thus was highly memorable. We believe that the households on which information was gathered were fairly representative of the entire *sección* of Juan Pablo at that time.

tural production and marketing. Five distinct social classes were situated within this local agricultural economy.[7] Some 7 percent of the households belonged to the capitalist class, as evidenced by their control of relatively large quantities of land and other capital, their heavy reliance on wage labor, and their ability to accumulate and reinvest capital on a regular basis. Most members of this capitalist class gained their livelihood by combining farming with commerce and moneylending. Another 15 percent of the households belonged to the petty-capitalist class. Members of this class controlled quantities of productive resources that exceeded the amount that could be worked solely by household labor. These households had sufficient capital to allow them to supplement household labor with wage labor on a periodic basis. The largest class, the household labor class, included some 47 percent of all Juan Pablo households. This class controlled sufficient land and other capital to support its household members, but did not have sufficient surplus to hire additional labor. The fourth class, the semi-proletariat, numbered approximately 22 percent of all Juan Pablo households in 1961. Those belonging to this class did not control sufficient resources to meet their household members' production and consumption needs without complementing subsistence farming with wage work. Finally, 9 percent of the population were members of the fully proletarianized class, relying exclusively on wages for survival.

The Class Composition
of the Emigrant Population

What impact has emigration had over the last few decades on the community's class structure and social relations of production? To answer this question we must begin by describing the emigrants' class backgrounds. Members of each of the community's five social classes had reasons to find emigration a solution to changed economic circumstances. Both modernization and dependency theories of migration lead us to suspect that the bulk of the emigrant population would have come, however, from the semi- and fully proletarianized households, since in many cases these domestic

7. In defining distinct social classes, we have slightly modified definitions developed by de Janvry (1982) and Bray (1983b).

units suffered from an absolute labor surplus. For households with little or no land, emigration represented a clear solution to the problem of land fragmentation, diminished productivity, and low-ered socioeconomic standing. These are not, however, the classes that produced the majority of the emigrants. Indeed, exactly the opposite was the case, as Table 25 shows.

Over the last two decades the capitalist and petty-capitalist classes have accounted for a little more than one-fifth of the total population, yet these households have dispatched over one-half of all the emigrants from Juan Pablo. Two concurrent factors serve to explain these data. First, since the households belonging to these two classes no longer had to rely on unmarried and married house-hold members for their labor needs, some began to reevaluate the kinship norm that encouraged fathers to furnish their sons with land at the time of their marriages in exchange for periodic contribu-tions of labor. This norm led to the fragmentation of family holdings and thus interfered with the senior generation's goal of expanding coffee production. For these households, then, the emigration of adult sons represented a solution to a new relative surplus in house-hold labor—a condition that will be discussed in detail in the next chapter. And, second and more generally, the money and social contacts needed to sponsor an emigrant were unequally distrib-uted, being far more available to members of the capitalist and petty-capitalist classes.

Migration and Class Relations

As Table 25 shows, major changes have occurred in Juan Pablo's class composition between 1961 and 1981. Before examining how emigration has affected this recomposition, we must point out one important difference in the types of economic activity available to households in 1961 and in 1981. As was mentioned earlier, in 1961 almost all of Juan Pablo's households were engaged in some facet of agricultural production and marketing. By 1981, however, house-holds were engaged in a range of economic activities. Two social classes, the household laborers and the proletariat, have been par-ticularly affected by this diversification.

In 1981 the household-labor class no longer included only subsis-tence farmers. Rather, twenty-three of the fifty-seven households

TABLE 25
Social Class Distribution of Juan Pablo Emigrant
Population, 1961–1981

	Total Population 1961 (%)	Total Population 1981 (%)	Emigrant Population[a] 1961–1981 (%)
Capitalist	7	5	26
Petty capitalist	15	16	25
Household labor	47	35	28
Semi-proletariat	22	14	14
Proletariat	9	30	7
N	(86)	(189)	(276)

Source. Household histories and 1981 census of the town of Juan Pablo and four hamlets.

[a]Based on the social class of the emigrant's household at the time of departure. An emigrant is defined as one who resided in Juan Pablo at the time of emigration or had once resided in Juan Pablo and continued to maintain regular economic contacts with family members or friends in Juan Pablo.

belonging to this social class derived the majority of their income from a specialized craft (e.g., carpentry, masonry) or operating a family ("mom and pop") business. Another fifteen households had abandoned most, if not all, work in agriculture, either as direct producers or as wage laborers, and were totally or almost totally dependent on emigrants' remittances.

The composition of the proletariat has also changed over these two decades. It is necessary now to distinguish between those wage workers who receive fixed salaries (*asalariados*), largely from jobs in the state sector (e.g., teachers, road workers), and those workers who are occasional laborers (*jornaleros, echa-días*). The latter group are employed predominantly in agriculture. In 1981, 30 percent of the sixty-six proletariat households received the majority of their income from salaried employment; the remaining 70 percent of these households gained their livelihood through occasional labor, predominantly in agriculture.

Let us now consider the role, both direct and indirect, that emigration has played in promoting the recomposition in Juan

Pablo's class structure. As Table 25 shows, the two highest social classes have experienced virtually no recomposition. The percentage of households belonging to the capitalist and petty-capitalist classes has remained basically the same over the twenty-year period. Migration has helped to maintain this condition.

The capitalist class now found in Juan Pablo is in many ways a product of international migration. It is comprised predominantly of transnational extended migrant households. The men who head these households were born into the elite families and remained in Juan Pablo while their siblings emigrated. As a consequence, these non-migrants have been given access to large family holdings. By working these tracts, many have been able to accumulate profits that have been invested in additional land, labor, and technology.

The petty-capitalist class is a truly transnational class. It is composed largely of absentee (emigrant) landowners who employ overseers to work large and medium-sized tracts of land. Production decisions concerning land use and hiring practices are for the most part made by the migrant-owner in the United States.[8]

Unlike these two classes, the household labor and semi-proletarian classes have failed to maintain their share of households in the overall structure. Their percentage decline is also a product of a migration of sorts. Over the years, household-labor and semi-proletarian households have sloughed off sons and brothers. Many of these disenfranchised individuals have moved into the town of Juan Pablo and have entered the ranks of the fully proletarianized.

In the next section we document how the production strategies of the capitalist and petty-capitalist households have been heavily influenced by emigration. It is our contention that some of their

8. In our 1980 census of Juan Pablo, we ensured against multiple counts of the same emigrant by having each household report only on members who had departed directly from their household rather than on non-resident relatives. Households with such members were classified as migrant households. This convention does have the limitation of categorizing many households as non-migrant even though their productive activities are directly influenced by emigrants in the United States. Our ethnographic research, however, has allowed us to recapture and analyze these links, as will be seen in our discussions of transnational extended migrant households and overseer households. Moreover, through our ethnographic research we have been able to collect valuable information on emigrant families totally missing from our survey data because the heads of their families both of orientation and of procreation no longer reside in Juan Pablo.

migration-influenced strategies have directly contributed to the disenfranchisement and proletarianization of members of the household-labor and semi-proletarian households.

Sharecropping

In the 1950s and 1960s, large landowners and members of household-labor, semi-proletarian, and proletarian households found in sharecropping a productive relationship that served both the owner and the sharecropper. The sharecropper provided the staples that the landowner's household members formerly grew when they engaged in household production, and the landowner provided the sharecropper with land on which to raise food for his family.[9] This mutually beneficial, albeit unequal, relationship has largely disappeared. Of the one hundred and eighty-nine households included in our 1981 census, only six derived the majority of their income through sharecropping. As members of Juan Pablo's poorest households explained, they themselves were the unwitting foot soldiers for the gradual disappearance of sharecropping. In the 1970s, large landowners (migrant and non-migrant alike) contracted sharecroppers to clear overgrown tracts of land. For the first year or two the sharecropper was permitted to prepare a *conuco* (a plot of land used to grow staples). However, once the crops were harvested and the land conditioned, the sharecropper was requested to plant the parcel in grass. This process went on for several years, until much of the available land suitable for sharecropping had been converted to pasturage and fenced in.

Emigration has indirectly spurred the abandonment of sharecropping and the transition to cattle raising. During the 1970s, a few incidents of land invasion took place in communities close to Juan Pablo, with sharecropping families refusing to abandon the land they had worked. Emigrants who sharecropped some of their land feared that their land might be similarly invaded.

Another blow to the practice of sharecropping came with an agrarian policy introduced in 1972 by the Balaguer government. A new law gave tenants the legal right to claim land they had been

9. In most cases the sharecropper provided all the labor and seeds and halved the harvest with the landowner.

working for several years. It also advised that owners and tenants/ sharecroppers enter into formal contractual relations. This law, although never enforced in Juan Pablo, nevertheless convinced many landholders, especially those who lived abroad, that sharecropping had become a complicated and risky endeavor that was no longer worth their while.

Finally, there was speculation that the Dominican government might claim unutilized land and redistribute it to the landless. Church-supported groups composed of smallholding and landless families who demanded access to land were also gaining strength in Juan Pablo in the 1970s. This development exacerbated fears of land seizures.

The many Juan Pablo families that had left their inheritable land with non-migrant brothers felt especially vulnerable to these new developments. In most cases, the non-migrant brother was able to work only a portion of the property intensively, leaving the remainder fallow or placing it in the hands of sharecroppers. Conversion of such "underutilized" land into pasturage became the landowners' hedge against takeovers by either sharecroppers or the government.

Semi-proletarian households were most deeply hurt by both the precipitous decline in sharecropping and the transition to cattle-raising. These households had generally been able to meet their basic consumption needs by combining household labor on their own land with sharecropping and agricultural wage labor. The following case history exemplifies how the decline in sharecropping and the transition to cattle-raising have caused many Juan Pablo households to sink into the ranks of the fully proletarianized:

In 1974, fifteen households sharecropped and worked regularly on Sosu Collado's farm. That year, since he was growing old and all his sons were in New York, Sosu decided to sell his farm. A relative, Milo Collado, who was residing in the United States, purchased the farm. Milo immediately hired an overseer and instructed him to remove all the sharecropping families, burn the coffee plants on the property, and sow grass seed. With the loss of access to land for sharecropping and the precipitous decline in labor demand, seven of the fifteen households were forced to leave their family land and settle elsewhere. Four of the households relocated to the town of Juan Pablo; the other three settled in rural communities in another *sección*. With this move, most of the disenfranchised households passed from the ranks of the semi-proletarianized to those of the fully proletarianized.

The strategy of raising cattle in lieu of growing food crops or producing coffee is a controversial one in Juan Pablo. Indeed, for many non-migrants, cattle-raising has become a symbol and a symptom of all that is wrong with emigration from Juan Pablo. Consider the words of two critics, the first a merchant and the second a day laborer:

The best land here, land that is well suited to agriculture [i.e., food crops], has been converted to pasture. It is the fault of those men who seek their livelihood in New York and do not care whether there is production and employment here.

I know, I am a storeowner. In the past there was plenty of food to go around. But now we shopkeepers have to bring beans, rice, and potatoes from warehouses in Santiago. And these staples are so expensive that the poor day laborer now fills his children's bellies with ten cents' worth of bread rather than thirty cents' worth of beans.

I look at a cow and I see my enemy. . . . Here in Juan Pablo a cow on thirty *tareas* [approximately two hectares] eats better than my children. And should I try to buy some beef for my family—a peso and a half per pound! Tell me how I can afford that, when I make a mere three pesos a day, if I'm lucky enough to find work. It's a curse, and I place the blame on those high and mighty gentlemen who have gone to New York.

The wisdom of the large-scale transition to cattle-raising has been questioned by officials connected with a national development project for the Sierra region. Agronomists working in Juan Pablo estimated that in 1981, approximately 80 percent of the land base was dedicated to cattle-raising. They have tried to convince landholders to make the conversion from cattle to coffee. They have explained that coffee is more profitable. For example, one cow raised on two hectares of land in 1980 yielded a net profit of 330 pesos. The same amount of land dedicated to coffee cultivation netted almost twice the profit—640 pesos. Agronomists have also argued that coffee production helps employ the local labor force, at an average of more than double the person-hours required for cattle. Finally, they have pointed out that coffee plants help retain topsoil, whereas grazing cattle deplete this valuable resource. These arguments have convinced some resident landowners to increase coffee production, but the agronomists have had virtually no success with the largest group of landowners—the absentee owners. As we shall see, most emigrants prefer cattle-raising because it is neither labor- nor capital-intensive, and it requires minimal supervision.[10]

Overseeing

The practice of overseeing the land of absentee owners is relatively new to Juan Pablo. There are three distinct forms of overseeing property. The first is the most preferential to the overseer. In this case, the landowner lends the overseer his property. There is often an understanding that the overseer will tend the owner's cattle in exchange for the free use of land for agricultural cultivation. Of the twenty-one households in our 1981 census that derived the bulk of their income from overseeing, twelve had arranged these terms. In almost every case, the overseer was a poor relative of the emigrant landowner. In the second form, adopted by six households, the overseer-owner relationship is patterned on the principles of sharecropping. The overseer receives property with fixed capital, such as coffee plants and cattle. He is responsible for contributing all the additional inputs necessary to produce a marketable commodity. The owner and overseer divide the profits from sales equally. In the last and least common form (followed by three households), the overseer is strictly an employee of the landowner. Under these conditions, the overseer receives a salary which, when calculated on a daily basis, is two to three times higher than a hired hand's daily wage of three pesos (U.S. $2.20).

The job of overseer is a coveted one. It guarantees full-time work and allows the overseer to enjoy a standard of living far higher than that enjoyed by most non-migrant households. When we collected a detailed annual household budget for an overseer, we learned the following: first, the overseer and his family raised the bulk of their food on the property they were working; second, even though the overseer had to assume all the production costs and split the profits,

10. It should be noted that the Dominican government has been promoting the policy of cattle-raising for export since 1966. Dominican cattle producers have been rewarded with a favorable price structure: between 1966 and 1977 the export price of beef rose tenfold (Georges 1990).

he realized a net profit of some 1,500 pesos (U.S. $1,100) from the sale of coffee; third, when the yearly household consumption costs were subtracted from the overseer's profits in coffee and milk, he ended the year with a total profit of 300 pesos (U.S. $220). We can better appreciate his success when we realize that most Juan Pablo household-labor and semi-proletarian households finish the year in debt.

Although emigration has brought direct economic and social benefits to the few overseer households, other non-migrant households have received few or no spillover benefits. In the overseer–absentee owner relationship, capital- and labor-intensive modes of production are avoided. The overseer, who is usually required to absorb all production and transformation costs, lacks sufficient capital to expand production by investing in additional technology and commodities (e.g., tractor, coffee plants, cattle). Furthermore, since the property is not his, he has no real incentive to improve the holding by investing in additional coffee or spending his savings on upgrading the land. Since cultivation of food crops, such as beans and rice, is highly labor-intensive, most overseers do not grow much beyond what is needed for household consumption. Overseers, like absentee owners, tend to favor cattle-raising, which requires minimal labor costs. For example, seven hectares dedicated to cattle-raising require an annual average of 500 person-days, while seven hectares planted in beans require 1,200 person-days over a year, if planting is done in four cycles. Overseers also attempt to keep labor costs low by relying heavily on household labor.

Property placed in the hands of an overseer does not provide agricultural laborers with the employment opportunities that would very likely exist if the migrant were managing his own land. This is the case because resident owners tend to complement cattle raising with the production of more labor-intensive commodities such as coffee, beans, and rice.

Capitalist and Petty-Capitalist Farmers and Agricultural Wage Workers

We have already noted that employment opportunities in agriculture have declined greatly. This lack of employment has been especially punitive to Juan Pablo's semi-proletarian and proletarian classes. The main cause of unemployment—the transition to cattle-raising—has not only deprived these classes of much needed employment, but has also deprived them of land to sharecrop and access to cheap, locally grown staples.

One group, however, has continued to employ local wage workers in relatively large numbers: the non-migrant siblings of transnational extended migrant households. Although their numbers are small—only five households among the one hundred and eighty-nine included in our 1981 census—they are the leading employers in the community. Each employs a year-round work force of three to ten employees while contracting more than sixty workers a day during the three peak months of coffee harvesting. This group engages in a mixed pattern of commodity production. The profitability of this comparatively labor-intensive strategy is evidenced by the fact that these men are the wealthiest and most entrepreneurial farmers in Juan Pablo.

On the positive side, emigration has allowed these men to work large tracts of family land. The profits they have made have given them the opportunity to invest in more land, hired hands, and technological improvements. On the negative side, emigration has played a role in dissuading many from increasing coffee production and consequently employing more workers. This is the case, because many emigrants continue to exert not only direct but indirect influence on the production decisions of their non-migrant kin in Juan Pablo. Members of transnational extended migrant households pride themselves on being united, by which they mean that despite the death of one or both parents, the heirs have not divided the patrimonial estate. This practice benefits non-migrant siblings who have invested heavily in cattle, since their herds are free to graze vast ranges. However, it has thwarted the desires of some of the most entrepreneurial non-migrant farmers to expand coffee production to neighboring tracts of land.

These farmers are constrained from extending coffee production to land which they may not be able to purchase in the future from migrant siblings, or their wives and children, when the patrimonial estate is formally divided. Theoretically, those who inherit land that has been improved with fixed capital, such as coffee plants, are expected to compensate the purchaser for the improvements. In practice, such improvements have often occasioned heated conflict among family members. Consequently, non-migrant members of migrant families are reluctant to make such investments on their own. When non-migrant siblings have made overtures to their emigrant relatives about dividing the land and then purchasing parcels, they have frequently heard the rebuff, "We are guests in the United States. There's no telling when we may be forced to leave. A family's most valuable security is land. Leave things as they are."

The gains to be made in cattle are less than those for coffee, but the costs and profits associated with cattle are far more predictable. Livestock is thus often chosen over coffee, to avoid accusations over the misuse of funds or the misrepresentation of profits. This decision is common in those cases where the migrant sibling receives one-half to one-third of the profits from the sale of the commodity produced on the land he or she will eventually inherit.

With reasonable profits to be made in coffee production, absent migrant family members might on the face of things have been expected to invest their locally derived profits in expanded coffee production on the land they stand to inherit. The explanation of their failure to do so serves as an illustration of why it is important to trace flows of labor, capital, and goods within and outside a migrant community. Our research shows that rather than reinvesting their profits from local agriculture in expanded production, migrants most commonly invest in construction of one or more homes in Santiago. These migrants are at once profiting from the comparatively cheap labor available in Juan Pablo and redirecting the surplus these workers afford them to commodities and activities that in no way benefit the local labor force.

From the perspective of inter-class relations, however, it is the landholding migrant households that are headed either by resident wives or by elderly parents that most constrain the employment of non-migrant semi-proletarian and proletarian households. These migrant households tend to cut back on almost all agricultural activities and instead use migrants' remittances to meet their members' consumption needs. These households, it should be noted, are far more numerous than the households headed by resident siblings of transnational extended migrant households.

We found in our 1980 census of the town of Juan Pablo that

migrant households were more likely than non-migrant households to report diminished levels of agricultural production over the last ten-year period or over a lesser period of time in which they had been engaged in agriculture—58.8 percent, as compared to 31.7 percent. Only 11.8 percent of the migrant households stated that their production levels had increased over the last decade, as compared to 29.3 percent of the non-migrant households. Finally, only 41.2 percent of migrant households with land stated that they cultivated all of their land, compared to 71.4 percent of the non-migrant households with land. Migrant households were also more likely than non-migrant households to report that they cultivate only approximately one-half or less of their total landholding—41.2 percent, as compared to 26.2 percent.

Although nonproductive migrant households derive little or no income locally, this shortfall is more than compensated for through the regular receipt of remittances. Nonetheless, some are clearly losers in their transition from commercial-farming household to remittance-dependent household. The losers are those members of non-migrant households who spend the bulk of their days unemployed and whose members are forced to make drastic cuts in their daily expenditures for food and other basic necessities. Daily household budgets and employment records were kept over a six-month period for eight households (see Table 26). The male heads of the fully proletarianized Almonte and Ríos households worked an average of only 2.8 days a week, and in consequence they could afford to spend little more than two pesos a day on food and other household staples. In comparison, the totally remittance-dependent Nuñez and Cruz families averaged a daily rate of 11.17 pesos and 13.22 pesos, respectively, on food and other staples. This marked contrast in daily expenditures between non-migrant and migrant households was not influenced by differences in family size: for example, the five-member Ríos family spent 49 centavos per capita, and the five-member Cruz family spent 2.64 pesos per capita.

Land Transactions and Property Values

Migration has had notable impacts on land sales and land values. In some cases, land transactions have led to changes in local households' class standing. First, several household-labor families lost

TABLE 26
Daily Average Expenditures of Selected Rural Households

Family	Major Source of Income	Members, by Age	Average Daily Expend. (D.R.$)	Average Daily Expend. Per Capita (D.R.$)
Non-migrant:				
Almonte	Agricultural wage labor	40, 34, 16, 12, 11, 9, 7, 5, 4, 2, 1	2.27	.21
Díaz	Farming	70, 35, 13, 11, 9, 3, 1	1.87	.27
Ríos	Agricultural wage labor	37, 32, 13, 9, 6	2.43	.49
Tavera	Carpentry, dressmaking	51, 51, 23, 17, 15, 14, 10, 8	6.46	.81
Migrant:				
Alvarez	Remittance	25, 22, 20, 19, 14, 12, 9	7.48	1.07
Cruz	Remittance	35, 13, 12, 10, 7	13.22	2.64
Nuñez	Remittance	50, 48, 20, 18, 17, 14, 5, 4, 2	11.17	1.24
Ureña	Remittance	72, 72, 39, 27, 26, 15, 8, 7	8.56	1.07

Source. Project data, Juan Pablo Ethnography.

most or all of their land to what they characterized as "the illusion of migration." These households had placed their property as collateral when borrowing money to underwrite a member's unsuccessful emigration. If they had not attempted to sponsor a member's emigration, most, if not all, of the brothers would have been able to subsist on the family land. With most or all of their land forfeited to the guarantor, these men have been forced to join the ranks of the semi- and fully proletarianized.

Second, in the first decade of migration some migrants chose to invest in land. They offered their Juan Pablo neighbors large sums of money, raising local land values by 400 percent or more. As the sellers now lament, "we were dazzled by all the money, but we have long since eaten those profits." These former members of the household-labor class must now rely on wages and self-employment to meet household consumption needs.

During the 1970s and 1980s, land sales have become less common as community members in Juan Pablo and abroad have come to recognize the social and economic security that property represents. As a result of this tight market, land prices are beyond the financial means of all but select members of the local capitalist classes and their migrant members.

In 1980, a local peasant association tried to break this monopoly on land sales by purchasing land with the help of a Santiago-based religious order. The peasant association hoped to provide fifteen poor households with land. At the last moment, the sale was held up over a problem with the deed to the property. Rather than postpone the sale until this matter could be resolved, the New York–based owners chose to sell their property immediately, to one of the largest resident landowners in Juan Pablo. This failure so disillusioned the association that more than half of the approximately twenty members ceased attending meetings and paying their dues.

For most members of Juan Pablo's semi-proletarian and fully proletarian classes, then, migration has exacerbated the problem of inadequate access to land and has contributed to reduced demand for agricultural workers. It has intensified the trend in the community that finds members of poor agricultural households forced to abandon the agricultural sector altogether. The migration-related transition to cattle-raising and the decline of sharecropping have meant that many semi-proletarian households have had to slough off members. Such individuals, who previously had maintained themselves and their dependents through subsistence agriculture on family and sharecropped lands combined with wage employment, now struggle to meet their basic consumption needs through self-employment and wage employment.

Some households, however, have maintained or improved their class position through migration. These households have been able to take advantage of emigration to slough off surplus members, and in this way the households have avoided the problem of land fragmentation. Although this capitalist class has provided some much-needed opportunities for employment, migration-related factors constrain local demand. The consistency in the 1961 and 1981 figures on percentages of households belonging to the capitalist and petty-capitalist classes points up the fact that migration has allowed several of the more prosperous extended families in Juan Pablo to maintain their pre-emigration status in the community. For most of these households, however, migration represents a holding operation, not a means to acquire capital for expansion of commercial agriculture and to increase employment opportunities throughout the community.

Finally, a third group of households have abandoned most, if not all, forms of local income-generating activities and have become dependent on remittances. At an earlier time, most of these remittance-dependent households had employed workers on a periodic basis. Now these households neither employ much labor nor do they have members who seek wage work in the local economy. For these reasons we have categorized remittance-dependent households as members of the household-labor class. While this shift in class has left no negative traces on the standard of living such migrant households enjoy, it has contributed significantly to the shrinking number of production alternatives in agriculture available in Juan Pablo for non-migrant households.

When we place these findings in our expanded framework of the migrant community, we find that migration has neither eased class inequalities within Juan Pablo nor improved the lot of the most disadvantaged households. Furthermore, the flow of migrants' remittances and savings has not resulted in beneficial changes for the majority of the population engaged in agriculture. In fact, this capital flow from abroad has often stimulated either a transfer of commercial farming profits away from Juan Pablo into the Santiago construction industry or a removal of fixed capital (land) from local production.

Migration and the Commercial, Craft, and Service Sectors

Migration can have positive impacts on a community if remittances and savings are invested in commercial ventures that create new income-generating activities and employment opportunities. Remittances can also increase household incomes, thus heightening the demand for local commodities and services.[11] Let us consider whether migration has brought such benefits to Juan Pablo.

Of the fifteen commercial establishments located in the town of Juan Pablo in 1980—establishments which ranged from coffee warehouses to "mom and pop" grocery stores—five were started either by a migrant silent partner or by a returned migrant. Four of these establishments provided employment only for the local owner-operator and his immediate family; the other employed one full-time worker.

Several emigrants have invested in pickup trucks, which they

11. Another way to redistribute capital within the migrant community is to pass remittances as gifts from migrant households to non-migrant households. Some such transfers occur in Juan Pablo between individual households tied through bonds of kinship, fictive kinship (*compadrazgo*), and friendship, but this exchange has been more formally instituted through the creation of a charitable association whose members reside in New York and in Juan Pablo. In 1979, after six years of operation, the association had collected approximately U.S. $14,500 and had expended some U.S. $7,000 on gifts of food, clothing, and money for the community's poorest households. Although this charity has helped many, it has, nonetheless, followed and reinforced class divisions within the community—a fact that was recognized by some of the poorer community members. One man described the association in the following words: "There are many here who are fooled by these gifts. They think these gifts are free, but I know better. The donors expect respect and submissiveness from the poor families who receive their 'charity.' Let any family, like my own, complain about the low wages these rich families pay us miserable souls and see when we will again get thrown one of their bones. . . . It's like the biblical story: if you really want to help the poor you must give them nets to catch their own fish, not just charity of fish and bread. If these grand families here really wanted to help us, they would sell land to us at a fair price, not give us Christmas baskets."

operate with a local partner/driver. Other emigrants have purchased trucks as gifts for close family members who reside in Juan Pablo. A weekly lottery is the only migrant business that has created multiple opportunities for employment. In any given week approximately twenty men and two women sell numbers. The commissions these vendors earn contribute approximately one-fourth to one-half of their annual household budgets.

The impact of migration on local commerce has been greater than is revealed by a simple focus on migrants' investments in business, however. As was discussed above, migration has contributed to a reduction in the opportunities available in the agrarian sector. In the face of these reduced opportunities, many displaced members of household-labor and semi-proletarianized families have resettled in the town of Juan Pablo. While most of "rural" Juan Pablo has been losing population over the last few decades, the number of households in the town of Juan Pablo has climbed from 28 in 1960 to over 100 in 1980—this, despite much emigration to the United States. Along with this increase in the town's population have come expanded opportunities for self-employment and wage employment in commerce, services, and the public sector.

In 1960 the town had only four small general stores. By 1980 the number had grown to ten. On the one hand, there were more men and women who were no longer engaged in farming and therefore had the time to operate a store with a tiny and inexpensive inventory. On the other hand, there were more households in 1980 that bought their food locally than grew much of it on their own property or sharecropped land. This was the case for fully and semi-proletarianized households as well as for migrant households that were dependent upon remittances for their consumption needs.

Practicing a trade is a central component of the multiple income-earning strategy pursued by many Juan Pablo households. Among the most popular occupations are those of carpenter, mason, seamstress, and tailor. The impact of migration on these occupations has been mixed. Emigrants have hired local carpenters and masons to rebuild the town's church and to remodel their own or their parents' homes in Juan Pablo. Santiago, however, remains by far the most popular site to build a new home: over fifty new houses have been built there by Juan Pablo emigrants. This is further evidence that large amounts of capital and employment opportunities are bypassing the community altogether.

Local tailors and seamstresses have been less successful than craftsmen in the building trades. Juan Pablo has been virtually inundated with store-bought clothing from the United States. This clothing is sent by emigrants to relatives and friends. It is later redistributed as hand-me-downs to poorer households.[12] Not only has this large supply of clothing reduced the absolute need for locally crafted apparel, but it has affected local tastes. When new articles of clothing are sought, handmade items are spurned in favor of mass-produced fashions imported from the United States and sold in Santiago shops.

Finally, in some migrant communities located elsewhere in the Dominican Republic, migrant households have afforded poor women the opportunity to work in domestic service (Castro 1985; Georges 1990). Our 1981 census revealed only one Juan Pablo resident, however, who worked full-time as a domestic servant in a migrant household. This woman cared for the four children left behind by a widow who had emigrated to New York. Other Juan Pablo women and teen-age girls did bring in occasional earnings by cooking, cleaning, and washing clothes, but such opportunities were as likely to be found in a non-migrant household where the woman worked full-time.

Neither the equilibrium nor the dependency view of migration, with their emphasis on a homogeneous community, proves adequate to account for the effects of emigration on the social classes of Juan Pablo. According to the equilibrium view, migration should have siphoned off the labor surplus from the community and narrowed the gap between rich and poor. In contrast, the dependency view would have us believe that migration indiscriminately siphoned off valuable resources from the community and impoverished most of the residents.

As we have seen, migration can indeed alter the class structure and composition of a community. Furthermore, as labor, capital, and commodities circulate within a migration network that stretches between the place of origin and new destinations (New York, Santi-

12. This practice can sometimes lead to incongruous outcomes. For example, a local man who is a catechist and known for his strict morals sported a hand-me-down shirt festooned with nude women in pin-up poses.

ago) certain families, social classes, and labor markets benefit disproportionately while others suffer the costs.

In Juan Pablo, the nature of the capital and labor flows and their
destinations within the migration network have led to a general
impoverishment of production alternatives within this community.
Most emigrants have not viewed the land, commerce, and workers
of Juan Pablo as economic assets to be cultivated. Emigrants' risk-
aversion strategies toward potential opportunities in Juan Pablo
have led to decisions that have reduced the range of alternatives
available to most local residents. Rather than investing their savings in Juan Pablo, most migrants have directed savings to homes
and commercial ventures in Santiago or in the United States. The
following case history exemplifies the fact that while valuable resources are circulating back and forth between the Dominican Republic and the United States, Juan Pablo has tended to be the
source rather than the recipient of investment capital:

Most of the children of Juan Pérez, one of the wealthier members of the
capitalist class in Juan Pablo, are either return migrants, who reside in
Santiago, or migrants living in New York. Juan Pérez used his profits from
coffee production and merchandising to sponsor his children's emigration.
He has since directed large sums of money to business ventures, such as
food markets and restaurants, which his sons and their partners have
initiated in New York. As a silent partner in these ventures, Juan has made
sizable profits, which he has channeled either into loans to other would-be
immigrant entrepreneurs in New York or into commercial ventures in
Santiago. For example, in order to purchase a Santiago pharmacy, Juan
entered into silent partnership with a son living in New York and another
son recently returned from the United States.

Most residents of Juan Pablo have not benefited from such instances of capital flows out of the community, but one social class
has realized certain advantages. Resident members of the social
class that contributes the majority of the migrants have benefited
from the reduction in the range of economic opportunities available
in Juan Pablo. These farmers have at their disposal a local labor
reserve that is hungry for employment and dependent on small
gifts of charity and loans. As a consequence, these desperate agricultural workers have largely turned their backs on local peasant associations that in the past were successful in extracting wage concessions from employers.

Rural Emigration in a National Context

To assess the national impact emigration has had on agrarian class relations and agricultural production and employment, we need to know whether Juan Pablo is a representative rural migrant community. Unfortunately, no national data on rural emigration exist that permit a definitive answer to this query. In the absence of such national data, we must compare our Juan Pablo findings with material from the few available studies of rural emigrant communities.

Detailed information is available for only four other rural emigrant communities: Licey, Los Pinos, San José de las Matas, and Tamboril (Grasmuck 1984a; Castro 1985; Georges 1987, 1990; Ravelo and del Rosario 1986). Some comparative material can also be gleaned from studies of La Aldea (Hendricks 1974) and La Amapola (Bray 1987).[13] All these communities are located in the northern section of the country known as the Cibao.[14]

Emigrant Classes

The one finding on which there is total agreement across all six community studies concerns the class composition of the emigrant population. In each case the researchers found that at the time of departure, the majority of the emigrants belonged to the large and medium-sized landowning classes of the region. For example, of the Amapola migrants who emigrated outside the country, 15 percent originated from the capitalist class, 2.7 percent were from the peasant class, and 1.5 percent were from the working class (Bray 1987: 101–2). The Licey and Los Pinos studies show that non-migrants are found at the two socioeconomic extremes: they are the landless poor and the comparatively large capitalists among the merchants and farmers.

In her study of Los Pinos, Georges presents us with an intriguing variation on these data. Although the majority of the community's emigrant population do originate from the large and medium-sized

13. Los Pinos, La Aldea, and La Amapola are pseudonyms.
14. Our attempt to compare three key elements, predominant emigrant classes, production and employment, and remittances, has been hampered by the fact that researchers employed various methods to study these elements; moreover, not all addressed these three features.

landowning classes, almost one-fourth come from landless or below-subsistence farming households. We can infer from Georges's research that many of these members of Los Pinos's proletarian and semi-proletarian classes were recruited through emigrant networks created by some of the community's working-class women. Georges reports that almost one-half of the female emigrants were wage workers (mainly domestics) in a Dominican city at the time of their departure to the United States. These women used their urban-based social contacts and meager savings to arrange for migration abroad (Georges 1990).

There may well be, then, greater class diversity in the emigrant populations of those rural communities like Los Pinos in which capitalist agriculture took hold in the early part of the twentieth century. In these communities, displaced peasants were forced to pursue non-agricultural work both within and outside their home community. Occupations such as petty commerce and urban-based domestic labor would have given these individuals the requisite social contacts for emigration—contacts inaccessible to most rural-based peasants and farm workers who sought to emigrate.

Production and Employment

In contrast to the consistency in the comparative findings on the class origins of rural emigrants, the research findings on the impact of emigration on agricultural production and productivity vary considerably. The most positive findings come from our Licey study, where emigration was associated with increased agricultural production. According to our 1980 survey, Licey migrant households with access to land were more likely than non-migrant households to report that their agricultural production had increased over the last ten years (50.1 percent, compared to 39.9 percent). While 31.1 percent of the non-migrants with land said that they had decreased production over the past decade, only 16.9 percent of the migrant households had done so. Finally, our survey revealed that migrant households in Licey were more likely than non-migrant households to cultivate all of their landholdings (91.7 percent and 83.8 percent, respectively).

In contrast, Georges's results from Los Pinos show far less agricultural success for migrants. First, she claims that agricultural production was far higher prior to large-scale emigration in the 1960s than it was in 1981. She infers that emigration is partially to blame and backs this argument with the finding that in Los Pinos, income from commercial and subsistence agriculture contributed only 5 percent of the aggregate community income in 1981. In contrast, in a neighboring non-migrant village, agriculture contributed some 26 percent of the total income base (Georges 1990).

Georges attributes much of this decline in agriculture to the massive transition to cattle-raising. In 1980, eight times as much land was in pasture as in agriculture. Georges is careful to delineate the national and international factors that have contributed to this new production strategy, but she does acknowledge that emigrants have been at the forefront in reducing agricultural production in favor of cattle-raising. As we found in Juan Pablo, in Los Pinos she observed that large-scale cattle-raising has promoted land concentration and a decline in local demand for agricultural wage laborers and sharecroppers. In fact, she reports that one of her informants who considers himself an agricultural wage laborer was able to find only thirty-four days of such work in 1980–1981.

Finally, in contrast to results from both Licey and Juan Pablo, Georges finds that for the reduced number of households that do engage in agriculture, the production levels and earnings of migrant and non-migrant households are basically equivalent. These select migrant households apparently compensate for shortages in household labor by employing hired hands.

In the cases of San José de las Matas and Tamboril, Ravelo and del Rosario report an inverse relationship between remittances and production. That is, the average income generated locally by households that do not receive remittances is two times higher in San José de las Matas and one and one-half times higher in Tamboril than the locally generated incomes of those households that obtain remittances (Ravelo and del Rosario 1986: 16). As might be expected, they also find that emigration has led to increased unemployment among members of emigrant households (Ravelo and del Rosario 1986: 15). Inasmuch as emigration draws disproportionately from the capitalist sector of these two communities, we can safely assume that, as in other migrant communities, the relative economic inactivity of the migrant households has contributed to reduced wage opportunities in agriculture for poor, non-migrant households.

How can we account for these contrasting community-level findings? It would appear that in Licey, favorable environmental conditions, relatively easy access to national and international markets, and local opportunities for investment in agriculture and other economic activities have encouraged migrant households to approach farming as a productive avenue for capital accumulation. That is, farming provides profits that, when added to migrant members' savings from work in the United States, contribute to the goal of advancing the household economically and permitting all of the members to be reunited in the Dominican Republic.

In contrast, in light of the deterioration in the position of the agricultural producer in the country as a whole (World Bank 1981; Rodríguez Nuñez 1984) it is not surprising that migration leads to reduced agricultural production and increased reliance on remittances in geographically and environmentally marginal communities such as Juan Pablo, Los Pinos, and San José de las Matas. What is surprising, however, is the reduction in production reported for Tamboril, a semi-rural community that shares many environmental and infrastructural features with Licey. Clearly, more research is needed to uncover those factors that promote either an increase or a decrease in agricultural production in Dominican emigrant communities.

Remittances and Local Income

Comparative research findings on remittances and emigrants' savings can be divided thematically into two issues: whether these monetary flows result in community investments that increase opportunities for local income acquisition; and whether remittances and savings have reduced income inequality in migrant communities. [15]

In assessing the impact of remittances and savings on income generating activities, it is useful to distinguish between the agrarian sector, on the one hand, and urbanized commercial, craft, and service sectors, on the other. In the majority of the communities for

15. For each of the communities, the pervasiveness of remittances is impressive. For example, in Juan Pablo, 44 percent of the households received some financial aid from migrants in the United States; the figure for Licey was 36 percent.

which we have information, remittances have promoted a reduction in agricultural production and employment. When migrants have invested locally, they have favored cattle and land. Such investments have reduced the income-generating options available to non-migrant families in the agrarian sector. For example, migrants often purchase land not in order to farm but to engage in land speculation, an activity that raises land values well beyond the reach of local, non-migrant households that seek to work the land.

In contrast, the infusion of remittance income does appear to boost local commerce and services (Castro 1985; Georges 1990). There is, however, a tendency for migrant households and return migrants to invest in the same few types of activity—e.g., taxis, pickup trucks, and small groceries. This can quickly lead to a glut in the market.

It must be noted that remittance-dependent local economies are highly vulnerable, because remittances are highly unstable. These transfer payments can easily fall victim either to economic downturns in labor-importing economies or to maturing immigrant communities abroad that require a higher proportion of investment in the new community than in the one left behind (Piore 1979).

Most of the community studies show that remittances have exacerbated rather than reduced income inequality. For example, the research in San José de las Matas and Tamboril showed that those migrant households with the highest levels of local income received the largest proportion of the remittance dollars entering the community (Ravelo and del Rosario 1986: 9). The authors conclude that out-migration and the influx of remittances are factors that "only serve to increase the gap between the rich and the poor in the two communities" (Ravelo and del Rosario 1986: 13). Only in Los Pinos have remittances decreased income inequality to some extent.[16] Georges attributes these findings to the fact that many relatively poor households have been able to dispatch a member abroad. And of those households, two-thirds receive between 75 and 100 per-

16. Georges (1990) notes that equal income distribution within a given community would result in a gini coefficient of 1. She finds that despite the selective emigration pressures that discriminate against the poorest households in Los Pinos, the distribution of income there is nonetheless more equal (.54) than in the neighboring community of El Guano, with its small emigration (.37), or in Santo Domingo (.44).

cent of their yearly income in remittances from abroad (Georges 1990).

Migration and National Trends in Dominican Agriculture

The available community studies of rural out-migration, though few in number, may suggest ways that migration may parallel, if not contribute to, some of the negative trends in Dominican agriculture. First, the 1981 national census data on landholdings in the Dominican Republic showed a growing trend toward increased inequality in land ownership and toward the fragmentation of the number of hectares members of the poorest group of landholders possess. Whereas 82 percent of all the landholders possessed only 10 percent of all the land, less than 0.3 percent of all landholders—some 200 persons—possessed 36 percent of the best land in the country (Rodríguez Nuñez 1984: 27). Furthermore, the average size of the *minifundio* (small, privately owned farm) has decreased from 29 *tareas* (slightly less than 2 hectares) in 1971 to 20 *tareas* in 1981. Observers of Dominican agriculture conclude that a peasant population no longer exists, having been replaced by a rural population comprised predominantly of paid agricultural workers (Rodríguez Nuñez 1984: 26).

Emigration often militates against land fragmentation and the subsequent proletarianization of household members. Yet this is a relief available principally to the already more secure members of rural communities. Given the tendency of migrant families to invest in additional land, usually at the expense of poorer community members, we must conclude that migration contributes to the related national trends of increased land concentration among more privileged families and land fragmentation among the poor.

Unemployment and underemployment plague Dominican rural areas. The rural labor force was estimated in 1981 to be about twice as large as the demand for rural labor (World Bank 1981: 37). As the community studies show, emigration does not siphon off members of the reserve army of labor in rural areas. Rather, the production strategies developed by many migrant households have added yet more members to this rural labor reserve.

Finally, there is reason to worry about the nation's ability to feed its people. Increasingly, the Dominican Republic has been forced to import staples such as rice and beans. In 1980, the Dominican Republic imported food worth some D.R. $280 million (Rodríguez Nuñez 1984: 31). At the same time, with the blessing of the Dominican government, the amount of exported farm commodities has grown, with sugar and cattle taking the lead. As of the late 1970s, fully 56 percent of all arable land was used to graze cattle (Dore y Cabral 1979: 19). Migration appears to be contributing to this national trend whereby land formerly dedicated to food production for the domestic market is reconverted to commodity production for external markets. Research in Juan Pablo, Los Pinos, and San José de las Matas documented that many migrant households have replaced mixed cropping of staples with cattle-raising.

Growing reliance on external markets for the sale of agricultural commodities is only one side of the uneasy dependency and vulnerability that are developing within the national agrarian sector. Another threat resides in the increasing dependence on remittances on the part of previously productive farming households. With respect to this growing dependence, Ravelo and del Rosario caution that with emigration the source for rural savings and investment has shifted from local, rural economies to the United States, where Dominican emigrants live and work. These Dominican researchers conclude: "Remittances are a factor that has worsened the 'fragmenting' of the rural economy, reproducing conditions that keep Dominican agriculture in a state of crisis" (1986: 14).

In sum, emigration has not proved to be the boon to the agrarian economy that many assume. Rather, emigration's impact on land distribution and use, production, and employment parallel general negative trends found throughout the country.

6

Households and International Migration

Dynamics of Generation and Gender

Studies of migration have generally focused on one of two extremes: macro-level trends in the political economies of labor-exporting and labor-importing societies that stimulate migration (Castells 1975; Sassen-Koob 1978), and micro-level processes influencing individuals' decisions to relocate (Sjaastad 1962; Rothenberg 1977). In recent writings on migration, however, several authors have recommended the inclusion of the household as a basic unit of analysis, since it contributes to and mediates both macro- and micro-level processes (Weist 1973; Dinerman 1978; Wood 1982; Selby and Murphy 1982; Roberts 1985). In this chapter we adopt this expanded mode of analysis, and at the same time we aim to correct those deficiencies in the household approach that threaten to diminish its potential for elucidating factors that precipitate migration and condition its effects.

Of the great variety of conceptualizations of the household in social science literature, two perspectives have had a disproportionate impact on migration literature. The first perspective portrays the household as a moral economy exhibiting social solidarity and income pooling among members. The second perspective, while not contradictory to the first, emphasizes the role households play in developing strategies for survival—which usually means strategies aimed at maximizing economic gains.[1] Our fundamental criti-

1. Some researchers have sought to make an analytical distinction between the household and the family, a distinction we also find useful. For example, Rayna

cism of these two perspectives is that they fail to take into account the hierarchies of power internal to the household, especially those based on generation and gender. This omission leads to a host of faulty assumptions about the relationship of households to the process of migration.

The Household as a Moral Economy: Or, Morality for Whom?

Central to a variety of perspectives on households—perspectives as divergent as neoclassical economics and Marxism—is the notion that the household is a "moral economy" organized according to principles of reciprocity, consensus, and altruism among members (Folbre 1988). For proponents of the "New Home Economics" model, households are homogeneous units. According to their theoretical framework, this homogeneity implies two fundamental household principles. First, household preferences must be shared; in economic terminology, households must take joint utility functions. Second, household members' economic resources must be pooled (Fapohunda 1988; Becker 1981). Although Marxist analyses of the household avoid the term *altruism,* they implicitly assume that altruism reigns (Folbre 1988). Moreover, they avoid analysis of materially based inequalities within domestic groups (Deere and de Janvry 1979; Humphries 1979).

Much of the literature dealing with migrant households shares this moral-economy view. In his very innovative work on migrant households, Wood defines the household as "a group that ensures

---

Rapp, following Jack Goody (1972), defines households as empirically measurable units within which people perform the tasks of production, reproduction, and consumption (1978: 280). The family, on the other hand, according to Rapp, is a normative construct which recruits people into households and organizes their relations and actions (Rapp 1978: 281). In our discussion, we refer to such normative constructs more broadly as kinship, gender, and class ideologies.

Some of the social scientists whose writings we review below may have chosen the term *household* in an attempt to escape from what Rapp calls the "heavy load of ideology" the concept of *family* possesses (Rapp 1978: 281). Most have, unfortunately, added normative ("family") elements to their depiction of households— elements which, we argue, are not universally applicable to household organization and behavior.

its maintenance and reproduction by generating and disposing a *collective* income fund" (emphasis ours) (1981: 339). Yet, this emphasis on a collective fund excludes the many domestic groups in which income is not pooled but, rather, jealously guarded and controlled by the individuals who generated the income (Guyer 1981, 1988; Dwyer and Bruce 1988; Fapohunda 1988). Among the Yoruba of Nigeria, to cite one example, a woman's income is kept separate from that of her husband (G. Marshall 1964: 189): hence there is no collective income.

Social scientists who adopt a political-economy framework of analysis commonly depict the household as a collective, income-generating unit whose members struggle together to stretch and supplement inadequate wages (Burawoy 1976; Humphries 1979; Dinerman 1978). Thus, Meillassoux (1981) makes the important observation that the indirect costs of absent migrant members are met through the income-generating activities of those members left behind. While acknowledging that women who engage in non-capitalist domestic activities within the household are in a contradictory and exploited relationship vis-à-vis the capitalist economy, this observation does not lead to an analysis of social and economic relations *within* the migrant household. Because Meillassoux sees the household as a collective, income-pooling unit, he maps power relations exclusively *between* the household and the workplace.

The idea of collective household budgeting minimizes the hierarchies of power around which income generation and allocation are organized in the household (Dwyer 1983; Fapohunda 1988; Wilk 1989). Not only does power go disproportionately to members who generate income but under capitalism, wages and wage workers are accorded higher status in the household than workers who receive in-kind income or who produce commodities for home use (Bach and Schraml 1982; Zavella 1987). With the emergence of capitalism, from about the sixteenth to the nineteenth century, patriarchal organization of households intensified as men increasingly came to work in the public sphere, and either women worked exclusively in the private sphere or their earnings in the public sphere provided below-family incomes (Tilly and Scott 1978; Hartmann 1981; Mann 1986). Thus, for several centuries men and women have generally experienced household and family life differently, and to assume a harmony of interests among members of a household glosses over the important differentiation of experience that has historically characterized the two genders.

Beyond its failure to account for internal power relations, the moral-economy perspective has been criticized for its portrayal of households as essentially passive, as social units whose members are collectively victimized by the market economy. Such a view does not lend itself to an exploration of how selected household members may resist the values and roles the larger political economy assigns to them. Ethnographic studies that examine social relations within migrant households show, for example, that women are not always compliant victims of capitalism and patriarchy (Lamphere 1987; Smale 1980; Watts 1983; Fernández-Kelly and García 1990). For one instance, Nelson reports that many Kikuyu women, left behind by husbands and fathers to maintain homes and land, have rejected these burdens by "voting with their feet" and migrating alone to nearby cities (Nelson 1978: 89). We will see that Dominican immigrant women's strategies to prolong their households' stays in the United States confound their employers' wishes for a vulnerable, cheap, and impermanent work force.

Household Strategies

In contrast to the passive household acted upon by external forces, a second perspective presents us with a household that continuously seeks to adjust itself to the larger socioeconomic and ecological system. Members of households are seen as developing strategies to alter the effects of their social and physical environment (Deere and de Janvry 1979; Wood 1982; Pessar 1982; Massey et al. 1987).

One group of writers characterize these strategies primarily in terms of economic motives. From this perspective, the household is basically an economic unit and household strategies are based on the principle of economic survival or maximization (Banck 1980; Becker 1981; Dandler and Medeiros 1988). This view is reflected in migration scholarship as well, where the migrant household is often described as an economic maximizing unit and migration as a purely economic act. Thus, Roberts writes: "The household, when its size and composition allow, engages in a strategy of risk minimization through the allocation of its labor to different economic sectors and regions" (K. Roberts N.D.: 7). Other writers suggest that high fertility and subsequent migration are integrated strategies poor households embark upon to meet their subsistence needs (Nutini and Murphy 1970; Weist 1973).

In attempting to recover the active component of human behavior, this perspective has tended to describe the household as relatively unconstrained by external conditions. A "veneer of free choice" is built into the concept of strategies (Wood 1982: 11). Such neoclassical assumptions overlook the many external, structural constraints limiting the range of strategies households can adopt (Wood 1982; Pessar 1982). Moreover, the model of the economic maximizing household fails to specify how strategies develop within the confines of the household (Bach and Schraml 1982). Just as we have seen in our criticism of the first perspective, failing a specification of the mechanisms of strategy evolution, the implication is that the unit has no dissension over objectives (Dwyer 1983; Rouse 1986; Schmink 1984).

As an alternative to the "unrestrained household," Wood has argued that household behavior should be conceptualized as a series of "sustenance strategies" by which the household strives to maintain a dynamic balance between its consumption necessities, its labor power, and the alternatives for generating monetary and non-monetary income (1981: 339). Migration thus becomes one of a series of options contingent on the balance between a household's consumption needs and productive capacity. We agree it is necessary to include the structural constraints that affect household strategies, but we must stress that the conceptualization of constraints should not be restricted to the strictly economic or material sphere. Sociocultural factors influence households strongly. Kinship, gender, and class ideologies guide the strategies of household members both as individuals and in concert (Rapp 1978; Weiss 1985; Fernández-Kelly and García, 1990). As we will see in our discussion of sons' and wives' migration, out-migration is sometimes the outcome of household members' attempts to adjust their situation to a lack of cohesion between traditional kinship or gender ideologies and new material circumstances. Moreover, what or who determines the desired quantity and quality of consumption and investment is not always immediately obvious. In order to answer such questions it is necessary to explore the beliefs surrounding consumption and investment, as well as the social relations within the household that govern the decision-making about these activities. As we shall document in the following section, the definitions of *consumption necessities, labor power,* and *alternatives for income generation* are social and, during times of social change, are particularly open to negotiation and manipulation by household members whose interests conflict. Consequently, the decision to sponsor a member's migration is often a politically charged event within a household.

If we are to increase our understanding of migration by the inclusion of the household in our analysis, then, we must take care to avoid a number of faulty assumptions found in the current literature. First, the social-solidarity view of the household must be tempered. While household members' orientations and actions may sometimes be guided by norms of solidarity, they may equally well be informed by hierarchies of power within households; thus, the tensions and coalition-building these hierarchies produce must be examined (Poster 1978; Barrett 1980; Barrett and McIntosh 1982; Thorne and Yalom 1982; Lamphere 1987). Second, the notion of household strategies must be broadened to include cultural considerations and not merely material or economic ones. Ideologies of kinship and gender, as well as production and consumption possibilities, condition the range of strategies available to households (Young 1978; Selby and Murphy 1982; Tilly and Scott 1978; Zavella 1987; Grasmuck 1991).

Many of our findings concerning Dominican migration contradict, or cannot be explained by, the premises found in conventional household analysis. These findings are understandable only when a conceptualization of the household that includes the internal divisions of the household along lines of generation and gender is applied.

Household Labor Surplus

In his cogent critique of neoclassical theories of migration, Standing (1981) argues that labor migration is not a "natural" condition freely available to the individual as one of an array of production options. Rather, it emerges as an alternative after historical transformations have produced the conditions and demand for a "free" work force that is obliged to sell its labor power.

Some researchers have correctly insisted that it is the household that mediates this flow of free labor to the labor market and employers (Wood 1982; Weist 1973; Humphries 1979; Lamphere 1987). It is necessary to extend our discussion of the mediating role of households further, however, by answering the question, How do historical transformations in the organization of production interact with the organization of domestic activities to release the labor power of *select* household members and to constrain or prohibit the productive activities of others? To answer this query, we must uncover the lines of authority within households that permit certain members, first, to decide that a domestic surplus does indeed exist and, second, to impose this decision on others. Here we explore the household political economy. We must also examine the norms that govern the decision that a labor surplus exists and that it can be resolved by dispatching a specific member or members from the household. Here we focus on class, kinship, and gender ideology.[2]

By taking these analytical steps, we avoid the common pitfall of starting our analysis with a tacit acceptance of the existence of a household labor surplus. The latter stance forecloses an examination of significant household decisions and strategies that may lead to migration and often condition its later effects.

Moving from the internal organization of the household to its placement within the larger political economy, it must be acknowledged that class-based opportunities and constraints influence the range of strategies a given household can adopt. These opportunities and constraints condition, for example, which households can amass the necessary social and economic resources to underwrite a member's emigration.

˙Emigration of Sons from Juan Pablo

Let us now apply this framework for the analysis of migration and labor surplus to the empirical case of the emigration of sons from Juan Pablo. We will describe a situation of out-migration which is

2. For discussions that are sensitive to these issues concerning labor surplus, see Tilly and Scott 1978; Young 1978; Lamphere 1987; and Stansell 1986.

not wholly comprehensible when we draw on conventional models of the migrant household. Stated simply, why should sons of commercial farming households have left Juan Pablo at exactly that moment when their families were experiencing a boom in local economic opportunities? To account for this, we must examine kinship ideology and social relations within capitalist farming households and link these to the new commercial opportunities that emerged in the late 1950s.

During the many decades when the Juan Pablo economy was based on subsistence farming, the patrilateral, extended household was a basic unit of production and distribution. Such a household was comprised of a senior couple, their unmarried children, and the couple's married sons and their wives and children. When a son married, the father was expected to give him land to work. Married sons were not, however, entirely independent of the parental holding. Rather, they and their dependents were expected to contribute labor to the parents' holding when it was needed.

According to informants, the traditional father-son relationship contained several conflicting elements. First, it was common for fathers to delay their sons' marriages in order not to have to share the youths' labor with the sons' newly formed families. Informants explained that this practice often caused sons to resent their fathers—a resentment that might linger long after the son was permitted to marry.

A second source of conflict revolved around a married son's rights concerning the patrimonial plot he was permitted to farm. Land in Juan Pablo, as elsewhere, varies in quality. For example, flat land was preferable to mountainous stretches and land planted in permanent cash crops, such as coffee, was more valuable than overgrown tracts of land. Fathers were known to give the better-quality lands to their favorites. This favoritism could be quite capricious. According to informants, in several cases a married son fell out of favor when he neglected to consult v ith the father on some matter in which the patriarch believed his counsel was required, or when the son disregarded the elder's advice. In these cases the displeased father forced the errant son to relocate the following year to an inferior tract of land.

Moreover, sons could be disenfranchised altogether from the patrimonial estate. It was not uncommon for elderly fathers to decide to sell all their land to one son. Under those circumstances, upon the patriarch's death the heirs divided the remaining profits from the land sale. This practice was allegedly aimed at mitigating conflict among heirs over competing claims. In practice, it has sometimes led to animosity among siblings, with accusations of favoritism.

The enduring power fathers exercised over sons and the social and economic vulnerability to which sons were subjected were, then, central elements in the political economy of patrilateral extended households. The domestic activities that provoked the greatest stress were production—the father's desire to monopolize his unmarried sons' labor—and distribution—the provisional nature of sons' access to patrimonial property while the father was still alive. These elements of conflict were tempered within several households during the late 1950s and early 1960s. This tempering developed in the context of a major change in the political economy of Juan Pablo: the transition from an economy based largely on subsistence farming to one in which commercial farming emerged as a viable alternative.

As was described in the preceding chapter, the movement in the late 1950s from subsistence production, based predominantly on household labor, to commercial farming with local wage workers created a peculiar labor problem for the newly emerging commercial farmers. Whereas many sons had formerly been an asset, they now represented a threat to the plan of expanding coffee production by clearing and working most of the property with the aid of paid laborers. If the traditional kinship norm were followed, large holdings would have to be subdivided among the sons, who would need to plant food crops destined for home consumption. Emigration provided a way out of this quandary. By sponsoring a son's emigration, fathers reasoned, they were meeting their obligation to provide sons with an economic stake while at the same time ensuring that the household would benefit from the new rewards of commercial agriculture.[3]

The decision to sponsor a son's emigration was often made unilat-

3. For a contrasting case which describes how ideology—the value placed upon the maintenance of the traditional three-generation household—promotes Mexican emigration, see Selby and Murphy 1982, and Nutini and Murphy 1970. For a discussion of how the migration of sons from the rural Ecuadorian sierra is related to changes in economic development and in fathers' mortality rates, as well as to delays in sons' inheritance of land and their limited access to labor arrangements accessible to fathers, see Weiss 1985.

erally by the head of the household. This step sometimes pitted a male household head against his wife and members of the son's new family. Older female informants explained that at first, when the United States was largely unknown, these women complained that their husbands were attempting to disenfranchise their own sons from the family holdings. As one woman stated:

A mother is always more protective of her children than the father is. When my husband first talked about our son moving to the United States, I cried. I claimed it was unfair to deny the boy the same rights to work the land that my husband's father had given to him, and my husband, in turn, was obligated to extend to our sons.

From this point of view, a father's decision that his son should emigrate did appear to be an act of disenfranchisement. The decision could also be seen, however, as a way for younger men to escape the hierarchy within the patrilateral household and the vulnerability to which young men were subjected. Interviews with male migrants who emigrated from commercial households in this early period revealed that most men viewed their opportunity for migration as a means of escape. Thus a coalition was forged between fathers and sons which overpowered the opposition to migration by other household members such as mothers and the wives of sons. These aspects of the household political economy were highlighted in an early migrant's account of his departure from Juan Pablo:

Back then fathers were real tyrants. I was young and wanted to be the head of my new family, but I always had to check things like what to plant and what to buy with my father. Because I wanted to establish myself on my own and not be under my father's thumb, I pretended that I sided with him—that I thought it was best for the whole family that he expand coffee production. But really I just wanted the chance to be independent. That was the case with all the young men who left when I did.

It should be noted that the objective act of sons leaving commercial farming households could be interpreted retroactively as a collective household strategy aimed at adjusting the household to changing economic circumstances. Such an interpretation would, however, miss the renegotiation over the control of sons' labor that contributed to this migration strategy and made it palatable for the "disenfranchised" young men. Moreover, by recognizing the changing nature of patriarchal control over sons' labor, we are in a position to understand why, as time progressed, fathers were unable to hold onto the household labor that was necessary for true economic maximization. Once the patriarchal values that governed the mutual obligations between fathers and sons had been renegotiated, the younger sons in migrant households felt less obligated to remain on the family land after they married, to contribute to the labor requirements of the patrilateral, extended household. Youngest sons, in particular, challenged the kinship norm that obliged the youngest and his family to care for the elderly parents in exchange for inheritance rights to the parental home.

In the case of capitalist farming households, elderly fathers often sought their youngest sons' help in managing the farm. Moreover, men who headed petty capitalist and household-labor households frequently found that they could not replace the productivity of the emigrant sons with paid labor. They were thus reluctant to lose the aid of other sons and their families through emigration. However, fathers who had encouraged their eldest sons' emigration were often unable to constrain the emigration of younger offspring. Migration ceased to function as a strategy to promote the economic maximization of the patrilateral, extended household. Rather, it became a strategy by which young men broke from the constraints of this domestic unit. In breaking away, young men often actually weakened the unit's economic base.[4]

It is often assumed that capitalism reinforces patriarchy (Nash 1976; Kuhn and Wolpe 1978). In Juan Pablo, however, the patriarchal control of fathers over sons was threatened by capitalism's tendency to reward individualism over kinship identity and loyalties. The following story told by an informant captures the tension that existed in Juan Pablo between the values of patriarchy and individualism:

Eduardo tried to hang onto his youngest son, Blanco. He lamented that he was growing old and he could no longer supervise the workers, who

4. For contrasting findings on how Mexican emigration fortifies the material base of the patrilateral, extended household and strengthens the senior male's authority, see Nutini and Murphy 1970. In our opinion, this contrasting finding is attributable to the fact that Mexican migration tends to be far more temporary than that of the Dominicans. Therefore, Mexican sons tend to leave wife and children behind under the protection of their father; and the temporarily absent sons direct remittances to their father for allocation.

would not work hard if they were not constantly watched. . . . Eduardo's sons and daughters [in New York] were sympathetic, but they all favored Blanco's emigration. They said there was no future for a young man like Blanco in Juan Pablo.

Many people in Juan Pablo criticize men like Eduardo. They say these men are being old-fashioned and egotistical in trying to hang onto their sons when progress is not in Juan Pablo but in New York. They criticize men like Eduardo who are taking advantage of their sons and keeping them from advancing in life.

We see, then, that the initial emigration of sons from Juan Pablo was predicated on expanding economic opportunities for one segment of the population and declining opportunities for those households that were forced to sell their labor to their more fortunate neighbors. The strategy that several large landholders adopted—to increase the amount of land in production and to employ wage laborers to grow and harvest cash crops—fostered a new perspective on household labor. Commercial farmers redefined their sons' labor as surplus. The manner in which power and economic resources were distributed among members of the patrilateral, extended household dictated that the father would make the decision that a son or sons should emigrate. The tensions such a household political economy engendered ensured that most sons accepted their father's decision willingly. However, once fathers released selected sons from the moral and physical confines of the patrilateral, extended household, the patriarchs found it difficult to prevent other sons from emigrating as well.

Emigration of Wives from Juan Pablo

Whereas many sons of commercial households were defined as a labor surplus and dispatched into a distant labor market, the wives of these households experienced a more contradictory fate. As is described below, although these women were also defined in the late 1950s as surplus labor, this determination served initially to restrict both their mobility and their participation in local productive activities. An analysis of the eventual out-migration of wives from Juan Pablo highlights again the importance of including the analytical elements of the household political economy, as well as class and gender ideology. This instance also points up the limitations of assuming that households' production strategies are guided first by the goal of income maximization.

The movement in the 1950s from subsistence agriculture to commercial farming had profound consequences for the women of Juan Pablo. At this time, women from capitalist and petty capitalist households ceased working in most phases of agricultural production. This occurred for two reasons: first, men and women from poor households were available to carry out arduous work at low wages; second, households gained prestige by "freeing" their female members from agricultural work. These households were able to put one Dominican proverb into practice: "Ladies do not soil their delicate fingers" (Tancer 1973: 224).

The household as a social unit may have benefited from this reallocation of female labor from agricultural production to the domestic sphere. Nonetheless, women lost the status they had enjoyed in the household by virtue of their role in producing certain food crops for household consumption and for exchange with other households. Since domestic activities neither were rewarded with wages nor generated a surplus that could be exchanged outside the household, these women became dependent on male-acquired income for their material well-being and their status.

Prior to the large-scale emigration of men from Juan Pablo, the allocation of female labor to reproduction, socialization, and household maintenance did not adversely affect the household unit's economic viability, and it did increase its prestige. However, once male household members began to emigrate, the practice of withdrawing women from agricultural production began to create economic problems.

Most men who emigrated left a wife behind on the farm. These women often did not have the skills to work the land, nor was such activity viewed positively by the community. Migration was a strategy commonly pursued by households that sought to accumulate wealth abroad specifically in order to purchase more land in Juan Pablo and thus to buttress the household's status in the community. The sight of women from migrant households laboring in the fields would have been a threat to the status aspirations of these domestic groups.

One way of getting around this labor problem might have been for women to hire agricultural workers. This option was rejected in most cases, because migrant husbands were reluctant to give their wives full administrative responsibility. As one man explained:

Women just don't have heads for managing things. They're too good-hearted, and these hired hands here take advantage. You pay them for a full day's work and they're sleeping most of the day. You can't have a woman overseeing men's work.

Agricultural production was drastically reduced in most migrant households where women remained behind as nominal heads. These units lost their capacity to produce use-values and contributed little to the total household income through the sale of agricultural products. In other words, the household members left behind were in many cases dependents rather than contributors to the total household budget.

This finding hardly fits the image of migrant households as income-maximizing units. Rather, it alerts us to the need to include in our household analysis elements such as the sexual division of labor and the way this gender system is used to differentiate households socially within a community. As in this ethnographic case, the sexual division of labor may militate against household economic maximization.

Nonetheless, many migrant households did find a way to overcome the contradiction between local gender and class ideology, on the one hand, and the goal of the migration strategy, on the other. This contradiction was sometimes overcome through the act of sponsoring the wife's emigration to the United States. The Dominican immigrant community in the United States demonstrates less resistance to women working outside the household for wages than does the sending community.

For many of these women from Juan Pablo, the decision to relocate involved other factors in addition to that of meeting the migration goal of accumulating savings. Women of Juan Pablo claimed that they resented the social barriers that kept most women of economically secure households from engaging in income-generating activities. They realized that their total dependence on men's earnings limited their ability to demand rights in decision-making within and outside the household. In migrating to the United States and acquiring employment there, wives of migrant men saw a way to escape that total dependence on their husbands. As the following quote illustrates, women often cloaked their desire to migrate under the ideology of household economic maximization:

On a visit to Juan Pablo, my cousin saw the way my husband was making me wait on him hand and foot, and the way he'd yell if everything wasn't perfect. She said she didn't see such behavior in New York. She said, "Wait till you get there. You'll have your own paycheck, and I tell you, he won't be pushing you around there the way he is here." After that I just kept reminding my husband about how expensive it was to keep a house in Juan Pablo and a house in New York. I also told him about how much money other women were making in New York.

For both sons and wives from Juan Pablo, we see that it is at best simplistic and sometimes empirically wrong to assume that migration is solely or primarily motivated by the economic goals of some abstract collectivity. It is also erroneous to assume that throughout the migration process all household members coordinate their domestic activities to realize such economic goals. Yet, it is easy to reach such faulty conclusions. In Juan Pablo, for example, household members sometimes publicly proclaimed that their migration was motivated by the collective household goal of income maximization. Often this was a calculated strategy on the part of politically weaker household members. These individuals sought to appear to be allying themselves with the senior male of the household. They did this by feigning support for the "collective" household interests which, according to Dominican kinship ideology, the male household head should represent. Nonetheless, this declaration of unity sometimes masked the divergent interests of household members.[5] In the two cases discussed here, son and wife were motivated by anticipated gains in personal autonomy. Both found in migration the promise of reducing the patriarchal control over their actions within and outside the household.

5. For an analysis of the rhetorical dimension of household members' interpretations of their own and others' involvement in Mexican migration, see Rouse 1986. Rouse reaches the same conclusion we do: researchers "treat the frequent references to the importance of family loyalties as simple descriptions of actions and intentions without considering how people might shape these accounts as they advocate and advance their positions in the debates to which their divergent projects give rise" (6).

Gains in Women's Status in the Household

Patriarchal control over household labor and its products is not only a contentious matter for household members in the Dominican Republic; it retains its importance for Dominican immigrants in the United States as well. Control over the household budget is a key arena in which Dominican immigrant women have achieved greater gender parity. To appreciate why and how household budgeting has become such an important arena, we must discard the definition of the household which maintains that it is a collective, income-pooling unit. Implicit in this definition is the notion of a democratic or egalitarian mode of decision-making concerning how household income is obtained and spent. Income pooling, with members contributing different sources of income and collectively, even consensually, deciding on uses of that income, is only one possible form of budgetary organization. Indeed, such a relatively egalitarian type of household is a variant of domestic organization that many Dominicans have experienced for the first time in the United States. Far from being a universal structure, this household form marks a change in domestic relations within many Dominican migrant households.

Observers of the family in the Dominican Republic have distinguished two basic forms of domestic organization, the single-mate and the multiple-mate patterns, each associated with specific forms of authority (see Brown 1972; Ferrán 1974; González 1970, 1976; Tancer 1973). In the single-mate pattern, authority resides largely with the senior male; in the multiple-mate unit, women tend to command authority (see Brown 1972; Ferrán 1974).

With Dominican migration to the United States, a third pattern of domestic authority has emerged in many immigrant households. The movement has been away from the hegemony of one sex over decision-making and control of domestic resources to a relatively egalitarian division of labor and distribution of authority. Our ethnographic data on patterns of household budgeting collected in New York, allowing comparisons of budgetary arrangements before and after migration, illustrate this transition. Interviews with fifty-five immigrant women disclosed that in the Dominican Republic, prior to emigration, men controlled the household budget in the large majority of these households—even though women contributed income in many of the households on a regular or semi-regular basis. Of the three types of budgetary arrangements uncovered, two can be considered male-controlled. The first type, the traditional, patriarchal form in which members gave all or part of their wages or profits to the senior male who, in turn, oversaw the payment of household expenses, constituted 18 percent. Approximately half, or 51 percent, operated with the second type, the household-allowance pattern, wherein the wife was given a housekeeping allowance to cover such basic expenditures as food and clothing. When women in households with the household-allowance pattern generated income, it was most commonly used for household rather than personal items of consumption, and these household purchases tended to be luxuries rather than staples. Both objectively and symbolically, the direction of these women's savings to nonessential, prestige items reinforced the image of the man as the breadwinner and the woman as, at best, the bestower of modern status goods and, at worst, the purchaser of frivolities. Finally, 31 percent of these pre-migration households were characterized by what we term a pooled-household-income pattern. All but two of this third category of household were headed by women, with no senior male present in the Dominican Republic. In most cases, then, the pooling of income and shared decision-making occurred among a female head and other income-contributing household members.

Dominican households in the United States have experienced a profound change in budgetary allocation. Far fewer households follow a patriarchal pattern of budgetary control, and many more pool their income. Not only is pooling more common in the United States, but it is increasingly found in households with a senior male present. Thus only 4 percent of the fifty-five migrant households in New York followed the traditional, patriarchal pattern of budgetary control. Also, in most of the households where women received a household allowance, the wife was either not employed or engaged in industrial homework. The dominant pattern, found in 69 percent of the households in New York, was to pool income. The majority (58 percent) of these income-pooling units were nuclear, with 42 percent headed by women. When nuclear households pool income, the husband, wife, and working children pool a specific amount of their wages or profits for shared household expenses such as food, rent, and electricity. The remainder of the income is usually divided between joint or individual savings accounts and personal items of consumption.

Income pooling within nuclear households brings women advantages that were unavailable to them in the Dominican Republic. Responsibility for meeting the household's basic subsistence costs is distributed among members regardless of gender, thus mitigating the invidious comparison between "essential" male contributions and "supplementary" female inputs. Moreover, according to informants, men's greater participation in domestic tasks generally assigned to women in the Dominican Republic—tasks such as developing strategies for stretching the food budget—has led them to appreciate more fully the experience and skills women bring to these activities.

How have Dominican immigrant households managed this transition from patriarchal to more egalitarian relations, not only in household budgeting but in other domestic activities? We believe that the answer lies in the material and cultural experiences of immigrants in the United States.

Most Dominican immigrants earn wages below the family-subsistence level. In practice, this has meant that few married-couple households can manage economically, at least in the early years of residence in the United States, if they adopt the traditional pattern of a sole male provider. Certainly this has been the case if the family has aspired to a secure working-class standard of living, or more desirable still, a middle-class one. Out of this experience of dual- or multi-wage-earning households has come a questioning of the efficacy and legitimacy of the traditional, patriarchal ideology which holds that the man should be the sole or at least the primary breadwinner.

Moreover, the fact that the wife is working, and often the older children as well, suits the Dominican migration ideology. Key values in this ideology are consistently articulated as progress through the concerted sacrifices of a united family. The fact that family members who traditionally did not work outside the home do so in the United States also reflects and reinforces the popular views among Dominicans that "one lives to work" in the United States, and "there is no life in New York." In this labor market, where Dominicans receive relatively low, unstable wages, many have agreed temporarily to submerge traditional familial values based on lack of equivalence and gender hierarchy to more "democratic" market values in which adult family members all represent labor power.

As Dominican immigrant women find themselves materially in a position parallel to wage-earning husbands, many have demanded that their husbands relinquish some of the self-gratification and privilege that have historically accrued to males who have "supported" the family (Kessler-Harris and Sacks 1987; Rubin 1976). Such renegotiation has been very clear in the matter of which family member or members have the right to assume the status of household head. For most Dominicans the status of household head is equated with the concept of "defending the household" (*defenderse la casa*). This "defense" is conceived of largely in material terms. As women have come to demonstrate their capacity to share material responsibility with men on more or less equal terms, they have begun to expect to be co-partners in heading the household. Thus in response to the questions "Who is the household head now?" and "Who was the head previous to emigration?" the words of this woman echo those of many respondents:

We are both the heads. If both husband and wife are earning salaries, then they should rule equally in the household. In the Dominican Republic it is always the husband who gives the orders in the household. But here, when the two are working, the women feels herself the equal of the man in ruling the home.[6]

Many Dominican couples have also renegotiated another feature of the household division of labor; namely, private housework and child care. At issue is the norm that assigns women exclusively to this unwaged labor. According to traditional family norms, the wife (often with assistance from daughters and a paid domestic worker) is expected to carry out housework and child care duties for her immediate family and for other kin domiciled in the home. These duties are dispatched in the name of femininity, obligation, and

6. In his study of Dominican immigrants in a small New England city, Andrew Gordon also found a change toward greater equality between working husbands and wives (1978: 80). In the words of one of Gordon's male informants: "[In the Dominican Republic, women] had to accept whatever the man did. In the U.S. the woman says *Yo poncho la tarjeta* (I punch the card; i.e., clock in the factory). She says, 'I contribute too.' She says what she wants" (Gordon 1978: 66).

love. In exchange, the husband is expected to provide financially for the family. Now that many wives share the latter duty with husbands, many of our female and male informants have come to question the legitimacy of the traditional division of labor that assigns only women to housework. Sometimes willingly and sometimes after domestic struggle, Dominican immigrant husbands and sons have come to assume a greater, but by no means equal, share of the housework and child care responsibilities.

Since household duties are not shared equally between the sexes, the double burden of wage work and domestic work falls hardest on women. As the following vignette from our fieldwork shows, the vast majority of our female informants, as well as many of our male informants, believed that when both partners worked outside the home, the husband should "help" with tasks such as shopping and washing dishes:

At the Collados' home, Tomás was preparing dinner. Tomás claimed he would never be found in the kitchen, let alone cooking, in the Dominican Republic. But, he added, there his wife would not be working outside the house; he would be the breadwinner. Tomás explained that since he made his living in the United States as a chef, it seemed natural that his contribution to running the household should include cooking at home. He joked that if he wore out more pairs of socks running about in the kitchen, it was all right because his wife worked in the garment trade and she could apply her skills at home by darning his socks.

Tomás and his wife said that soon after they were both working they realized that "if both worked outside the house, both should work inside, as well. Now that we are in the United States, we should adopt Americans' ways."

Dominican women mentioned such male assistance in housework and child care when they spoke positively of changing relations between wives and husbands in the United States. None of our informants believed, however, that men could or should act as equals to women in the domestic sphere. The following quote captures the beliefs held by many Dominican immigrant women: "I know of cases where the man assumes the housekeeping and child care responsibilities. But I don't believe a man can be as good as a woman; she is made for the home and the man is made to work."

In analyzing women's household labor, feminist theorists have drawn our attention to the fact that under capitalist relations of production, employers depend on this unpaid female labor to reproduce labor power on a daily and generational basis (Bentson 1969; Dalla Costa 1975; Fox 1980; Hartmann 1981). Although wages cover the costs of many of the commodities needed to sustain household members, a certain amount of supplementary labor is required to transform, replenish, and maintain these commodities. Historically, women have been assigned to these activities of social reproduction. Moreover, kinship ideology has tended to mystify the true productive nature of these activities by classifying them as women's "labor of love," as distinct from men's wage labor. Some of our female informants have begun to challenge such classification, as is attested by the following disagreement:

Bolívar: After killing myself at work each day I long to return home, where love resides. It is here in my home that I can bask in love's warmth.

Criselda: Don't think for an instant that work stops and love takes over as soon as people punch the time clock and return home. I have my own time clock here, Bolívar. Dinner must be on the table for the children at 6:00, for you at 8:00. The children must be bathed by 8:30 and in bed by 9:00. Sure, I love my children and would do anything for them, but let me assure you that the work that confronts me at home when I come back from the factory is every bit as demanding as my work on the assembly line.

Finally, a small minority of our female informants have come to challenge the dual notion that domestic work is both women's work and a type of activity that is separate from the capitalist sphere. As our interviews with these informants revealed, in most cases what led to this challenge was the women's recognition that many of the men and women without close kin in the Dominican community had to pay for the domestic services that our informants provided freely to family members. As the following incident shows, this realization usually emboldened our informants to request more assistance in housework and child care duties from other household members:

We were all sitting around the dinner table, having just finished the meal, when Pablo came home. His brother, Sergio, told his wife, Elvira, to prepare another plate for Pablo. Elvira was clearly agitated as she clanged the pots and pans in which the food was being reheated.

After wolfing down his food, Pablo departed for his evening job at a gas station. As soon as the door closed behind him, Elvira began shouting.

She told Sergio that she was not his family's slave. She said that, like Sergio and Pablo, she too put in long hours at work and did not plan to add further to her labors by providing for "extra people" like Pablo. Moreover, she added, she was not about to help Pablo's employer, as well, by freely providing housekeeping services that the employer should be forced to compensate adequately in his payment to his workers. Elvira concluded her argument by declaring that Pablo would have to pay her a fair wage for her cooking and cleaning on his behalf, share in these duties as an equal member of the family, or find his own place.

Within two months, Pablo had rented an apartment with a male friend. He had also changed to a higher-paying job in order to be able to afford his added household expenses.

In an attempt to interpret the emergence of more egalitarian households among Dominican immigrants, certain analogies may be drawn between middle-class American families and Dominican immigrant families aspiring to middle-class status. First, many of our informants claimed, like Tomás, that they self-consciously patterned their more egalitarian relations on what they believed to be the dominant U.S. model. They viewed this change in orientation as both modern and a sign of progress. Second, as Elvira's complaints about providing for "extra" family members attests, many of our upwardly mobile informants sought to slough off kin and friends. That is, they abandoned a pattern more common in the initial phase of migration—resource pooling among kin and friends and the consequent leveling of resources. What Rayna Rapp says about middle-class American families is applicable to Elvira and many others of our informants: they have selected a pattern of family relations "which is consistent with resource accumulation, rather than dispersal" (1978: 297).

In significant ways, however, the Dominican experience does not parallel the American one. In the United States, gender and class ideology can be reinforcing, as in the model of the relatively egalitarian, middle-class professional family where, ideally, partners share in salaried work and housework does not fall exclusively to women. The Dominican immigrant woman faces a far more contradictory set of gender and class norms and values. The bourgeois standard of living the female Dominican immigrant and her family hope to emulate is a standard informed by Dominican values. These hold that the woman shall remain in the home and the man shall be the sole breadwinner. For Dominicans, this represents a material and social accomplishment analogous to that of early generations of American workers whose men symbolized and actualized their material well-being and social mobility by earning a "family wage." Thus, most of our female informants spoke of their tenure of work outside the household as temporary. Even the most ardent supporter of joint status as household head could be heard to say that she was working "to help her husband out."

In this regard, perhaps a more apposite group within U.S. society with which to compare Dominicans is Cuban immigrants. In their research among Cuban women in South Florida, Fernández-Kelly and García (1990) found that women entered the labor force to buttress their households' declining socioeconomic status and to maintain the integrity of patriarchal families by, in their informants' words, "helping their husbands." However, the bourgeois class aspirations of these Cuban households, coupled with the association of patriarchy with middle-class standing, have dictated a temporary period of wage work for Cuban women. According to the researchers, once Cuban immigrant households attained their desired socioeconomic standing, wives were receptive to husbands' urgings to abandon wage employment.

The Dominican and Cuban cases share the norm of relegating middle-class women to the domestic sphere in the name of household mobility, but at least in the Dominican experience we find indications of a growing tension between previously reinforcing gender and class ideologies. At issue for Dominicans is the greater gender equality brought about by migration to the United States and wage work. For most of our Dominican female informants, an improvement in gender relations has been an unintended outcome of the immigrant experience.[7] And once this improvement has become available to women, it has emerged as an attainment or a goal in its own right—one that is incompatible with women's "retirement" to the domestic sphere in order to support the bourgeois norm of a sole, male breadwinner.[8]

7. For additional studies that show how migration has improved women's status within the household, see Abadan-Unat 1982; Brettell 1982; Morokvasic 1984; Lamphere 1987; Watts 1983; and Whiteford 1978.

8. For a discussion of how women's seasonal, wage employment affects domestic relations in Chicano households, see Zavella 1987.

The irony is that, for many women, the struggle to gain greater parity has not led to a more egalitarian household but, rather, to the dismantling of the union. Of the fifty-five senior, female members in our New York ethnographic sample, eighteen were divorced or separated from a partner while in the United States. Fourteen cited the struggle over domestic authority as the primary factor leading to the disbanding of the union. Not only have they lost the battle for a more equitable union, but without a husband's financial contributions these women have also severely compromised their goal of attaining a middle-class standard of living. The median income reported in the 1980 U.S. census for Dominican households in New York City was $12,156, but the corresponding figure for female-headed households was only $5,933 (Mann and Salvo 1984). In the next chapter we will describe in greater detail the disadvantages associated with marital disruption and female-headedness.

The Gender Politics of Settlement
versus Return

The decision regarding the household's return to the Dominican Republic has become an arena in which women struggle to maintain the gains that migration and employment have brought to them. Women tend to postpone return, because they realize that Dominican gender and class ideology, as well as the sexual division of labor in the Dominican economy, militate against wage employment for women of their training and class background. It will be recalled from our discussion of return migration that, in the thirty-five households comprising our Santiago ethnographic survey, only one of the wives was working.

In their attempt to postpone their return and likely "retirement," many women have embarked on an income-allocation strategy whereby large amounts of money are spent on expensive, durable goods, such as a home and home furnishings. This strategy serves both to root the family securely and comfortably in the United States and to deplete the funds needed to relocate. By contrast, men were commonly reported as planning ways of reducing their time in the United States, as is reflected in the often repeated refrain, "Five dollars wasted today means five more years of postponing the return to the Dominican Republic." In this struggle over return, migration loses its character as a collective and unifying household project for social mobility. Rather, the conflict over return revolves around traditional gendered privileges for middle-class and upper-working-class men, privileges that migration has challenged and many men seek to regain back home.

Migration has brought societal- and household-level changes to many Dominican immigrant men. Immigrants' first jobs tend to be on the lowest rung of the prestige hierarchy, and the status associated with these jobs may contradict the immigrants' self-identity and sense of worth (Piore 1979). This is particularly likely for Dominican men, whose pre-migration employment often placed them in the ranks of the middle class or the upper working class. Although such men experience a decline in status by migrating, they are urged by others to subsume their individual identities and goals within the larger sphere of the household.

Herein lies a major tension in the immigrant experience of many Dominican men. As noted above, the purpose behind migration—according to most Dominicans, it is the desire for economic and social progress—may not be realized by an individual, but is often achieved collectively. The wages migrants receive and the level of consumption this income makes possible permit the domestic unit to enjoy, by its members' standards, a middle-class life-style. Notwithstanding the social mobility realized at the household level, however, Dominican men in the United States sometimes become frustrated by their inability to translate these household gains into public prestige. This observation underscores what is for men an uneasy balance between becoming first among equals in the immigrant household, and the prevailing gender ideology and sex roles in the Dominican Republic, which promote patriarchy in the home and prestige and privilege for middle-class men in the public sphere.[9]

With this tension as a major catalyst, some men choose to pursue

9. Gordon also notes that men's social relations have become "atomized, making the household, rather than the kin or friend network, the primary unit of social relations" (Gordon 1978: 80).

a financial strategy in which frugal living and savings are emphasized to ensure that the household will eventually return to the Dominican Republic. Not infrequently, this places the man at odds with his spouse, who has embarked on an opposing financial course. In five of the eighteen cases of divorce we studied, what ultimately precipitated the breakup was the man's return to the Dominican Republic with sufficient savings to reestablish himself, while the woman elected to remain in the United States.

This ethnographic material clearly illustrates the fallacy of assuming that the household is a unit that is defined by its members' contribution to and management of an undifferentiated, collective income fund. To fully understand the profound changes in household authority within Dominican immigrant households and women's strategies to prolong their household's stay in the United States, we must recognize two elements that are absent from this conceptualization. First, wage income is assigned greater value and rewarded differentially from the use-values that women often contribute to household budgets. Second, under some circumstances, such as when they gain regular access to wages, women are able to use this income as leverage to modify the terms that dictate decision-making about household budgeting and other domestic activities. When previously excluded members of the household are permitted control over this household activity, they are reluctant to give up this newfound power.

Our discussion of the collective household project of social mobility, as well as the divergent projects concerning settlement versus return, underscore one of our fundamental claims regarding households. While we do not deny the existence of collective household projects, we do question the tendency to view them as typical and unchanging.

Migrant Households and the Workplace

Researchers frequently argue that migrant households possess certain features that make them especially suited to meeting employers' goals of capital accumulation (Burawoy 1976; Meillassoux 1981; Griffith 1985). Foremost among these features is the existence of household members back home who subsidize the migrants' low wages and provide for the dependents left behind. Under these conditions, the migrant purportedly is willing to accept low-paying, insecure employment. This situation does characterize most immigrant populations at some phase of the migration process, and for some groups it may prevail until the migrant returns home for good. Nonetheless, as our studies of Dominicans clearly show, this portrayal relies on an essentially static conceptualization of relations within migrant households and between these domestic groups and the larger political economy. Little attention has been paid, for example, to the changing social relations and strategies that lead members of temporary migrant households to change the location where dependent household members are raised.

These concerns lead us to a reconsideration of Dominican settlement in the United States. Women's strategies for rooting the household in the United States include bringing dependents from the Dominican Republic.[10] This strategy carries implications for the type of jobs immigrant household members will remain in or accept. First, U.S. residents who wish to sponsor the immigration of a relative must demonstrate that they have savings—an accomplishment that usually requires steady employment at higher than minimum wages. These savings are needed to convince U.S. immigration officials that the children being sponsored will not become wards of the state. They are also needed to meet the actual costs of sponsoring the children's migration. Second, since tax records are part of the portfolio of successful petitioners, the decision to recruit additional family members greatly reduces immigrants' incentives or willingness to work for employers who pay "off the books." Indeed, we knew of many Dominicans who quit such jobs when they began to contemplate sponsoring their children's emigration. Finally, of course, the costs for maintaining children in the United States are usually higher than they were in the Dominican Republic.

The high rates of marital instability and of female-headedness among Dominicans in New York, which were uncovered in our ethnography and confirmed by others (Gurak and Kritz 1982: 20; U.S. Bureau of the Census 1984), also influence the types of employment Dominican immigrant workers are willing to accept. Do-

10. This strategy also fulfills the desire of many women to care for their children themselves.

minican immigrant women who head households rarely conform to the pattern of the migrant target earner who accepts unfavorable working conditions in order to maximize savings and return quickly to gainful employment back home (Piore 1979). In most cases, the female head shares the dream of eventual return to the Dominican Republic with all the material accoutrements of a solid, middle-class standard of living. To realize this dream, however, the woman realizes that she must toil for many more years in the United States than must members of dual-wage-earning immigrant households. She also recognizes that her goal will be achieved more easily if she finds secure, reasonably well-paying employment. As is described in the next chapter, this employment goal is made problematic by a discriminatory labor market, which assigns to immigrant women the least desirable jobs. As our ethnographic research uncovered, over time many such women become resigned to a stable working-class lifestyle in New York, and a lesser number enter the ranks of the underclass as welfare recipients.

To summarize, our ethnographic material challenges the common depiction of a passive migrant household whose members essentially respond to the needs of employers, allowing the latter to exploit not only the migrant worker but his or her household members as well. We have focused on the dynamic actions of Dominican female immigrants, many of whom, in pursuit of their own goals, have confounded the wishes of some U.S. employers for a cheap, impermanent source of labor.[11]

Conclusion

In order to understand how the global transformations of the international economy have stimulated emigration, it is essential to consider those social organizations that mediate these transformations. In this chapter we have focused on the role assumed by households and have made a number of observations regarding the

11. Fernández-Kelly and García (1990) find that a change from on-site production in garment factories to industrial homework is a way that economically secure Cuban immigrant women can resolve the pull between their dedication to children and husbands and their desire to bring in additional income. This strategy, which is tied to Cuban family ideology and mores, has confounded apparel factory owners' requirements for on-site workers, according to the authors.

social relations found in households. An appreciation of these social relations, we maintain, is essential to a better understanding of the way opportunities for migration are realized and how certain migration effects occur.

With an eye to encouraging further study of the role of households in migration, we criticized some of the inadequate or faulty premises found in the literature on households in general and migrant households in particular. In their place, we offer the following formulation. First, households are organized according to social relations based on principles of generation and gender. Second, these principles are converted into sentiment through kinship, gender, and class ideology. Third, tension and conflict within households are likely when hierarchy and inequality rather than complementarity characterize domestic relations and ideology. Fourth, conflict is likely to surface when new strategies are devised to readjust the unit to changing conditions in the larger socioeconomic system: in rejecting old strategies and searching for new ones, an opportunity is opened for household members to renegotiate both their role in decision-making and their access to valued resources such as wage income. The ways these tensions get resolved are highly significant for such migration outcomes as the decision to sponsor migrants, the decision to return to the home community, and the nature of ties between international migrants and their home community. Although households can never be indifferent to the broader socioeconomic environment in which they operate, attention to the way these complex units mediate these broader processes helps to explain certain migration outcomes not comprehensible using conventional analyses.

7

Dominican Workers in the New York City Labor Market

Between 1975 and 1980 the Dominican Republic ranked first among countries of origin for New York City immigrants entering the United States (Bogen 1987: 37). These 35,860 Dominican newcomers joined the 353,900 foreign-born persons who settled in New York City during this period (Bogen 1987: 39). Why did such large numbers of Dominicans and other immigrants head for New York City at exactly the moment when unemployment peaked at 11.5 percent of the city's labor force? Just as we have been able to account for large-scale Dominican out-migration within the context of overall national growth by focusing on class relations and particular occupational sectors, so we can understand the growth of immigrant labor in a time of high unemployment and overall job loss if we examine evolving class relations in New York City and the recomposition of its economy.

Even within the context of demand for immigrant workers in New York City, immigrants are not a homogeneous category of labor (Portes and Stepick 1985). Through both survey and ethnographic findings, we explore how the legal status and the gender of a Dominican immigrant worker influence such work-related outcomes as wages, the size of firm that hires the immigrant, workplace conditions and benefits, and the likelihood of the immigrant being employed in a unionized firm and taking part in workplace struggles.

We believe that a fuller appreciation of Dominican immigrant workers' contributions to New York City's restructuring hinges also upon a textured account of how Dominicans conceive of their work in New York and how they reproduce the social relations required to maintain the small, informal workplaces in which many Dominicans are employed.

Dominicans in New York City

According to the 1980 United States census, 169,100 persons of Dominican birth were residing in the United States, and of those, 124,100 (73 percent) lived in New York City (Kraly 1987: 68). Dominicans in Manhattan are concentrated in Washington Heights and the Lower East Side. In the other boroughs the largest numbers of Dominicans are found in the South Bronx, the Greenpoint section of Brooklyn, and the Jackson Heights section of Queens. The population is youthful: the median age for males is 23.3; for females, 27.1.

The percentage of married-couple households among Dominicans is significantly lower than the New York City average: 52 percent, compared to 69 percent. Approximately 42 percent of Dominican households were female-headed. As reported in the 1980 census, the median incomes of Dominican married-couple and female-headed households were $12,156 and $5,933, respectively (Mann and Salvo 1984). These are well below the median citywide average of $20,625 for married-couple households and $8,516 for female-headed units (Bogen 1987: 48). The relatively low level of the Dominicans' household incomes can be attributed partially to the fact that over 23 percent of these households drew public assistance income, as compared to the city's 14 percent average for such recipiency (Mann and Salvo 1984: 19).

On the whole, Dominicans demonstrate relatively high rates of labor-force participation: 79.9 percent for Dominican men and 49.9 percent for Dominican women, according to the 1980 census (Gurak and Falcón-Rodríguez 1987). Dominicans' labor-force participation rates exceeded the overall rates for New York City of 69.2 percent for men and 47.1 percent for women (Mann and Salvo 1984: 18). As Table 27 shows, the predominant occupations for Dominicans lie in the manufacturing and service industries. This in

TABLE 27
*Occupational Distribution of Dominicans
by Sex, New York City, 1980*

	Males (%)	Females (%)
Professional	2.8	2.0
Semi-prof./technical	0.9	0.5
Managers	6.4	1.6
Clerical	10.6	18.6
Sales	3.4	3.0
Artisans	13.2	6.1
Operatives	32.6	55.1
Personal service	23.5	11.5
Laborers (except farm)	6.2	1.4
Agricultural laborers	0.2	0.0

Source. Adapted from Gurak and Falcón-Rodríguez
1987 and based on Public Use Microdata Samples of the
1980 Census, Five Counties in New York City Area.

itself is not surprising. What is noteworthy is their relatively low representation in professional and semi-professional occupations and their high representation in operative jobs (and, for males, services), compared to other Hispanics in New York. Table 28 compares Dominicans to other Hispanics with respect to their participation in these occupations and their levels of education. Dominicans' comparatively low education attainments—9.2 years for men and 8.2 years for women—may help to account for their positioning in lower-skilled occupations than other, better-educated Hispanic populations. However, we will see shortly that even well-educated Dominicans do not tend to find employment consistent with their higher education and prior professional employment in the Dominican Republic. One may speculate that, in comparison to other Hispanics in New York City, immigrant status (in contrast to Puerto Ricans) and especially race (in contrast, for example, to Colombians) further exacerbate the disadvantages that comparatively low education brings to Dominicans when they compete for jobs in the New York City labor market (cf. Reimers 1983). It should be added

TABLE 28

Occupational Distribution and Education of Hispanics by Sex, New York City, 1980

	Puerto Rican	Cuban	Dominican	Colombian	Mexican	Other Spanish-Speaking
Males						
Professional	4.7	12.9	2.8	9.9	11.9	9.9
Semi-prof./technical	1.4	2.9	0.9	2.0	1.2	1.0
Operatives	22.5	13.9	32.6	23.5	18.5	20.3
Personal service	22.6	21.1	23.5	20.3	28.9	18.8
Median education	9.9	11.5	9.2	11.7	10.7	11.6
Females						
Professional	7.7	11.5	2.0	7.0	16.6	9.4
Semi-prof./technical	2.4	2.1	0.5	2.6	1.0	2.3
Operatives	24.6	22.5	55.1	29.8	22.6	27.1
Personal service	13.2	14.2	11.5	20.3	13.1	20.1
Median education	9.6	10.8	8.2	11.6	10.6	11.7

Source. Adapted from Gurak and Falcón-Rodríguez 1987 and based on Public Use Microdata Samples of the 1980 Census, Five Counties in New York City Area.

that social networks reinforce this pattern by channeling newly arrived Dominican immigrants into the low-skilled occupations of their compatriots.

Our own and other researchers' surveys show that the majority of adult male Dominicans emigrated to the United States in order to work. By contrast, family unification was an especially important motivation for Dominican women (Gurak and Kritz 1984: 9). The comparatively high rates of labor-force participation of Dominicans show that they were generally successful in finding work, despite the economic downturns characterizing New York City during the 1970s.

The Role of New Immigrants in the New York City Economy

Between 1970 and 1980, New York City lost over 270,000 jobs and employment fell by 8.6 percent (Waldinger 1987: 377). Native-born whites were the group that both quantitatively and proportionally lost the greatest number of jobs over the decade, with a decline in employment of about 22 percent. Much of this job loss can be attributed to migration to the suburbs and to the Sunbelt, as well as to the retirement of an aging white population. There were other, smaller losers in this declining labor market. During the same time period, employment fell for native-born black and native-born Hispanic workers by 5 percent and 4 percent, respectively (Waldinger 1987: 381).[1] Waldinger has documented that all minorities, but especially non-white immigrants, have benefited from the marked decline in the proportion of whites in the New York City labor market. The exodus of whites has caused an ethnic realignment in the city. The Asian foreign-born saw an approximately 350 percent increase in employment (31,200 to 108,740 jobs); black foreign-born (predominantly Haitians, Jamaicans, and other black Caribbeans) realized a 307 percent increase in employment (from 55,500 to

1. See Waldinger 1987 for a discussion of the industries and occupations in which job increases and decreases occurred over the 1970s and various native-born and immigrant groups' proportional shares in these industries and occupations. Waldinger also examines the extent to which these populations' changes in employment were proportional to changes in the group's overall growth over the decade and to changes in the composition of occupations in New York City.

170,320); and foreign-born Hispanics experienced a more modest gain of 155 percent (132,700 to 205,520) (Waldinger 1987: 376).

As the non-white population replaced whites, the former began to specialize in distinct economic spaces. Immigrants realized gains in every New York City industry, but they came to be heavily overrepresented in the declining manufacturing sector.[2] This was especially the case for Hispanic immigrants. For example, between 1970 and 1980 manufacturing lost 117,740 jobs but during that same period Hispanic immigrants increased their share of jobs in manufacturing by 11,568 (Waldinger 1987:382).

To account for the apparent increase in demand for immigrant labor within the declining manufacturing sector, we must consider the restructuring that has occurred and examine the role that immigrants have played in this restructuring. In the face of heavy competition from other domestic and international markets, many New York industries would not or could not afford to hold onto native-born workers by increasing wages and improving working conditions; neither did they invest in modern equipment and technology. New immigrants represented an alternative. They were willing to accept prevailing wage levels and working conditions, thus placing a brake on escalating wages and operational costs. For example, in the apparel industry—a major beneficiary of immigrant labor—average hourly wages declined by 10 percent between 1965 and 1980 (Waldinger 1983: 111). Immigrants also had skills needed in traditional manufacturing industries. Adriana Marshall (1983, 1987) convincingly argues that the large number of new immigrants has actually increased the demand in manufacturing for these workers, since employers have come to rely on labor-intensive techniques and older forms of production organization, such as subcontracting and industrial homework, that depend on a cheap and unorganized work force.

Self-employment, especially in firms that cater to immigrant clients, is also often an important part of the immigrant settlement

2. Waldinger writes, "Where the white proportion declines as radically as it did in New York, we can expect ethnic realignment as opportunities open for nonwhites to take over better jobs" (1987: 377). Hence his argument is that immigrants' replacement of whites in manufacturing is central to understanding their gains.

process in places where immigrants abound (Light 1972; Bonacich and Modell 1980; Portes and Bach 1985; Waldinger 1986b). In 1980, the self-employment rate for foreign-born males in New York City was 12.7 percent, compared with 3.3 percent for native black males; and the rate of self-employment among immigrants climbs with the length of stay in the United States (Waldinger 1987: 394). Immigrant enterprises are aided by the growth of the immigrant population, which creates its own demand for immigrant-specialized services, and, as we shall see, by the existence of a pool of undocumented immigrants who need the sponsorship, employment, and protection that immigrant firms sometimes offer.

The restructuring and decentralization of manufacturing have also brought opportunities for the immigrant entrepreneur. Such operations as apparel subcontracting shops require relatively little start-up capital and thus are within the reach of the immigrant entrepreneur.[3] Network hiring further cuts operating costs and ensures a relatively committed and compliant work force. The pattern of network hiring benefits co-immigrant workers while reducing opportunities for native-born workers. For example, the Dominican owner of a small lamp factory stated:

At least once a week a Puerto Rican walks off the street looking for a job. But unless one of my workers can vouch for him, I'm not interested, even if there's work. Puerto Ricans just have too many smarts. Come a union organizer and they're the first ones to join. I simply cannot afford those extras—social security taxes, overtime, paid vacations. God save me from Puerto Ricans and the unions!

The importance of having trusted, compliant workers is especially pronounced for immigrant entrepreneurs, because native-born owners have conceded to them the most volatile and risky niche in manufacturing (Waldinger 1986b; Wong 1987).

Whereas manufacturing's share of the New York labor market has decreased, the service industry has expanded. In 1950, manu-

3. In the early 1980s, a would-be owner of a new apparel firm needed as little as $25,000 to purchase a twenty-five- to thirty-worker factory with a boiler adequate to generate steam for pressing, as well as the necessary electrical and gas hookups. Moreover, generous financing terms could be obtained. As Waldinger's (1986b) study of the New York City garment industry documented, a down payment of $6,000 to $7,000 usually sufficed, with the remainder amortized over an eighteen- to twenty-four-month period at below-market interest rates (138).

facturing supplied almost one job in three, while services supplied only one in seven. By 1980 these figures were reversed (Sassen-Koob 1981: 28). The shift to a service economy has increased income polarization and created a much larger share of low-wage jobs than was the case when New York had a strong manufacturing-based economy (Sassen-Koob 1986: 96). In 1980, almost 11 percent of all jobs in finance, insurance, and real estate were low-waged and required few, if any, technical skills or language abilities; similarly, 24 percent of all jobs in business services and 18 percent in the remaining service industries were of this caliber (Sassen-Koob 1986: 97). Sassen-Koob has identified a relationship among the expansion of the number of high-income service workers, residential and commercial gentrification, and the demand for consumer services. Well-paid service workers establish in everyday living new cultural forms associated with gentrification that depend on the availability of a vast supply of low-wage workers (Sassen-Koob 1986: 97).

Immigrant workers have also been recruited in large numbers into the lowest tiers of the expanding service economy. According to the 1980 census, immigrants were overrepresented in several economic activities in the service industry. Among these were eating and drinking places (Latin American men, Asian men and women); wholesale trade (Asian men); personal and household services (Latin American and non-Hispanic Caribbean women); and professional services (non-Hispanic Caribbean women). Table 29 lists the thirteen industries in which post-1965 immigrants constituted almost one-quarter of the labor force. As is the case with manufacturing, immigrants predominate in the labor-intensive segments of service delivery.

Undocumented Dominicans
in New York City

The preceding discussion of the role of immigrant workers in the declining manufacturing sector challenges the neoclassical assumption that immigrant labor is needed to meet labor shortages per se. It is very clear that employers in labor-intensive industries seek a special category of worker—one who is relatively inexpensive and docile. Among those authors who adopt a historical-structural ap-

TABLE 29
New York City Industries with Concentrations of New Immigrants, 1980

	New Immigrant Employment	Total Employment	% New Immigrants to Total
Apparel	42,760	118,540	36.1
Hospitals	41,660	185,820	22.4
Eat./drink. establishments	36,820	110,640	33.3
Banking	21,540	125,320	17.2
Construction	15,120	77,960	19.4
Real-est./bldg. management	11,540	71,660	16.1
Private households	11,520	30,620	37.6
Nursing facilities	9,820	30,960	31.7
Misc. manufacturing	9,520	32,080	29.7
Grocery stores	8,920	47,040	19.0
Insurance	8,720	76,980	11.3
Motels/hotels	7,860	25,420	30.9
Printing/publishing	7,760	74,280	10.4
Total, 13 indus.	233,560	1,007,320	23.2
All other indus.	259,200	1,890,560	13.7
Total	492,760	2,897,880	17.0

Source. Bogen 1987: 85, based on 1980 U.S. Census Public Use Microdata File.

proach to migration, it has frequently been argued that although most immigrants meet these specific labor needs, undocumented immigrants are preferred, because of their special vulnerability (Portes 1978b; Sassen-Koob 1981). Through our survey and ethnographic research, we sought to determine the ways that undocumented workers differ from their documented counterparts and the factors that reinforce the former's vulnerability and compliance as workers. In seeking this clarification, we have considered not only the personal attributes and actions of our respondents, but also the organization of work in the businesses in which they are employed.

Let us begin by examining the popular proposition that undocumented workers embark on the migration process with vulnerabilities they bring with them from home, such as less education and lower skills than their documented compatriots. Our New York survey data reveal a profile of the illegal Dominican immigrant population that is significantly at odds with prevailing stereotypes of the illiterate and unskilled undocumented worker. When we compare the undocumented Dominican immigrant population included in our 1981 snowball sample with its legal counterpart, we find the following contrasts. The illegal Dominican is more likely than the documented Dominican to come from an urban background (85.9 percent and 75.4 percent, respectively); the illegal has a somewhat younger median age (31.7, compared to 34.2); and the illegal is on the average somewhat better educated (8.4 years of schooling versus 7.9 years).

Contrary to conventional wisdom, illegal Dominican immigrants do not originate from the ranks of the least skilled. On the contrary, our survey reveals that the undocumented workers held more prestigious jobs prior to emigration than did their documented counterparts. Undocumented women and men were far more likely to have worked as professionals or managers in the Dominican Republic than were documented immigrants (see Table 30). Almost 30 percent of the female illegal immigrants had been professionals prior to emigration, compared to 21.5 percent of the documented women. Similarly, approximately 30.3 percent of the undocumented men compared to 15.3 percent of the legal males had worked as professionals in their last job in the Dominican Republic. By contrast, the documented population clustered in unskilled occupations. More than 20 percent of the documented women held unskilled jobs such as operative or laborer: the ratio drops to roughly 8 percent for undocumented women. Among the men, 40 percent of the legal immigrants had worked in the Dominican Republic as drivers, craftsmen, operatives, or laborers, compared to 27.3 percent for the undocumented men.

What might account for the relatively higher skill levels of undocumented Dominicans in our survey? In our conversations with undocumented and previously undocumented Dominicans, we learned that the vast majority were visa abusers, persons who had overstayed the period of their tourist visas. A smaller percent had

TABLE 30
Occupational Distribution of Dominican Immigrants in Home Country and New York City, by Legal Status and Sex

	Females				Males			
	Undocumented		Legal		Undocumented		Legal	
	U.S. (%)	D.R. (%)	U.S. (%)	D.R. (%)	U.S. (%)	D.R. (%)	U.S. (%)	D.R. (%)
Professional, technical, managers, proprietors	2.3[a]	29.2	2.9[a]	21.5	13.1	30.3	6.5	15.3
Clerical and sales	6.8[a]	45.8[a]	17.7	28.6	7.9	21.2	24.0	20.8
Drivers, artisans, operators, laborers (except farm)	70.5	8.3[a]	63.2	21.4	55.2	27.3	51.1	40.2
Personal service (including private household)	20.5	16.7	16.2	21.4	23.7	13.6	18.5	5.6
Agricultural laborers	0.0	0.0	0.0	7.1[a]	0.0	7.6	0.0	18.1
N	(44)	(24)	(68)	(28)	(76)	(66)	(92)	(72)

Source. Project data, New York Survey, 1981.
[a]Fewer than 5 cases.

assumed the identity of a Dominican legal resident who was not living in the United States at that time. Consulate officials stationed in the Dominican Republic are selective in issuing tourist visas. They favor individuals with characteristics similar to those we found for our undocumented respondents—applicants who are productively employed in the Dominican Republic, have accumulated assets, and, most important, have incentives to return back home after a brief visit to the United States.

Just as selectivity occurs at the level of the U.S. consulate, it also occurs at the level of the would-be illegal and his or her referent group. Two vignettes from our fieldwork illustrate the latter claim:

Enrique beamed as he left the U.S. consulate office in Santo Domingo. He had just secured a tourist visa to travel to the United States. The smile revealed not just pleasure in the anticipation of his journey but equally the satisfaction that comes from having met a difficult challenge successfully. The challenge had been to convince the immigration officials that he had every intention of returning to his home in the urban area of Licey after his brief trip to visit his relatives in New York. As a young student of accounting struggling unsuccessfully to meet expenses while attending classes in Licey, he had no permanent job and certainly no savings. Yet, he had learned from countless friends that immigration officials insisted on a history of well-paid employment and proof of the intention to return.

Enrique's strategy consisted of the following. First, he opened a bank account with money borrowed from three different relatives and held the account for one month in order to receive a monthly statement of his balance. Second, one of his uncles who managed a money-exchange house reluctantly wrote a letter stating that Enrique had been an employee for several years and would return to his job after his holiday.

On the day of the visit to the U.S. consulate in August, 1981, Enrique and his wife, dressed in their finest and armed with the confidence and "cultural capital" bestowed on university students, successfully received a temporary non-immigrant visa for recreational travel. One week after their arrival in New York, they both secured work as sales clerks in the clothing discount store managed by Enrique's cousin—a store that catered almost exclusively to Hispanic clients. They remained in the United States for the next ten years.

Irma resembled a first cousin who was a U.S. temporary resident. The first cousin was planning to stay in the Dominican Republic for the four months until her first child was born. Irma had convinced this cousin to lend her the latter's green card so that Irma might travel to New York in search of work. Once Irma was settled, she would send the card back with a family member who was planning to travel.

When Irma's friends heard of her intention, they repeated the cautionary tale of another unschooled resident of Juan Pablo, Tito, who had also attempted to travel with another person's green card. Tito's undoing came at the ticket counter in Santo Domingo. There an agent with a handful of customers' airline tickets was trying to return the tickets to their proper owners; she enquired whether Tito was Euclides Rodríguez, the man whose identity Tito had temporarily assumed. Apparently interpreting this question as a challenge, Tito became flustered and soon admitted that he was not Euclides, but a poor *campesino* who was trying to help his large family by migrating to the United States. The story has it that Tito was apprehended by airport officials and lost the money he had spent on his ticket and other travel expenses.

Irma explained that after having heard Tito's tale repeated several times, she became frightened about her future interrogations at the Santo Domingo and New York airports. She concluded that the officials were far more intelligent and worldly than she and were likely to entrap her into admitting, like Tito, that she was not the person she claimed to be.

What is notable about these two case histories, one of success and the other of fear of failure, is the extent to which the success of the deception required both a sophisticated sense of how bureaucracies work and considerable social confidence, traits that migrants are more likely to possess if they are relatively well educated.

Beyond the selectivity that operates at the level of tourist visas, it may also be the case that as the economic crisis in the Dominican Republic has worsened, the migratory flow draws progressively more heavily from the middle class. In addition, the undocumented population is likely to be concentrated among the more recent arrivals in the United States, since the tendency is for the undocumented eventually to regularize their status (Pérez 1981). Thus, it may well be the case that the data on the higher degree of education and higher class backgrounds of the illegals demonstrate not that undocumenteds are always more educated than documented aliens but, rather, that out-migration from the Dominican Republic has become progressively more selective as wages of professionals increasingly prove inadequate for maintaining a middle-class lifestyle in the home country.

Our survey and ethnographic data indicating that undocumented Dominicans often have higher levels of education and skills than their documented counterparts raises the question as to whether this training and experience are rewarded in the New York City labor market or whether the immigrants' illegal status nullifies these advantages. Here our findings are for the most part negative. Despite their variety of occupational experiences in the Dominican Republic, our survey revealed that most Dominicans—legal and undocumented alike—are concentrated in blue-collar jobs (see Table 30). For example, more than 60 percent of the documented and undocumented women (70.5 percent of the undocumented and 63.2 percent of the legal women) were working as craftsmen, operatives, or laborers in New York at the time of the survey. By contrast, less than 3 percent of both groups had found employment as professionals in the United States. Among the male migrants the process of channeling into the lower-skilled jobs, although less extreme, is similar. More than 40 percent of both the undocumented and documented male migrants worked as craftsmen, operatives, or laborers in New York. A somewhat greater percentage of the legal men than the legal women held sales and clerical jobs (24.0 percent, compared to 17.7 percent) and there were somewhat more professional undocumented men (13.1 percent) than professional undocumented women (2.3 percent). It should be noted that Table 30 permits only an overall occupational profile of the Dominican population in terms of legal status; a more refined analysis that controls for the educational level of migrants is needed.

Table 31 presents the effects of education on the occupational success of migrants. If it were true that illegal aliens experienced greater degrees of economic exploitation than the legal alien population, we would expect illegals, compared to legal immigrants with similar levels of education, to be concentrated in the smaller competitive firms and, within those sectors, to be holding the most undesirable jobs. One of the most striking differences between the documented and undocumented groups evident in Table 31 is the much greater likelihood that documented Dominicans work in clerical and sales occupations than undocumented Dominicans at the same educational level. In fact, almost one-third of the relatively educated, legal males hold clerical or sales jobs. Relatively less-educated men and women of both educational and legal-status categories concentrate in manual jobs, with over 50 percent in the category of craftsmen, operatives, and laborers. Breakdowns within this category reveal that both documented and undocumented Dominicans most typically work as operatives engaged in the manufacturing of textiles or packing. Second to operatives, we find almost a fifth of immigrants of both educational-level groupings working in service jobs, especially in the restaurant and hotel sector. The contrasting situation faced by relatively educated, documented women will be discussed when we turn to gender differences among Dominican immigrants.

Undocumented Dominicans find jobs in industrial sectors of the city that resemble those of the legally employed Dominicans (see Table 32). The overwhelming majority of both groups of women, but, among the less well educated, particularly the undocumented,

TABLE 31

Occupational Distribution of Dominican Immigrants in New York City, 1981, by Legal Status, Sex, and Educational Level

	Females				Males				Total Sample (%)
	0–8 Years Education		9 or More Years Education		0–8 Years Education		9 or More Years Education		
	Undocu- mented (%)	Legal (%)	Undocu- mented (%)	Legal (%)	Undocu- mented (%)	Legal (%)	Undocu- mented (%)	Legal (%)	
Professional, technical, managers, proprietors	0.0	0.0	4.3[a]	15.3[a]	9.6[a]	2.0[a]	17.6	11.9	6.8
Clerical and sales	0.0	16.3	13.0[a]	21.1[a]	7.2[a]	18.0	7.8[a]	31.0	15.4
Drivers	0.0	0.0	4.3[a]	0.0	14.3	2.0[a]	8.8[a]	4.8[a]	4.6
Artisans, operators, laborers (including farm)	81.0	63.3	56.5	63.2	45.2	60.0	41.2	33.3	53.6
Personal service (including private household)	19.0	20.4	21.7	5.3[a]	23.8	18.0	23.5	19.0	19.6
N	(21)	(49)	(23)	(19)	(42)	(50)	(34)	(42)	(280)

Source. Project data, New York Survey, 1981.
[a]Fewer than 5 cases.

TABLE 32

Industrial Sector of Employment of Dominican Immigrants in New York City, by Legal Status, Sex, and Educational Level

	Females				Males					
	0–8 Years Education		9 or More Years Education		0–8 Years Education		9 or More Years Education		Total Sample (%)
	Undocu-mented (%)	Legal (%)	Undocu-mented (%)	Legal (%)	Undocu-mented (%)	Legal (%)	Undocu-mented (%)	Legal (%)	
Manufacturing	81.0	62.5	68.2	68.4	46.3	44.9	57.6	43.9	55.8
Commerce, restaurants and hotels	4.8[a]	16.7	4.5[a]	10.5[a]	31.7	36.7	21.2	39.0	24.1
Personal and social services	14.3[a]	18.8	18.2[a]	10.5[a]	4.9	4.1[a]	6.1[a]	9.8[a]	10.2
Construction, transportation, communication, other	0.0	2.1[a]	9.1[a]	10.5[a]	17.1	14.3	15.2	11.8[a]	9.9
N	(21)	(48)	(22)	(19)	(41)	(49)	(33)	(41)	(274)

Source. Project data, New York Survey, 1981.
[a]Fewer than 5 cases.

are employed in manufacturing, especially textiles. The principal difference in the industrial-sector concentration of the documented and undocumented groups is the greater tendency for legal than for undocumented immigrants to find jobs in commerce, restaurants, and hotel trades. This is particularly true of the more educated Dominican men, with 39 percent employed in this sector compared to 21.2 percent of their undocumented counterparts. This is probably an expression of the fact that service-sector jobs are likely to be more visible and to require a higher level of proficiency in English than jobs in manufacturing.

Although, according to our research, undocumented Dominicans do not bring inferior human capital to the New York labor market, they nonetheless find themselves in a somewhat more precarious, down-graded work environment than their legal counterparts. As was noted in the preceding section, New York City has recently experienced a scaling down and "informalization" (Sassen-Koob 1986) of production in manufacturing and services. This change has entailed a movement away from firms that were relatively high-paying, vertically integrated, and union-organized to businesses that have a small work force, are informally organized, specialize in the most risky and most labor-intensive phases of production, and are difficult to organize. Our survey data indicate that although large numbers of all groups of Dominican immigrants have found work in New York's proliferating small businesses, it is the undocumented, in particular, who predominate in such workplaces. Thus, whereas 44 percent of our documented respondents were employed in businesses with fewer than 50 workers, the number rose to almost 60 percent of our undocumented respondents (see Table 33). By contrast, more than one-fourth of the legal immigrants worked in firms with more than 200 employees, while only about one-tenth of the illegals did so.

An association exists between small firm size and the tendency to operate a highly informal business in which employees are paid "off the books" in cash rather than by check. This "off the books" practice allows employers to cut costs by avoiding contributions to social security, unemployment insurance, and other workers' benefits. According to our survey, 43 percent of our undocumented respondents were paid in cash, as compared to only 19 percent of our legal respondents. Indeed, our data suggest that a sizable

TABLE 33
*Size of Firm of Employment of Dominican Immigrants
in New York City*

No. of Employees	Undocumented Immigrants (%)	Legal Immigrants (%)	Total Sample (%)
50 or fewer	59.1	44.4	50.7
51–100	16.1	16.1	16.1
101–200	12.9	12.9	12.9
201 or more	11.8	26.6	20.3
N	(93)	(124)	(217)

Source. Project data, New York Survey, 1981.

proportion—29.1 percent—of the Dominican work force may work in unreported jobs. In any case, even if all of the employers who pay our respondents in cash were in fact to report this activity, the cash payments in themselves indicate the informal nature of the labor contract.

The firms in which illegals were employed were not only smaller and more informal than the firms employing legal immigrants, but they also tended to pay lower wages. Table 34 presents the weekly wages of Dominicans in our sample, controlling for legal status and sex. Only 21.5 percent of the documented men earned less than $150 per week, but the ratio increased to 43.8 percent for undocumented men. In the case of women, 48.4 percent of the documented earned less than $150, as against 58.1 percent of the undocumented women. It should be noted that the minimum wage for a forty-hour week in 1981, the time of the survey, was $134.

We found that undocumented Dominicans were more likely to work in an ethnic niche than were their legal counterparts. Table 35 presents data on the ethnicity of the coworkers, supervisors, employers, and clients of the firms in which Dominicans in our sample were employed. Over one-third of all Dominicans work in firms in which their coworkers are predominantly other Dominicans (34.9 percent) and the overwhelming majority work alongside other Hispanics (67.3 percent). If we include blacks, then almost 85 percent of the Dominicans work with other minority or immigrant

TABLE 34

Weekly Wages of Dominican Immigrants in New York City, 1981,
by Legal Status and Sex

	Males		Females		
	Undocu-mented Immigrants (%)	Legal Immigrants (%)	Undocu-mented Immigrants (%)	Legal Immigrants (%)	Total Sample (%)
Less than $150	43.8	21.5	58.1	48.4	40.1
$150–174	15.1	21.4	18.6	22.6	19.4
$175–199	12.3	13.1	7.0	14.5	12.2
$200 or more	28.8	44.1	16.6	14.5	28.3
N	(73)	(94)	(43)	(62)	(262)

Source. Project data, New York Survey, 1981.

groups. This pattern is somewhat more dramatic for the undocumented workers, with 37.3 percent working with Dominicans, 42.2 percent working in mixed Hispanic work groups and 13.2 percent with blacks. Under 7 percent of illegal immigrants are employed alongside non-Hispanic or non-black workers. In contrast, over 20 percent of the legal Dominicans work in firms where the majority of workers are non-minority. Moreover, 23.2 percent of all Dominicans have an immediate supervisor who is also Dominican, and more than one-third report supervision by someone belonging to another Hispanic ethnic group.

Our data reveal a considerable amount of ethnic sponsorship: 22.5 percent of undocumented Dominicans work for other Dominicans. This compares with 13.1 percent of the legal Dominican immigrants. An additional 30.4 percent of the undocumenteds work for other Hispanic employers. Taken together, these data indicate that undocumented aliens are much more likely to be employed in ethnically homogeneous firms than are documented Dominicans (52.9 percent, compared to 32.4 percent).

Approximately one-third of the Dominicans work in firms that provide services or goods predominantly to the Hispanic commu-

TABLE 35
*Ethnicity of Workplace of Dominican Immigrants
in New York City, 1981*

	Undocumented Immigrants (%)	Legal Immigrants (%)	Total Sample (%)
Coworkers' ethnicity (majority)			
Dominican	37.3	33.1	34.9
Dominican and other Hispanic	42.2	25.2	32.4
Dominican and black	13.2	20.1	17.4
Other Non-Hispanic	6.9	21.6	15.4
N	(102)	(139)	(241)
Immediate supervisor's ethnicity			
Dominican	32.5	17.6	23.3
Other Hispanic	36.1	33.1	34.2
Non-Hispanic	31.4	49.3	42.5
N	(83)	(136)	(219)
Employer's ethnicity			
Dominican	22.5	13.1	17.0
Other Hispanic	30.4	19.3	23.9
Non-Hispanic	47.1	67.6	59.1
N	(102)	(145)	(247)
Clients' ethnicity			
Hispanic	36.1	27.2	31.1
Non-Hispanic	23.1	36.8	30.7
Don't know	40.7	36.0	38.1
N	(108)	(136)	(241)

Source. Project data, New York Survey, 1981.

nity itself. Again, this is somewhat more likely in the case of the illegals than of legal immigrants (36.1 percent to 27.2 percent respectively). The large number of "don't knows" probably corresponds to those immigrants who work in manufacturing industries where they rarely come in contact with the distributor or consumer of the product. Yet the fact that at least one-third of the immigrants work to provide goods or services for other Hispanics makes it apparent that the consolidation of an ethnic colony can eventually create its own limited demand. Ethnic groceries (the many *bodegas* of Manhattan) and small *criollo* restaurants are examples of enterprises catering to an ethnic clientele.

Our findings thus far point to clear differences between labor-market incorporation of legal and of undocumented Dominicans. The documented Dominicans appear more successful than their undocumented counterparts in locating employment in that tier of New York City's economy where native-born employers are able and willing to meet basic labor law requirements, such as payment of the minimum wage and social security benefits. The undocumented workers are more likely to be found in those largely Hispanic-owned firms where employers attempt to remain competitive by denying workers benefits that earlier generations of organized workers have secured from employers.

We must ask, then, how so many employers of undocumented workers have been able to avoid compliance with labor requirements. This leads to a discussion of differences in levels of worker organization and militancy in the firms that employ Dominican documented workers versus those that employ undocumented workers. Our survey data show that undocumented Dominicans predominate in businesses where the levels of worker organization and militancy are low. For example, almost 65 percent of our undocumented respondents were found in non-union firms, as compared to 30.6 percent of the legal immigrants. Of the undocumented workers employed in a union business, only 58 percent had opted to join a union, as compared to 83 percent of the documented Dominican immigrants.

The political docility of the immigrant population as a whole and the undocumented group in particular is further illustrated by information we collected on workplace struggles. All respondents were asked if their fellow workers, as a group, had taken steps to improve their working conditions or salaries since the respondent had worked at his or her place of employment. If the answer was yes, they were then queried about whether they had personally taken part in any of these activities. The great majority, 63.9 percent, reported that no such workplace struggle had occurred. The workplaces of undocumented workers were particularly manageable by employers: some three-fourths had undergone no efforts to improve conditions whatsoever, compared to 56.9 percent of the firms where legal immigrants worked. In those relatively few places where workplace confrontations of some type had taken place, the two groups appear to have behaved in a similar fashion: approximately 68 percent of both documented and undocumented workers participated.

These survey findings support the prevailing view that the undocumented are a particularly controllable category of worker. Our in-depth interviews with undocumented workers also revealed that these workers internalize and react to their vulnerable legal and material situation. As the following quote illustrates, the legal stigma undocumented workers acquire in the United States and the material disadvantages this stigma brings make illegals especially reluctant to participate in collective workplace struggles. One undocumented worker explained his decision not to sign a petition to support the unionization of his workplace:

Sure, I sign the petition with my assumed name, the one they know me by in this country. But how do I know it will stop there? The owner has hired some crafty lawyers to break the union. So how do I know that they won't start investigating all the names on the list and learn from some informer that I am not the person whose name is on my green card? . . . As jobs go, this is not such a bad one. Without good papers, you can't afford to be so picky. . . . I have a lot of people I still owe back home who helped me get over. How can I risk being fired if the boss decides to retaliate against all the people who turned against him and toward the union? Let others take the risk who don't have my debts and my problems with the *migra* [Immigration Service].

The undocumented are clearly highly vulnerable and thus likely to be more manageable than legal workers. There are, however, more factors to compliance in the workplace than simply undocumented status. As was reported above, our survey research points to a convergence between undocumented status and employment in small, ethnic-owned firms. It is our contention that the docility of undocumented workers is also conditioned by the organization of work in these ethnic-owned firms.

Through in-depth interviews with twenty-six undocumented

workers and participant-observation in five immigrant-owned work-places, we learned that personalism and patronage commonly struc-ture the working relations between undocumented workers and immigrant owners. In theoretical writings on the organization of work in immigrant-dominated workplaces, personalism has been interpreted as a direct and repressive form of control. For example, Sassen-Koob (1980) proposes that personalism allows employers to be far freer than owners of union or bureaucratically structured firms to fire workers who express dissatisfaction or demonstrate militancy. Our interviews and observations showed the personal-istic control of immigrant-owners operating in a different fashion, to curtail rather than repress dissatisfaction and antagonism.

In our opinion, immigrant owners would risk exacerbating the volatility of their businesses were they to secure undocumented workers through fear and coercion. A subcontractor in the garment trade, for example, must manage periods of little work as well as of high demand. As we personally observed, an undocumented mi-grant who has received small loans from his boss during slow peri-ods is far more likely to recruit family members and friends when production speeds up than are the undocumented workers whose overbearing employer has verbally abused them into accelerating their pace.

The patron-client ties between immigrant owners and workers also mitigate solidarity among workers. In place of a united work force, we observed a collection of individuals, each with a discrete set of problems and goals which defined his or her particular rela-tionship to the owner and to the workplace. The following cases, drawn from our ethnographic fieldwork, illustrate this point:

Isidro, an undocumented restaurant worker, negotiated a raise (from $3.50 an hour to $3.80) and a lengthened workday (from 10 hours to 12). He needed these concessions in order to begin to pay back the $5,000 he had borrowed to finance his illegal emigration. In his words, "I explained my special needs to the boss and he understood because he too had come over illegally [*con papeles sucios*] many years ago. . . . The boss told me not to tell anyone in the restaurant—not even my cousin—about my raise, because they would ask for one too. He told me he had helped me out because I am a hard worker and some of the others are not."

Rosario, an undocumented apparel worker, was allowed to take sewing home so that she could both work and care for her elderly mother, who had suffered a stroke. Rosario believed that her Dominican employer had done her a favor, and consequently she accepted without comment the five to ten cents reduction in the piecework rates she received for work done at home. Rosario's teen-aged niece criticized her aunt for being too passive and respectful "an abusive boss." She urged her aunt to speak to the other homeworkers from the factory and try to get all of them to demand, not only the same wages as women who sewed in the factory, but also reimbursement for supplies, such as thread and needles. Rosario retorted that, first, she was not about to interfere in other people's lives, and, second, she felt that to ask her employer for more money was both ill-mannered [*mal educada*] and a sign of ingratitude.

How patronage creates loyalty and trust as it reduces the likelihood that immigrant-owned workplaces will be successfully organized is illustrated in the following case:

Domingo, a young Dominican labor organizer of office workers, learned from friends that the Cuban restaurant in which he worked on weekends was soon going to be targeted by a restaurant union. He explained his dilemma: "I'm pro-union, of course. But I also had to acknowledge in my heart that Señor Riós had given jobs to many in my own family and others from my town when they first came to New York. . . . So I went to my friends and asked them to persuade their boss not to organize the restaurant. I never told Señor Riós, but I think he found out anyway. . . . I realize my actions were contrary to my commitment to working people. It just came down to trust [*confianza*]. I know Señor Riós has trust in me, and I have trust in him. And in this one case trust took precedence over organizing workers.

The success of immigrant-owned firms, then, is not solely based on a highly vulnerable, undocumented work force, but such workers do prove valuable to their employers. The special vulnerability that many illegals feel can keep them from leaving immigrant-owned businesses. The work histories we collected for adult members of fifty-five Dominican households showed that most quite quickly left a job with an immigrant employer for one with an American employer. In explaining their departure from immigrant-owned firms, most of these informants reported that they left because of inferior pay, benefits, and working conditions in the immigrant-run firms. Those informants who remained with immigrant employers tended either to be relatives or close friends of the owner or to have particular vulnerabilities, such as being undocumented or the recipient of welfare and therefore legally prohibited from working for wages.

According to our undocumented informants, upon their arrival they sought a Hispanic (preferably Dominican) employer who had already established a bond of trust with a close relative or friend. Over time, however, the ties between undocumented workers and immigrant owners became predicated less on the former's insecure status than on bonds of patronage that created a sense of loyalty and obligation to these employers. Indeed, for a small minority of our informants these ties were so strong that workers who had been successful in legalizing their status chose to remain with low-paying immigrant employers. Unfortunately, such manifold ties can hide a sinister reality. In many cases, it is precisely the low wages and lack of benefits, as well as the absence of collective bargaining, that create an immediate need for the patron-client tie between the immigrant owner and the immigrant worker.

Finally, our survey findings on the low wages of undocumented Dominican immigrants add credence to the claim that undocumented workers create downward pressures on wage levels within industries that depend heavily on an immigrant work force. We do not, however, believe that the brunt of this pressure is found at the workplace per se, where undocumented workers impede efforts aimed at unionization. Immigrants weaken the bargaining position of native workers in a less direct, yet powerful way. As our ethnography of workplaces revealed, the existence of a large pool of immigrant labor, willing to work under subcontracting conditions with no benefits, gives employers more leverage in their efforts to defeat organizing efforts. They effectively use the threat of closing firms and subcontracting production against unionized and unionizing workers who seek to improve salaries and working conditions. Immigrants domesticate native-born workers, then, by meeting the labor needs of those industries, such as apparel and electronics, where increasingly those segments of production that are most susceptible to worker discontent and militance can easily be passed on to small, non-union subcontracting firms.

Gender Differences among Dominican Immigrant Workers

Undocumented workers are not the only ones to suffer from a devaluation of their labor in the New York City labor market.

Women in general and immigrant women in particular are similarly victimized.[4] Women's labor, although it may be devalued, is in demand in New York City, where many industries are undergoing deskilling and the domestication of their work force.[5] Before examining how gender influences Dominican immigrants' work experiences and orientations toward work, let us briefly review some of the patterns of gender segregation and discrimination in the U.S. labor market.

Labor market research in the United States has documented a clear pattern of gender-stereotyping, with employers often excluding women from, or at least discouraging them from entering, higher-status jobs (Epstein 1970; Oppenheimer 1973; Almquist 1979). This segregation falls hardest on Latin American immigrant women, according to a recent study. In a comparison of data from the 1970 and 1980 U.S. censuses, Tienda et al. (1984) found an increasing disparity in the industrial and occupational allocations of native-born versus immigrant women. For example, they found a relative increase over the decade in the proportion of immigrant

4. Several authors have noted that migrants and female workers share the status of devalued labor. For example, Fernández-Kelly writes, "It must be emphasized that the reasons why women (and migrants) enter the work force as bearers of inferior labor have less to do with their particular training (or lack of it) than with the fact that they are female (or migrants)" (1983: 89). Historically, both women and migrants have functioned as a reserve army of labor. That is, they allow employers flexibility in hiring, but they are exempted from the benefits that organized (male) workers have extracted from employers and the state. The tendency has been to recruit migrants and women during periods of labor shortage, for part-time or seasonal work, and to discipline a work force that is organized against employers. It has been proposed that migrants can support themselves on low, irregular wages (a sub-subsistence wage), because they leave household members behind who also generate income needed to maintain the migrant worker and his or her dependents (Burawoy 1976; Meillassoux 1981). The ideological justification employers and the state have used to legitimate the lower and more irregular wages paid to women makes the assumption that women's wages supplement those of a male relative. In practice, working-class women have often stretched inadequate wages by pooling resources with other poor women who form support networks (Stack 1974; Rapp 1978).

5. The shift in the job market from goods to services over the course of the 1970s increased the access of all women to the labor force. Nonetheless, when we compare rates of employment and labor-force participation among native-born and immigrant women, we find that the latter apparently enjoyed a competitive advantage over their native-born counterparts (cf. Waldinger 1987: 292–93). For a discussion of how the de-industrialization of the U.S. economy has and will affect women and families, see Kuhn and Bluestone 1987.

women in the least-skilled, manual jobs, alongside a movement up from these jobs for native-born women. Latin American immigrant women in particular were concentrated in such low-paying, insecure occupations as apparel or electronics operative or domestic service. The authors identified a process of occupational succession wherein immigrants in general and female immigrants in particular were channeled into the least desirable jobs vacated by native-born workers.

With regard to wages, female Latin American immigrants are also disadvantaged. For example, one study based on 1980 census data found that Hispanic women earned only an additional $271.93 for each year of education acquired, whereas Hispanic men earned an additional $524.84 for each year (Verdugo 1982: 8). When the researchers controlled for all demographic, education, and workplace variables except gender and ethnicity, Hispanic women earned $3,256 less than white men. In other words, an earning gap of 29 percent existed between Hispanic women and white men, whereas one of only 14 percent existed between white and Hispanic males (Verdugo 1982: 9). From these data we may conclude that gender discrimination accounts for approximately one-half of the wage differential between Hispanic women and white men, and ethnicity accounts for the other half.

Our survey and ethnographic materials reveal a similar pattern of gender discrimination. Indeed, in several instances, gender appears to have a stronger negative impact on wage levels and working conditions than legal status does.

Consistent with the national pattern for Latin American immigrant women of occupational succession into the least desirable jobs, our findings indicated that the vast majority of our female respondents were employed as operatives in New York's declining manufacturing sector (see Tables 31 and 32). Moreover, in competing for jobs requiring higher skills, Dominican women, regardless of legal status, were at a greater disadvantage than their male counterparts. It will be recalled that 23.1 percent of our female respondents had been professionals in the Dominican Republic. Yet, less than 3 percent were able to match this level of employment in New York.

Not only are Dominican women channeled into manual jobs that demand low skill levels, but they are also paid very low wages (see

Table 34). Indeed, the association between wages and gender appears to be stronger than the association between wages and legal status. That is, both documented and undocumented women are overly represented in the lowest wage categories when compared to both groups of men. Even undocumented males out-earned documented females; whereas only 43.8 percent of the undocumented males earned less than $150 a week, 48.4 percent of the documented females and 58.1 percent of the undocumented females received wages below that level. The ordinal stratification of wages moves from undocumented females, to documented females, to undocumented males, to documented males.[6]

Given the fact that Dominican women's wages are significantly below men's, it is noteworthy that our ethnographic research revealed a pattern of greater job satisfaction among women than men. Women showed a greater tendency than men to associate their work with the migration goal of economic and social mobility for the entire household. This was the case even for those women who had experienced downward occupational mobility subsequent to emigration; indeed, such women argued that their own and other household members' improved wages compensated for any loss of job status. The following quote from a female head of household is typical:

Sure, my job as a sewing machine operator is not in itself a big thing. But I'm more than satisfied, because with this job I've been able to send my son to college, and my son's successes in college are mine, too. One day, when he becomes a lawyer, I too will feel like an important person in this country.

The economic vulnerability we have noted for women with regard to types of employment and wage levels is not replicated in

6. The amount of time the migrant had spent in the country was added as a control but did not alter the patterns established here, with the exception that the differences between undocumented and documented workers' earnings at the higher wage levels were somewhat less dramatic. It is also noteworthy that the migrants as a whole are concentrated at the lowest end of the wage scale, with 40.1 percent of the total sample earning less than $150 a week, which in most cases means below the legal minimum wage.

Another, more recent study of undocumented workers in the New York Metropolitan Area also found marked differences in earnings between women and men. The majority of the undocumented women (65 percent) received less than $5.00 an hour in 1983. In contrast, only 40 percent of the undocumented men received such low wages (Papademetrios and Di Marzio 1986: 145).

our survey findings on unionization. As is reflected in Table 36, Dominican women are more likely to work in union firms than men and are also more likely than men to become union members. Furthermore, a woman's legal status, unlike a man's, does not affect her likelihood of union membership; more than 80 percent of both the legal and illegal female migrants joined the union at their workplace. It might be tempting to conclude from these data that the women are more militant than the men, were it not for the fact that in the garment factories, where women workers are concentrated, the unions tend to be closed shops. The high rates of membership among the women undoubtedly reflect this condition rather than an inherently greater radicalism. In fact, our survey reveals that the female migrants are less likely than men to be employed in a workplace where there are collective struggles and less inclined than men to join such struggles (see Table 37). As might be suspected from our earlier discussion, both undocumented women and undocumented men are more docile when it comes to collective struggles than are their documented coworkers. What is noteworthy is that gender exerts a more powerful influence on this workplace behavior than does legal status. In those firms where workplace struggles occurred, 61.5 percent of the legal Dominican men participated, whereas only 50 percent of their female counterparts did so. Despite relatively high levels of unionization, undocumented and legal women alike are extremely disciplined workers, little given to collective efforts to improve their working conditions. Whereas legal status and unionization may operate to empower men for increased confrontations in the workplace, these conditions in themselves do not compel women to join in such efforts.

To account definitively for these gender differences we would have had to conduct more in-depth and systematic research on Dominicans' attitudes toward workplace struggle, and we would have needed to increase the number of cases of workplace struggles documented. What we can offer, instead, are informed speculations.

First, our survey data indicate that Dominican immigrant women face a far more restricted job market than Dominican men, and women apparently tailor their actions in the workplace accordingly.

TABLE 36

*Level of Unionization of Dominican Immigrants in New York City,
by Legal Status and Sex*

	Males		Females		
	Undocumented Immigrants (%)	Legal Immigrants (%)	Undocumented Immigrants (%)	Legal Immigrants (%)	Total Sample (%)
Non-union workplace	70.8	39.2	57.1	27.3	47.3
Union workplace	29.2	60.8	42.9	72.7	52.8
Migrant members	35.0	77.4	83.3	80.9	73.2
Migrant nonmembers	65.0	22.6	16.7	19.1	26.8
N	(65)	(79)	(42)	(66)	(252)

Source. Project data, New York Survey, 1981.

We found women to be more concerned than men about the likelihood that participation in workplace struggles might result in them being fired. Our female informants voiced the concern that garment work was virtually the only avenue of "honorable" employment opened to female immigrants with little or no proficiency in English. They also observed, correctly, that jobs in the apparel industry were becoming scarcer.[7] Although male garment workers also acknowledged that participation in a workplace struggle might lead to dismissal, they recognized that employment opportunities were available in other industries, such as restaurants and building maintenance.

Second, because women's wages tend to be lower than men's, women are less likely to have the monetary reserves to support themselves and their dependents during a strike or lockout. This is

7. Between 1969 and 1975, employment in the New York garment industry declined at a rate of 12,500 annually. Between 1969 and 1981 some 86,000 jobs were lost (Waldinger 1983: 103–4).

TABLE 37
Militancy at Workplace of Dominican Immigrants in New York City,
by Legal Status and Sex

	Males		Females		
	Undocumented Immigrants (%)	Legal Immigrants (%)	Undocumented Immigrants (%)	Legal Immigrants (%)	Total Sample (%)
No struggles at workplace[a]	67.4	55.9	81.3	57.8	63.3
Struggles at workplace	32.6	44.1	18.8	42.2	36.7
Migrant participated	42.3	61.5	41.7	50.0	39.7
Migrant did not participate	57.7	38.5	58.3	50.0	60.3
N	(43)	(68)	(32)	(45)	(188)

Source. Project data, New York Survey, 1981.

[a]The wording of the questionnaire items was: (a) "Have the workers in your workplace made efforts to improve their working conditions or salaries?"; (b) If yes, "Did you personally participate in any of these activities?"

particularly likely to affect women who live alone and those who are heads of households. In one of the three cases of unsuccessful union-organizing drives we investigated, the union organizers gave the vulnerability of the predominantly female work force as the reason behind the union's decision to dissuade the activist workers from striking. The organizers had believed, incorrectly, that they had enough votes to unionize the factory peacefully, without disrupting the workplace and jeopardizing the workers' receipt of wages.

Finally, it appears that Dominican women's overall satisfaction with the household gains employment brings to them as wives and daughters constrains their militancy. Women often viewed workplace struggle, with its risk of job loss or of protracted unemployment, as a threat to the more egalitarian roles wage work had allowed them to assume in the household. Neither concern was unfounded. The three union drives we observed at businesses with large Dominican female work forces (two garment shops and one lamp factory) all ended in the union's defeat and the shutdown of either several departments or the entire business. Furthermore, several of the unemployed women we interviewed indicated that their husbands reverted to a more authoritarian control over budgetary decisions when the women's financial contributions lessened. For example, Pessar witnessed a fight in which a laid-off worker's husband railed at his wife for having supported a union drive. He then forbade the woman to send part of her unemployment benefits to her widowed sister in the Dominican Republic, although the woman had always set aside a small part of her salary for her sister.

In his discussion of the distinct fractions of the working class, Edwards (1979) names blacks, Hispanics, females, teenagers, and the undocumented as those groups that are overrepresented in secondary-sector jobs. They are, in his words, the "working poor" who are subject to "super-exploitation." While this claim is valid as a broad generalization, it does not capture degrees of discrimination among the working poor. Our survey and our ethnographic research reveal a hierarchy of vulnerability and receptivity to employers' "super-exploitation," with the documented Dominican male in the least insecure position and the undocumented female in the worst position. Furthermore, we have found that in several exploitative aspects of work, gender is more significant than legal status.

These latter findings are troubling for many reasons. Legal standing, of course, is an achieved status, whereas gender is an ascribed one. As was mentioned earlier, Glauco Pérez concluded that an illegal Dominican worker takes approximately seven years to adjust his or her status to that of legal alien (Pérez 1981). This is usually accomplished through acquiring working papers or marrying a permanent resident or citizen. A Dominican woman, however, has no way to alter her gender status.

The implications of gender discrimination against immigrant women are particularly troubling when we take into account the rather high rates of marital instability that characterize Dominican households in New York. It will be recalled that, at the time of the last census, 41 percent of all Dominican households were female-headed. Indeed, among the more recent immigrant groups to New York, Dominican females stand out as particularly disadvantaged: they have relatively low levels of education and a higher probability of being in single-parent, female-headed households. Whereas 50 percent of Colombian females in New York City are in stable marriages, for example, only 41.3 percent of Dominican women are. Marital disruptions occur for about 43.8 percent of Dominican females, compared to only about 25 percent for Colombians of both sexes and for Dominican males (Gurak and Kritz 1984: 8). It is Puerto Rican women, with female headship rates of 44 percent, who most closely approximate Dominican women in the United States. This comparison carries ominous implications for Dominicans. Of all Hispanic ethnic groups, Puerto Ricans have had the highest increase in female headship since 1960 (an 83 percent jump). Moreover, the high female headship rate, combined with low labor-force participation rates, has placed Puerto Rican family income among the lowest in the country (Gurak and Falcón-Rodríguez 1987).

We have noted above that some Dominican women have been able to negotiate greater autonomy and decision-making rights within their households as a result of wage employment in New York. This has increased their marital satisfaction and encouraged them to think of New York as a permanent home. Yet, the success of the migration venture for them is dependent on the preservation of household bonds of solidarity, albeit renegotiated ones. When the household bonds are severed, the migration project often falters, because the individual resources of single members, especially women, are insufficient to sustain it. Indeed, the census report that 23 percent of all Dominican households drew public assistance income may reflect the fact that a significant proportion of Dominican women have already accepted periods of unemployment and state dependency rather than toil in low-paying, insecure jobs that net little more than welfare payments.[8] The pic-

8. In their 1981 probability survey of Dominicans in New York City, Gurak and Kritz found that women were more likely to be in the labor force if they were living with their spouses than if they were female heads. The differential was 25.4 (1988: 12).

ture is even bleaker for the illegal Dominican woman, who cannot avail herself and her family of state-supported assistance. These women face long hours of low-wage work in illicit businesses, which are not likely to pay the cost of the social services needed to supervise children and other dependent household members. There is a painful irony associated with the fact that the newfound autonomy of many migrant women may come at the cost of the collective mobility project of the household and in many cases lead to poverty.

How Dominican Immigrants Perceive Their Material Circumstances

The 1980 census and our New York survey present us with a Dominican population that clusters in the lowest tiers of the labor market and ranks among the lowest-paid groups of workers. Within this overall population, two categories are especially disadvantaged: undocumented workers and female workers. When these economic and social facts are juxtaposed against our informants' perceptions of their situation in New York, we find a perplexing situation. The majority of our ethnographic informants, undocumented and women included—68 of 100 informants—declare themselves to be middle-class.

How do we explain the fact that these occupants of largely dead-end, poorly remunerated jobs view themselves as middle-class? Critical factors may be the meanings and symbolic markers of social mobility and middle-class identity Dominican immigrants embrace. As was described in the introductory chapter, it is characteristic of an increasingly interdependent world economic system that social status is measured and marked by access to prestigious consumer goods available on the international market. As a way of extending markets for commodities and labor, core capitalist countries export new consumer goods and create a demand for them. Consequently, a transnational symbolic system of stratification based on commodity consumption has emerged. However, these consumer goods are distributed unequally, not only among social classes in each country, but, more significantly, among the same social classes in different countries. Many consumer goods enjoyed by poorer-class Americans, for example, are completely beyond the reach of members of the lower class in less developed countries. It is this disparity between the United States and less developed countries, such as the Dominican Republic, over access to prestigious consumer goods that makes emigration a viable strategy for social mobility (cf. Grant and Herbstein 1983). For example, as Kessler-Harris observes, consumerism in the United States has for many decades "raised the level of 'necessary' goods to the point where telephones, refrigerators, and automobiles were rarely optional" (1981: 145), but these commodities, deemed necessities in most American households, are out of the reach even of many members of the middle class in the Dominican Republic.

The precarious hold many of our Dominican informants had on a middle-class standard of living, as measured in household income and commodities, has been strengthened in the United States. Thus, when Dominican workers move to the United States and acquire "prestigious" consumer goods such as modern kitchen appliances, color televisions, and automobiles, many feel they have solidified, if not improved, their status, and they accordingly perceive themselves as middle-class.[9]

Job satisfaction and loyalty are enhanced by the belief of many Dominicans that employment in the United States has solidified their middle-class standing. This middle-class identification among Dominican immigrants has not escaped the attention of union organizers. In conversations with us, several organizers contrasted Puerto Ricans, whom they claim are receptive to union-organizing arguments based on the premise of class struggle, with Dominicans, whom they claim frequently reject the idea that they are members of the working class. In the words of one organizer, "You just don't talk about social class with Dominicans. It falls on deaf ears, or, worse, it turns them off completely. I just get down to bread-and-butter issues, higher wages to send the kids to college and to make a down payment on the house back home."

The fact that the majority of our informants identified them-

9. Prior research has shown that many native-born blue-collar workers in the United States also identify themselves as middle-class (Hodge and Treiman, 1974). It is possible, therefore, that some of our Dominican informants may have "assimilated" U.S. conceptions of social class; however, we believe that most Dominicans draw on Dominican referents.

selves as middle-class and drew on Dominican-based referents in arriving at this self-attribution is emblematic of the fact that Dominicans do indeed remain between two islands. On the one hand, they embrace U.S.-manufactured items of consumption, transmogrified into Dominican models of consumption and standing, to shield themselves from a more objective, or at least U.S.-centered, measure of their class position in New York. Stocked with expensive gifts and plenty of cash, they also use visits and investments in the Dominican Republic to reinforce their identity as middle-class. Yet, as our discussion of return migration shows, this middle-class identity often cannot stand the test of permanent or full-time settlement in the Dominican Republic. On the other hand, most Dominicans have yet to make the full social and cultural transition to permanent settlement in the United States. An important step in this direction might be more active participation in working-class institutions such as unions. Another could be a greater involvement in neighborhood and city coalitions rather than the more usual participation in Dominican social clubs and political parties (cf. Georges 1984; Torres-Saillant 1989).[10]

Conclusion

This chapter has examined one of several seeming paradoxes concerning Dominican international migration. We have explored why in the 1970s, despite mounting, city-wide unemployment, Dominicans headed in ever larger numbers to New York City and found employment, for the most part, in the industrial sector—which was experiencing the greatest job loss. To account for this seeming paradox, we have described the restructuring and ethnic realignment that has characterized the New York City economy during this period. This restructuring has led to the expansion of small, secondary-sector firms which have assumed many of the production functions earlier performed in large, union factories. Immigrant entrepreneurs have also flourished with the growth of the immigrant population. Our research revealed a significant amount

10. For more contemporary studies of the evolving Dominican community in the United States, see the new journal *Punto 7 Review: A Journal of Marginal Discourse*, edited by Ramona Hernandez and Silvio Torres-Saillant, two Dominican-born scholars residing in New York.

of "sponsorship" (in the form of employment at extremely low wages) of undocumented Dominicans by fellow Dominican entrepreneurs. Owners of secondary-sector businesses and immigrant employers alike have found a cheap, compliant work force among immigrants in general, and undocumented workers and female immigrants in particular.

8

Conclusion

In our treatment of Dominican migration to the United States, in order to illustrate the multidimensional nature of international labor migration we have focused principally on four levels of analysis: (1) the international division of labor; (2) domestic state policy of the sending society; (3) social class relations in both the sending and the receiving communities; and (4) gender, generations, households, and migrant social networks.

We found the concept of an international division of labor useful in explaining Dominican emigration as a response to interrelated economic and political developments in the Dominican Republic and the United States. The notion of an international division of labor, associated with the perspective of a world system, emphasizes the external constraints imposed on developing societies, and especially the role of foreign capital and the unequal terms of trade between developed and developing societies. The Dominican Republic, as a country oriented to the external world market and with a high dependence on a narrow range of traditional exports, is marked by disincentives to internal market expansion and consequent high income inequality.

We argued, however, that external constraints and dependency have conditioned, rather than determined, emigration outcomes. Much greater emphasis should be placed on internal institutional factors such as repeated domestic state policy decisions that serve to reproduce external market conditions and income inequality. In the Dominican Republic, since the early 1970s we have witnessed a critical worsening of international export prices, accompanied by persistent official and international reports on the need to diversify out of sugar. Yet despite two radically different political regimes since the mid-1960s, Dominican state policymakers have not taken the measures necessary for diversification. Restrictive food policies have been used to discriminate against rural producers, and terms of trade between agriculture and industry have deteriorated over time. The deterioration of agriculture has provoked high rates of migration from rural to urban areas. Import-substitution policies have favored the interests of large-scale business through tariff policies that tax agriculture, through exchange-rate policy, and through price, credit, and wage policies. The high dependence on traditional exports is continually reinforced by officeholders and by state policymakers who stand to benefit personally and politically by bolstering inefficient state enterprises and by favoring the interests of a politically powerful group of industrialists. Moreover, unprecedented growth in higher education in urban areas has resulted in an oversupply of relatively highly skilled persons with raised expectations for social mobility and the life-styles of the middle class. These internal structural factors have predisposed the Dominican Republic to emigration.

By focusing on social class as an essential category of analysis in our study, we have avoided a sterile debate over whether migration is beneficial or harmful to sending societies as undifferentiated entities. Too often this question has been asked as though migrant communities were classless or populated solely by members of one social class (Griffin 1976). The question is not whether, but, rather, to whom migration is beneficial or harmful. The issue must be recast in class terms because decidedly different conclusions might be drawn regarding the impact of migration, depending on the focal group chosen. In rural areas, for example, we suggest that out-migration has benefited the social class that dispatched members abroad while at the same time it contributed to the deterioration of productive options for those social classes unable to take advantage of labor emigration.

In our treatment of Dominican emigration as it appeared in the early 1980s, we have emphasized that migration from the Dominican Republic, as well as elsewhere in the Caribbean and Latin America, is not an effective remedy for unemployment and underemployment. Dominican emigrants do not represent a labor surplus. Through emigration from urban areas the Dominican Republic is losing valuable human resources—people with training, skills, and experience that far exceed national averages. We are not arguing that the out-migration of such workers has heretofore resulted in actual shortages of skilled, experienced workers in the Dominican Republic. Yet, relatively high rates of investment in the higher education of such a migration-prone stratum are a questionable use of scarce state resources. Moreover, emigration in rural areas has not resulted in less unemployment in agriculture. To the contrary, out-migration contributes to national declines in farm employment and in rural people's access to land.

Dominican out-migration has become a strategy of income accumulation for middle-class or aspiring middle-class households that cannot solidify their class position within the confines of the Dominican national economy. So strong is this association between middle-class standing and emigration that many Dominican workers in the lowest-paying and lowest-status jobs in New York insist they are members of the middle class in the United States. And they dramatize this standing by bringing relatives high-status goods such as color television sets and by investing in expensive homes in the Dominican Republic—homes in which the emigrant owner often cannot subsequently afford to reside. From the point of view of the non-migrant, emigration seems an easier way to achieve material gains than does any attempt to improve economic standing within the Dominican Republic. However, if changes in U.S. immigration law make migration more difficult, more resident Dominicans may politically resist domestic development strategies that rely on out-migration to stimulate economic growth and assure political stability.

Finally, just as the notion of social class has often been missing in studies of migration's impact on labor-exporting countries, so has any consideration of the role of gender in the migration process (Morokvasic 1984; Pessar 1986). Until quite recently the status of labor migrant has been treated as if it were predominantly male or neuter, despite the fact that legal immigration to the United States, the largest of the international flows, has been female-dominated for the last fifty years (Houston et al. 1984: 909). Even those women who do not migrate but remain behind in transnational migrant households play a role in influencing how emigration alters local patterns of production, consumption, and investment. Based on our New York research, we have also concluded that gender influences Dominican immigrants' attitudes toward settlement, return, and workplace struggle.

At first glance, Dominican immigrant women present a paradox. Although they receive lower wages than documented and undocumented men, and although they have access to less occupational mobility than men, Dominican women are generally more satisfied workers than men, and women are far more likely to be the instigators of settlement in the United States. To account for this paradox and other migration puzzles, we have analyzed Dominican migration within the context of migrant households. The household, as we conceive it, has its own political economy, in which access to power and other valued resources is distributed along gender and generational lines. We have seen that in numerous cases emigration represented a way for wives and adult sons to reduce the control husbands and fathers had over their labor and products. Wage employment in New York has allowed some married women to forge a more egalitarian partnership with their husbands. Women associate this gain directly with paid work. Consequently, they are reluctant to jeopardize this advance either through participation in collective workplace struggles that might lead to prolonged unemployment in New York or by acceding to a husband's decision to return to the Dominican Republic.

Although migration can prove liberating to subordinate household members such as women and the younger generation of adults, the success of the migration project may hinge on the maintenance of household structures that permit the pooling of several rather low incomes. If the newfound autonomy of employed immigrant women leads to marital disruption rather than altered power relations in the traditional household, the collective mobility project is likely to fail, leading to poverty either in the Dominican Republic or in the United States. The proliferation of single-parent households and consequent "Puerto Rican–ization" of the New York Dominican community could well be the outcome. This condition is exactly opposite to that reported for successful entrepreneurial minorities such as Greeks, Japanese, Koreans, and Chinese, whose economic mobility has depended on the preservation of strong, usually patriarchal, kinship bonds (Light 1972; Nakano Glenn 1984; Bin Yim 1984).

We have examined the two-way flow of people, cash, goods, services, and ideology between the Dominican Republic and the United States in terms of social networks. These networks are constructed by Dominican workers and their families who have struggled to extend their economic options beyond the confining boundaries of communities, regions, and nation-states. Through the building and maintenance of such structures as transnational households and transnational social networks, these Dominicans have helped create what Uzzell calls a "social village spread over thousands of miles" (1979: 153). These "social villages" are organized by transnational structures that maintain two-way flows of people, goods, money, and production and consumption circuits. As a consequence of these transnational structures, even those households that cannot afford to dispatch a migrant, or do not choose to do so, are directly affected by the actions of migrants and their resident household and family members.

The transnational network that Dominicans create and help to maintain is not only a locus for economic opportunity, it is also a kind of space that contains multiple, sometimes contradictory, social statuses and cultural elements. We have seen these multiple social and cultural elements come into play, and sometimes transmute or collide, as individuals and households try to make such important decisions as whether to participate in a workplace struggle or whether to settle or return.

Future Trends

The Dominican immigrant community in New York is, of course, growing and maturing. If current immigration trends continue, by the 1990 census Dominican-born New Yorkers should outnumber the Italian-born—the largest bloc of foreign-born residents in New York City for most of the twentieth century (Bogen 1987: 81). Certain of the newly evolved characteristics of the Dominican immigrant population we have observed are likely to pose challenges to the New York Dominican community and to modify its role within the city's economy. Let us briefly consider two of these characteristics: the presence of second-generation Dominicans in New York, and the existence of large numbers of female-headed households.

We have seen that many Dominican immigrants are satisfied and accommodating workers, in part because they evaluate their employment and social mobility against Dominican sociocultural standards. Our conversations with and observations of second-generation Dominicans reveal a distinctly different pattern emerging, however. This new generation tends not to evaluate types of employment in the United States in terms of social class categories relevant for the Dominican Republic. Nor will this second generation be likely to resign itself to low-status, low-paying jobs. And in this, paradoxically, they are in agreement with their parents. Dominican immigrants are no different from earlier waves of European immigrants who aspired to meaningful social mobility for their children and who used different standards of success for their children than for themselves.

Yet, the aspirations of immigrant households for a middle-class standard of living are unlikely to be matched by the employment opportunities available to their children. Although many Dominicans view their children's education as a primary vehicle for the family's continued social mobility, two factors militate against this goal. First, many of the parental generation intend their educated children to return to the Dominican Republic to apply their U.S. training. There is, unfortunately, little reason to believe that the Dominican economy will develop sufficiently to absorb large numbers of this foreign-educated cohort. As we have seen, the level of unemployment among highly educated youth in the Dominican Republic is high. Many of these underemployed or low-paid individuals have left their native land for the United States, where they have secured jobs beneath their level of training. Moreover, immigrant children tenaciously resist leaving their childhood residence, regardless of how many relatives live in their parents' homeland.

Second, as a consequence of the shift to a service economy from one dominated by manufacturing, the last two decades have witnessed a greater inequality in the income distribution of workers in the United States—particularly in urban areas, such as New York City, that receive immigrants. Broadly speaking, we can expect an increase in the supply of low-wage jobs, particularly jobs for which females are generally hired (Applebaum 1987). The sources of these increases are multiple. For one, the fastest-growing service-sector industries contribute to further polarization of income because they are marked by a high concentration of low-wage jobs and high wage jobs, with relatively few middle-income jobs (Singleman 1978; Stanback and Noyelle 1982). For another, a general down-grading of skills in the manufacturing sector has occurred. This is a result both of the entrance of high-technology industries with large concentrations of low-wage jobs in production and of the reorganization of traditional manufacturing, which is turning increasingly to subcontracting of contingent labor and to industrial homework (Sassen-Koob 1984: 1153; Martella 1989).

We have seen that Dominican immigrants are concentrated in low-paying operative and service occupations. Given the increased polarization of the United States economy described above, there will likely be severe structural constraints on the mobility of immigrant children. The latest wave of second-generation immigrants may find that their social mobility will be much more circumscribed in the United States than was the case for the earlier waves of immigrants.

If Hispanic workers in secondary-sector firms continue to be deprived of the higher wages, greater job security, and other social benefits unions have historically brought to laborers, it is likely that the economic vulnerability of Hispanics will be attributed by many Americans to "immutable" racial and ethnic characteristics of this work force. Any rebuttal of anti-immigrant and anti-Hispanic sentiments will have to make the American public aware that the probable limited mobility of the new wave of immigrant workers and their children as compared to earlier European groups stems from new political-economic constraints—constraints that will be faced by a large segment of United States workers, immigrants and non-immigrants alike.

Beyond the structural or macroeconomic obstacles to social mobility, some of the emerging characteristics of Dominican households are also grounds for concern about the economic welfare of immigrant children. Data from the 1980 census and Gurak's survey of Colombians and Dominicans in New York City confirmed our ethnographic findings of high rates of marital disruption of Dominican women, reflected in the fact that over 40 percent of Dominican households with children under the age of eighteen were female-headed (Gurak 1987; Gurak and Falcón-Rodríguez 1987). Mother-only families have had substantially higher poverty rates than other groups in the United States for the past fifteen years. Indeed, approximately one out of every two mother-only families in the United States today falls below the poverty level as defined by the U.S. government (Garfinkle and McLanahan 1986: 12). Low income is a significant factor behind the intergenerational transmission of poverty because of its effect on educational attainment and occupational status. The obstacles that Dominican children growing up under such circumstances will face are likely to be considerable.

While the Dominican immigrant community is at once maturing and beginning to face the challenges posed by second-generation Dominicans, the community is at the same time receiving new members. Moreover, Dominican legal immigration to the United States is likely to continue at current levels for the indefinite future. For one thing, deteriorating economic conditions in the Dominican Republic continue to provide a strong emigration incentive for those with the means to leave. For another, the continued consolidation of the Dominican community in the United States attracts aspiring Dominicans who benefit from the social capital afforded by networks (Massey et al. 1987) and the social and occupational sponsorship that immigrants need. Thus, regardless of conditions in the home society, the immigration process, once firmly established, as it is in the Dominican case, can become relatively self-sustaining.

It is worth reiterating that the survey and ethnographic data presented in this study reflect the conditions of the early 1980s in the Dominican Republic. Over the decade of the 1980s the economic crisis has intensified dramatically, as it has all over Latin America. Since 1988, for example, the inability of the government to pay for its needed oil imports has resulted in electrical shortages ranging from two to ten hours a day over the entire island, a situation with devastating consequences for poor and rich alike. Given these developments, our impression is that more recent outflows have tapped simultaneously a more affluent group and a more impoverished group of emigrants. Even the most privileged have been extremely inconvenienced by the failure of the Dominican state to provide a minimal range of public services such as electricity and adequate sources of fuel. The poor, more desperate than ever, have a wider range of social contacts in the United States than was the case in the early 1980s. There is evidence that over the course of the eighties large numbers of poor Dominicans have emigrated illegally to Puerto Rico, as well (Duany 1990). Some have remained, whereas others have attempted successfully to resettle in the United States by claiming at U.S. customs to be Puerto Rican nationals, and thus U.S. citizens. It is plausible, then, to argue that the Dominican outflow may have become more diversified over the decade of the 1980s as a result of large numbers of professionals having become desirous of escaping the inconvenience of an increasingly ill-managed society and of large numbers of poor Dominicans having become willing to take large risks to escape an increasingly precarious situation.

In the ideological discourse between the citizens of the "two islands," U.S. citizens are likely to assume that Dominicans, like all new immigrants, will settle permanently in the United States and exercise their rights to citizenship. Yet, Dominicans rank quite low among immigrants in their rate of naturalization. Only 16,000, or 7.8 percent, of the 204,000 Dominicans who were admitted for permanent residence in the United States between 1960 and 1980 had become U.S. citizens by 1980. By contrast, immigrants from many Asian countries have naturalization rates above 50 percent during this time period (Warren 1988: 4). We believe this reflects the deep interdependence which still exists between the Dominican communities on the two sides of the border. Some leaders in the Dominican community in New York have called for a change in U.S. and Dominican law to allow dual citizenship. Such an outcome is currently unlikely, but it reflects a desire to broaden political participation to protect interests that bridge the two societies. It is tempting to view these new pioneers as individuals inspired by a postmodern vision and mission. Clearly, there are indeed many whose plans and actions are not limited by historical structures and statuses such as the nation-state and one-country citizenship.

As the migration networks linking the Dominican Republic and the United States mature, we can expect even greater economic interdependence between petty capitalists on the two sides of the border. Indeed, very recent research has uncovered many instances of New York–based Dominicans investing in small businesses back home, as well as returnees traveling regularly to New York to sell their merchandise to fellow Dominicans and purchase goods from them (Portes and Guarnizo 1990).

It may not even be too great a leap to suggest that a situation somewhat analogous to Mexico-U.S. border industries and border culture may be emerging between the Dominican Republic and the United States. Some *dominicanos ausentes* are beginning to join U.S. investors in backing transnational projects in the Dominican Republic such as free zones and tourist centers. In fact, current and aspiring Dominican immigrant investors have begun to join U.S. businesspersons in lobbying the Dominican government for needed infrastructural development, such as improved electrical generating systems and roads.

Some years ago a German politician, exasperated by the independent spirit and actions of guest workers in Germany, concluded, "We called for workers and we got people." His words capture the fact that labor is not comparable to the other commodities that are exchanged on a global scale by members of a transnational capitalist class. Workers come equipped with ideologies, visions, strategies, social statuses, and social relations; they are exposed to new, sometimes contradictory, versions in the places where they settle. Out of this encounter, contemporary immigrants, like the Dominicans we have featured in this study, are fashioning a place for themselves in a global society where national identities, cultures, and institutions are becoming increasingly permeable.

References

Abadan-Unat, Nermin
  1982   "The Effects of International Labor Migration on Women's
            Roles: The Turkish Case." In Cigdem Kagitcibasi, ed., *Sex
            Roles, Family, and Community in Turkey*, 207–36. Bloo-
            mington: Indiana University Turkish Studies Series 3.
Acosta, Mercedes
  1976   "Azúcar e inmigración haitiana." In André Cortén et al.,
            eds., *Azúcar y Política*. Santo Domingo: Taller.
Acosta, Pablo Antonio
  1986   "Movilidad laboral en la República Dominicana." In Con-
            sejo Nacional de Población y Familia (CONAPOFA), ed.,
            Población y Sociedad: Seminario Nacional, 1983, 343–353.
            Santo Domingo: Impresora Gerardo.
Aguayo, Sergio, and Patricia Weiss Fagen
  1988   *Central Americans in Mexico and the United States*. Wash-
            ington, D.C.: Hemispheric Migration Project, Center for
            Immigration Policy and Refugee Assistance, Georgetown
            University.
Alba, Francisco
  1978   "Mexico's International Migration as a Manifestation of Its
            Development Pattern." *International Migration Review* 12
            (4): 502–13.
Alemán, José Luis
  1975   "Ciencia, tecnología y política de inversiones en R.D.,
            1966–72." *Estudios Sociales* (Santo Domingo) 8 (9).
Almquist, Elizabeth
  1979   *Minorities, Gender and Work*. Lexington, Massachusetts:
            D. C. Heath.

Amin, Samir
1976   *Unequal Development: An Essay on the Social Formations of Peripheral Capitalism.* New York: Monthly Review Press.
Anderson, Patricia
1988   "Manpower Losses and Employment Adequacy Among Skilled Workers in Jamaica, 1976–1985." In Patricia Pessar, ed., *When Borders Don't Divide: Labor Migration and Refugee Movements in the Americas,* 96–128. Staten Island: Center for Migration Studies.
Applebaum, Eileen
1987   "Restructuring Work: Temporary Part-time and At-Home Employment." In Heidi Hartmann, ed., *Computer Chips and Paper Clips: Technology and Women's Employment.* Washington, D.C.: National Academy Press.
Arizpe, Lourdes
1978   *Migración, etnicismo y cambio económico.* México D.F.: El Colégio de México.
Atkins, G. Pope, and Larman Wilson
1972   *The United States and the Trujillo Regime.* New Brunswick, New Jersey: Rutgers University Press.
Bach, Robert L.
1978   "Mexican Immigration and U.S. Immigration Reforms in the 1960's." *Kapitalistate* 7: 63–80.
1983   "Emigration from the Spanish-Speaking Caribbean." In Mary R. Kritz, ed., *U.S. Immigration and Refugee Policy,* 133–53. Lexington, Massachusetts: D. C. Heath.
1985a   *Western Hemispheric Immigration to the United States: A Review of Selected Trends.* Washington, D.C.: Occasional Paper Series, Georgetown University and the Intergovernmental Committee for Migration.
1985b   "Political Frameworks for International Migration." In Steven Sanderson, ed., *The Americas in the New International Division of Labor,* 95–124. New York: Holmes and Meier.
Bach, Robert L., and Lisa Schraml
1982   "Migration, Crisis, and Theoretical Conflict." *International Migration Review* 16 (2): 320–41.
Báez Evertsz, Franc
1978   *Azúcar y dependencia en la República Dominicana.* Santo Domingo: Universidad Autónoma de Santo Domingo.
Báez Evertsz, Franc, and Frank D'Oleo Ramírez
1985   *La emigración de Dominicanos a Estados Unidos: Determi-*

nantes socio-economicos y consecuencias. Santo Domingo: Fundación Friedrich Ebert.

Bailey, Thomas, and Marcia Freeman
1981   "Immigrant and Native-Born Workers in the Restaurant Industry." Conservation of Human Resources, Columbia University. Mimeo.

Banck, Geert
1980   "Survival Strategies of Low-Income Urban Households in Brazil." *Urban Anthropology* 9 (2): 227–42.

Baran, Paul
1957   *The Political Economy of Growth.* New York: Monthly Review Press.

Barrett, Michèle
1980   *Women's Oppression Today.* London: Verso.

Barrett, Michèle, and Mary McIntosh
1982   *The Anti-Social Family.* London: Verso.

Baučić, Ivo
1972   *The Effects of Emigration from Yugoslavia and the Problems of Returning Emigration Workers.* The Hague: Martinus Nijhoff.

Becker, Gary S.
1981   *A Treatise on the Family.* Cambridge, Massachusetts: Harvard University Press.

Bell, Ian
1981   *The Dominican Republic.* Boulder, Colorado: Westview Press.

Benería, Lourdes, and Martha Roldán
1987   *The Crossroads of Class and Gender: Industrial Housework, Subcontracting and Household Dynamics in Mexico City.* Chicago: University of Chicago Press.

Benería, Lourdes, and Catherine Stimpson
1987   *Women, Households, and the Economy.* New Brunswick, New Jersey: Rutgers University Press.

Bennett, Douglas
1986   "Immigration, Work and Citizenship in the American Welfare State." Paper presented at the Annual Meeting of the American Political Science Association.

Bentson, Margaret
1969   "The Political Economy of Women's Liberation." *Monthly Review* 21 (4): 13–27.

Bin Yim, Sun
1984   "The Social Structure of Korean Communities in California,

1903–1920." In Lucie Cheng and Edna Bonacich, eds., *Labor Immigration Under Capitalism: Asian Workers in the United States Before World War II.* Berkeley and Los Angeles: University of California Press.

Black, Jan Knippers
1986   *The Dominican Republic: Politics and Development in an Unsovereign State.* Winchester: Allen and Unwin.

Bogen, Elizabeth
1987   *Immigration in New York.* New York: Praeger.

Böhning, W. R.
1974   "The Economic Effects of the Employment of Foreign Workers, with Special Reference to the Labour Markets of Western Europe's Post-Industrial Countries." In W. R. Böhning and D. Maillat, eds., *The Effects of the Employment of Foreign Workers*, 41–123. Paris: Organization for Economic Co-operation and Development.

1975   "Some Thoughts on Emigration from the Mediterranean Basin." *International Labour Review* 3 (3): 251–77.

1981   "Elements of a Theory of International Economic Migration to Industrial Nation States." In Mary Kritz, C. Keeley, and S. Tomasi, eds., *Global Trends in Migration*, 28–43. Staten Island: Center for Migration Studies.

1984   *Studies in International Labour Migration.* London: Macmillan.

Bonacich, Edna, and Lucie Cheng
1984   "Introduction: A Theoretical Orientation to International Labor Migration." In Lucie Cheng and Edna Bonacich, eds., *Labor Immigration Under Capitalism: Asian Workers in the United States Before World War II*, 1–78. Berkeley and Los Angeles: University of California Press.

Bonacich, Edna, and John Modell
1980   *The Economic Basis of Ethnic Solidarity: Small Business in the Japanese-American Community.* Berkeley and Los Angeles: University of California Press.

Bosch, Juan
1979   *Composión social dominicana: historia e interpretación.* Santo Domingo: Alfa y Omega.

Bray, David
1983a   "Agricultura de exportación, formación de clase, y fuerza de trabajo excedente: El caso de la fuerza de trabajo migratoria en la República Dominicana." Paper presented to the Con-

ference on Dominican Migration to the United States, El Museo del Hombre Dominicano, Santo Domingo.

1983b   "Dependency, Class Formation and the Creation of Caribbean Labor Reserves: Internal and International Migration in the Dominican Republic." Ph.D. dissertation, Brown University.

1984   "Economic Development: The Middle Class and International Migration in the Dominican Republic." *International Migration Review* 18 (2): 217–36.

1987   "La agricultura de exportación, formación de clases y mano de obra excedente: El caso de la migración interna e internacional en la República Dominicana." In José del Castillo and Christopher Mitchell, eds., *La inmigración dominicana en los Estados Unidos*, 92–108. Santo Domingo: Editorial CENAPEC.

Brettell, Caroline
1982   *We Have Already Cried Many Tears.* Cambridge, Massachusetts: Schenkman.

Brown, Susan
1972   "Coping with Poverty in the Dominican Republic: Women and Their Mates." Ph.D. dissertation, University of Michigan.

Burawoy, Michael
1976   "The Functions and Reproduction of Migrant Labor." *American Journal of Sociology* 81 (March): 1050–87.

Bustamante, Jorge, and Gerónimo Martínez
1979   "Undocumented Immigration from Mexico: Beyond Borders but Within Systems." *Journal of International Affairs* 33 (Fall/Winter): 265–84.

Cabral, Manuel José
1975   "Inflación, distribución del ingreso y empleo." *Ciencia y Sociedad* 1 (1): 1–4.

Calder, Bruce
1974   "Some Aspects of the U.S. Occupation of the Dominican Republic, 1916–1924." Ph.D. dissertation, University of Texas, Austin.

1978   "Caudillos and Gavilleros versus the United States Marines: Guerilla Insurgency During the Dominican Intervention, 1916–1924." *Hispanic American Historical Review* 58 (4): 649–75.

1982   "The Dominican Turn Toward Sugar." *Caribbean Review* 10 (3): 18–21.

Cardoso, Fernando Henrique, and Enzo Faletto
1979   *Dependency and Development in Latin America.* Berkeley and Los Angeles: University of California Press.

Casasnovas, Nicolás
1981   "Evaluación de la industria azucarera en la República Dominicana." In *La industria azucarera y el desarrollo dominicano.* San Pedro de Macoris: Universidad Central.

Cassá, Roberto
1982   *Capitalismo y dictadura.* Santo Domingo: Universidad Autónoma de Santo Domingo.

Castells, Manuel
1975   "Immigrant Workers and Class Struggles in Advanced Capitalism: The Western European Experience." *Politics and Society* 5 (1): 33–66.

Castillo, Enmanuel
1981   "Bases y perspectivas de la democracia en la República Dominicana." Paper presented at Seminario Década del 80, Universidad Católica Madre y Maestra, Santiago.

Castles, Stephen, and Godula Kosack
1973   *Immigrant Workers and Class Structure in Western Europe.* London: Oxford University Press.

Castro, Max
1985   "Dominican Journey: Patterns, Context, and Consequences of Migration from the Dominican Republic to the United States." Ph.D. dissertation, University of North Carolina, Chapel Hill.

Catrain, Pedro
1980   "Estado, hegemonia y clases dominantes en la República Dominicana, 1966–1978." Paper presented to the Second National Sociological Congress of the Association of Dominican Sociologists, Santo Domingo.

Ceballos, Zeñon
1986   "Dinámica de la población dominicana en el período 1950–1980 y perspectivas futuras." *Población y Desarrollo* (Santo Domingo), 5 (14): 14–17.

Chaney, Elsa
1985   *Migration from the Caribbean Region: Determinants and Effects of Current Movement.* Washington, D.C.: Occasional Paper Series, Georgetown University and the Intergovernmental Committee for Migration.

Clausner, Marlin
1973   *Rural Santo Domingo: Settled, Unsettled, and Resettled.* Philadelphia: Temple University Press.

Coontz, Stephanie, and Peta Henderson, eds.
1986   *Women's Work, Man's Property: Origins of Gender and Class.* London: Verso.
Cordero, Walter, José del Castillo, Miguel Cocco, Max Puig, Otto Fernández, and Wilfredo Lozano
1975   *Tendencias de la economía cafetalera dominicana, 1955– 1972.* Santo Domingo: Universidad Autonóma de Santo Domingo.
Cornelius, Wayne
1976   "Mexican Migration to the United States: View from Rural Sending Communities." Massachusetts Institute of Technology, Center for International Studies. Mimeo.
1982   "Interviewing Undocumented Immigrants: Methodological Reflections Based on Fieldwork in Mexico and the U.S." *International Migration Review* 6 (2): 378–411.
1990   *Labor Migration to the United States: Development, Outcomes, and Alternatives in Mexican Sending Communities.* Washington, D.C.: Working Papers, Commission for the Study of International Migration and Cooperative Economic Development.
Cortén, André, Mercedes Acosta, and Isis Duarte
1976   "Las relaciones de producción en la economía azucarera dominicana." In André Cortén, Carlos Vilas, M. Acosta, and Isis Duarte, eds., *Azúcar y política.* Santo Domingo: Taller.
Crassweller, Robert D.
1966   *Trujillo: The Life and Times of a Caribbean Dictator.* New York: Macmillan.
Dalla Costa, Mariarosa
1975   "A General Strike." In Wendy Edmond and Suzie Fleming, eds., *All Work and No Pay: Women, Housework, and the Wages Due.* Bristol, Eng.: Falling Wall Press.
Dandler, Jorge, and Carmen Medeiros
1988   "Temporary Migration from Cochabamba, Bolivia to Argentina: Patterns and Impact in Sending Areas." In Patricia Pessar, *When Borders Don't Divide: Labor Migration and Refugee Movements in the Americas,* 8–41. Staten Island: Center for Migration Studies.
Deere, Carmen Diana, and Alain de Janvry
1979   "A Conceptual Framework for the Empirical Analysis of Peasants." *American Journal of Agricultural Economics* 61 (4): 601–11.

DeFreitas, Gregory, and Adriana Marshall
1984   "Immigration and Wage Growth in U.S. Manufacturing in
            the 1970s." In Industrial Relations Research Association,
            36th Annual Proceeding, 148–56.
de Janvry, Alain
1982   The Agrarian Question and Reformism in Latin America.
            Baltimore: Johns Hopkins University Press.
del Castillo, José
1978   La inmigración de braceros azucareros en la República Do-
            minicana, 1900–1930. Santo Domingo: Universidad Auto-
            nóma de Santo Domingo.
1981   Ensayos de sociología dominicana. Santo Domingo: Taller.
del Castillo, José, Miguel Cocco, Walter Cordero, Max Puig, Otto
Fernandez, and Wilfredo Lozano
1974   La Gulf y Western en la República Dominicana. Santo Do-
            mingo: Universidad Autonóma de Santo Domingo.
del Castillo, José, and Christopher Mitchell, eds.
1987   La inmigración dominicana en los Estados Unidos. Santo
            Domingo: CENAPEC.
Dinerman, Ina R.
1978   "Patterns of Adaptation among Households of U.S.-Bound
            Migrants from Michoacán, México." International Migra-
            tion Review 12 (4): 485–501.
Dore y Cabral, Carlos
1979   Problemas de la estructura agraria dominicana. Santo Do-
            mingo: Taller.
Duany, Jorge
1990   Los Dominicanos en Puerto Rico: Migración en la semi-
            periferia. Río Piedras, Puerto Rico: Ediciones Huracán.
Duarte, Isis
1983   "Fuerza laboral urbana en Santo Domingo, 1980–1983."
            Estudios Sociales 16 (53): 31–53.
Dwyer, Daisy
1983   Women and Income in the Third World: Implications for
            Policy. International Programs Working Paper no. 18. New
            York: The Population Council.
Dwyer, Daisy, and Judith Bruce, eds.
1988   A Home Divided: Women and Income in the Third World.
            Stanford: Stanford University Press.
Edholm, F., O. Harris, and K. Young
1977   "Conceptualizing Women." Critique of Anthropology 3 (9–
            10): 101–30.

Edwards, Richard
  1979   *Contested Terrain: The Transformation of the
            the Twentieth Century.* New York: Basic Book
Epstein, Cynthia
  1970   *Women's Place: Options and Limits in Pr*ᵤ.
            reers. Berkeley and Los Angeles: University of California
            Press.
Espinal, Rosario
  1986   "An Interpretation of the Democratic Transition in the Do-
            minican Republic." In Giuseppe Di Palma and Laurence
            Whitehead, eds., *The Central American Impasse,* 72–90.
            New York: St. Martin's Press.
  1987a   "Labor, Politics and Industrialization in the Dominican Re-
            public." *Economic and Industrial Democracy* 8: 183–212.
  1987b   *Autoritarismo y democracia en la política dominicana.* San
            Jose, Costa Rica: Centro InterAmericano de Asesoría y
            Promoción Electoral.
Etienne, Mona, and Eleanor Leacock
  1980   *Women and Colonialization: Anthropological Perspectives.*
            South Hadley, Massachusetts: Bergin and Garvey.
Evans, Peter
  1979   *Dependent Development: The Alliance of Multinational,
            State, and Local Capital in Brazil.* Princeton: Princeton
            University.
Fapohunda, Eleanor
  1988   "The Nonpooling Household: A Challenge to Theory." In
            Daisy Dwyer and Judith Bruce, eds., *A Home Divided.*
            Stanford: Stanford University Press.
Felix, David
  1983   "Income Distribution and the Quality of Life in Latin Amer-
            ica: Patterns, Trends and Policy Implications." *Latin Ameri-
            can Research Review* 18 (2): 3–33.
Fernández-Kelly, María Patricia
  1981   "Feminization, Mexican Border Industrialization, and Mi-
            gration." Ph.D. dissertation, Rutgers University.
  1983   *For We Are Sold, I and My People: Women and Industry in
            Mexico's Frontier.* Albany: State University of New York
            Press.
Fernández-Kelly, María Patricia, and Anna García
  1990   "Power Surrendered, Power Restored: The Politics of Home
            and Work Among Hispanic Women in Southern California
            and Southern Florida." In Louise Tilly and Patricia Guerin,

eds., *Women and Politics in America*, 130–49. New York: The Russell Sage Foundation.

Ferrán, Fernando

1974   "'La familia nuclear' de la subcultura de la pobreza dominicana." *Estudios Sociales* 27 (3): 137–85.

Folbre, Nancy

1984   "Cleaning House: New Perspectives on Households and Economic Development." Manuscript, Department of Economics, New School for Social Research.

1988   "The Black Four of Hearts: Toward a New Paradigm of Household Economics." In Daisy Dwyer and Judith Bruce, eds., *A Home Divided*, 248–62. Stanford: Stanford University Press.

Fox, Bonnie

1980   *Hidden in the Household*. Toronto: The Women's Press.

Franco, Franklin

1966   *República Dominicana: Clases, crisis y comandos*. Havana: Casa de las Americas.

Frank, Andre G.

1970   *Latin America: Underdevelopment or Revolution*. New York: Monthly Review Press.

Frank Canelo, J.

1982   *Dónde, porqúe, de qué, y cómo viven los dominicanos en el extranjero: un informe sociológico sobre la e/inmigración dominicana, 1961–62*. Santo Domingo: Alfa y Omega.

Frobel, Fölker, Jürgen Heinrichs, and Otto Kreye

1979   *The New International Division of Labour*. New York: Cambridge University Press.

Furtado, Celso

1971   *Development and Underdevelopment: A Structural View*. Berkeley and Los Angeles: University of California Press.

Garfinkle, Irwin, and Sara McLanahan

1986   *Single Mothers and Their Children*. Washington, D.C.: Urban Institute Press.

Garrison, Vivian, and Carol I. Weiss

1979   "Dominican Family Networks and U.S. Immigration Policy: A Case Study." *International Migration Review* 12 (2): 264–83.

Georges, Eugenia

1984   *New Immigrants and the Political Process: Dominicans in New York*. Occasional Papers 45, Center for Latin American and Caribbean Studies, New York University.

1987 "Distribución de los efectos de la emigración internacional sobre una comunidad de la sierra occidental dominicana." In José del Castillo and Christopher Mitchell, eds., *La inmigración dominicana en los Estados Unidos*, 77–91. Santo Domingo: Editorial CENAPEC.

1990 *The Making of a Transnational Community: Migration, Development, and Cultural Change in the Dominican Republic.* New York: Columbia University Press.

Gerson, Kathleen

1986 *Hard Choices: How Women Decide About Work, Career and Motherhood.* Berkeley and Los Angeles: University of California Press.

Gleijeses, Piero

1978 *The Dominican Crisis: The 1965 Constitutionalist Revolt and American Intervention.* Baltimore: Johns Hopkins University Press.

Gómez, Luis

1979 *Relaciones de producción dominantes en la sociedad dominicana, 1875–1975.* Santo Domingo: Alfa y Omega.

González, Nancie

1970 "Peasants' Progress: Dominicans in New York." *Caribbean Studies* 10 (3): 154–71.

1976 "Multiple Migratory Experiences of Dominicans in New York." *Anthropological Quarterly* 49 (1): 36–43.

Goody, Jack

1972 "The Evolution of the Family." In Peter Laslett and Richard Wall, eds., *Household and Family in Past Time*, 103–24. Cambridge: Cambridge University Press.

Gordon, Andrew

1978 "Hispanic Drinking After Migration: The Case of Dominicans." *Medical Anthropology* 2 (4): 61–84.

Grant, Geraldine

1983 "The State and the Formation of a Middle Class: A Chilean Example." *Latin American Perspectives* 10 (2–3): 151–70.

Grant, Geraldine, and Judith Herbstein

1983 "Immigrant Mobility: Upward, Downward or Outward?" Paper presented at the Annual Meeting of the Society for Applied Anthropology, San Diego, California.

Grasmuck, Sherri

1982 "Migration Within the Periphery: Haitian Labor in the Dominican Sugar and Coffee Industries." *International Migration Review* 16 (2): 365–77.

1983   "International Stair-Step Migration: Dominican Labor in
           the United States and Haitian Labor in the Dominican Re-
           public." In R. Simpson and I. H. Simpson, eds., *Peripheral
           Workers.* Greenwich, Connecticut: JAI Press.

1984a   "The Impact of Emigration on National Development: Three
           Sending Communities in the Dominican Republic." *Devel-
           opment and Change* 15 (3): 381–404.

1984b   "Immigration, Ethnic Stratification, and Native Working
           Class Discipline: Comparisons of Documented and Undocu-
           mented Dominicans." *International Migration Review* 18
           (3): 692–713.

1991   "Bringing the Family Back In: Towards an Expanded Under-
           standing of Women's Subordination in Latin America." Pa-
           per presented to the Latin American Studies Association
           Meetings, Washington, D.C.

Griffin, Keith
1976   "On the Emigration of the Peasantry." *World Development*
           4 (5): 353–61.

Griffith, David
1985   "Women, Remittances and Reproduction." *American Eth-
           nologist* 12 (4): 676–90.

Gurak, Douglas
1981   "Dominicans and Colombians in New York City." Paper pre-
           sented to the New York Forum on Migration, New York.

1987   "Family Formation and Marital Selectivity Among Colom-
           bian and Dominican Immigrants in New York City." *Interna-
           tional Migration Review* 21 (2): 275–97.

Gurak, Douglas, and Luis Falcón-Rodríguez
1987   "The Social and Economic Situation of Hispanics in the
           United States and New York City in the 1980's." In Office of
           Pastoral Research, ed., *Hispanics in New York: Religious,
           Cultural and Social Experiences*, vol. 2. New York City:
           Office of Pastoral Research.

Gurak, Douglas, and Mary Kritz
1982   "Dominican and Colombian Women in New York City:
           Household Structure and Employment Patterns." *Migra-
           tion Today* 10 (3–4): 14–21.

1984   "Kinship Networks in the Settlement Process: Dominican
           and Colombian Immigrants in New York City." *Hispanic
           Research Center Bulletin* (Fordham University) 7 (3–4): 7–
           11.

1988   "Household Composition and Employment of Dominican and Colombian Women in New York and Dominican Women in the Dominican Republic." Paper presented at the Annual Meeting of the American Sociological Association.

Gurak, Douglas, and Roger Lloyd

1980   "New York's New Immigrants: Who and Where They Are. The Hispanics." *New York University Education Quarterly* 11 (4): 19–28.

Gutiérrez, Carlos María

1972   *The Dominican Republic: Rebellion and Repression.* New York: Monthly Review Press.

Guyer, Jane

1981   "Household and Community in African Studies." Paper commissioned by the Social Science Research Council.

1988   "Dynamic Approaches to Domestic Budgeting: Cases and Methods from Africa." In Daisy Dwyer and Judith Bruce, eds., *A Home Divided*, 155–72. Stanford: Stanford University Press.

Hartmann, Heidi

1981   "The Unhappy Marriage of Marxism and Feminism: Towards a More Progressive Union." In Lydia Sargent, ed., *Women and Revolution*, 1–41. Boston: South End Press.

Hendricks, Glenn T.

1974   *The Dominican Diaspora: From the Dominican Republic to New York City. Villagers in Transition.* New York: Teachers College Press.

History Task Force, Centro de Estudios Puertorriqueñas

1979   *Labor Migration Under Capitalism: The Puerto Rican Experience.* New York: Monthly Review Press.

Hodge, Robert W., and Donald J. Treiman

1974   "Class Identification in the United States." In Joseph Lopreato and Lionel Lewis, eds., *Social Stratification: A Reader*, 182–92. New York: Harper and Row.

Hoetink, Harry

1965   "Materiales para el estudio de la República Dominicana en la segunda mitad del siglo XIX." *Caribbean Studies* 5 (3): 3–21.

1971   *El Pueblo Dominicano: 1850–1900.* Santiago: Universidad Católica Madre y Maestra.

Houston, Marion, Roger Kramer, and Joan Mackin Barrett

1984   "Female Predominance of Immigration to the United States Since 1930: A First Look." *International Migration Review* 18 (4): 908–63.

Humphries, Jane
  1979   "Class Struggle and the Persistence of the Working Class Family." *Cambridge Journal of Economics* 1 (3): 241–58.
Iglesias, Enrique
  1981   "Development and Equity: The Challenge of the 1980s." *CEPAL Review* (15): 7–46.
  1983   "Reflections on the Latin American Economy in 1982." *CEPAL Review* (19): 7–49.
Inter-American Development Bank (IDB)
  1987   *Economic and Social Progress in Latin America*. Washington, D.C.: Inter-American Development Bank.
International Labour Organization (ILO)
  1975   *Time for Transition*. Geneva: International Labour Organization.
Jalee, Pierre
  1973   *Imperialism in the Seventies*. New York: Third World Press.
Johnson, D. L., ed.
  1983   *Intermediate Classes: Historical Studies of Class Formations on the Periphery*. Beverly Hills: Sage.
Jones, Richard, ed.
  1984   *Patterns of Undocumented Migration: Mexico and the United States*. Ottowa: Rowman and Allanheld.
Kayal, Philip M.
  1978   "The Dominicans in New York: Part II." *Migration Today* 6: 10–15.
Kearney, Michael
  1986   "From the Invisible Hand to Visible Feet: Anthropological Studies of Migration and Development." *Annual Review of Anthropology* 15: 331–61.
Keeley, Charles
  1979   "Immigration Policies of the Overseas Anglo-Saxon Democracies: The United States of America." In Daniel Kubat, ed., *The Politics of Migration Policies*, 51–66. Staten Island: Center for Migration Studies.
Kessler-Harris, Alice
  1981   *Women Have Always Worked*. Old Westbury, New York: Feminist Press.
Kessler-Harris, Alice, and Karen Brodkin Sacks
  1987   "The Demise of Domesticity in America." In Lourdes Benería and Catherine Stimpson, eds., *Women, Households, and the Economy*, 65–84. New Brunswick, New Jersey: Rutgers University Press.

King, Russell
1986   "Return Migration and Regional Economic Development: An Overview." In Russell King, ed., *Return Migration and Regional Economic Problems*, 1–37. London: Croom Helm.
Klatch, Rebecca
1987   *Women of the New Right*. Philadelphia: Temple University Press.
Knight, Franklin
1981   *Migration, the Plantation Society and the Emergence of a Pan-Caribbean Culture*. Occasional Papers 1, Center for Latin American Studies, University of Florida, Gainesville.
Knight, Melvin
1928   *The Americans in Santo Domingo*. New York: Vanguard Press.
Kraly, Ellen Percy
1987   "U.S. Immigration Policy and the Immigrant Populations of New York." In Nancy Foner, ed., *New Immigrants in New York*, 35–78. New York: Columbia University Press.
Kritz, Mary
1981   "International Migration Patterns in the Caribbean Basin: An Overview." In Mary Kritz, Charles Keeley, and Silvano Tomasi, eds., *Global Trends in Migration: Theory and Research on International Population Movements*, 208–31. Staten Island: Center for Migration Studies.
Kritz, Mary, ed.
1983   *U.S. Immigration and Refugee Policy: Global and Domestic Issues*. Lexington, Massachusetts: Lexington Books.
Kuhn, Annette, and Ann Marie Wolpe, eds.
1978   *Feminism and Materialism: Women and Modes of Production*. London: Routledge and Kegan Paul.
Kuhn, Sarah, and Barry Bluestone
1987   "Economic Restructuring and the Female Labor Market: The Impact of Industrial Change on Women." In Lourdes Benería and Catherine Stimpson, eds., *Women, Households, and the Economy*, 3–32. New Brunswick, New Jersey: Rutgers University Press.
Laite, Julian
1981   *Industrial Development and Migrant Labour in Latin America*. Austin: University of Texas Press.
Lamphere, Louise
1987   *From Working Daughters to Working Mothers*. Ithaca, New York: Cornell University Press.

Larson, Eric M.
1984   "A Study of the Patterns of Labor Absorption by Occupation
            in the Dominican Republic Using 1970 and 1981 National
            Population Census Data." Unpublished monograph.
1987a   "Patterns of Labor Absorption by Occupation in the Domini-
            can Republic." *International Journal of Sociology and So-
            cial Policy* 7 (3): 67–77.
1987b   "International Migration and the Labor Force: A Study of
            Members of Migrant Households Versus Members of Do-
            mestic Households in the Dominican Republic." Ph.D. dis-
            sertation, University of Texas at Austin.
Larson, Eric M., and Wolfgang Opitz
1988   "Sex Ratio and Vital Statistics–Based Estimates of Emigra-
            tion from the Dominican Republic." Paper presented at
            Conference on Dominican Migration to the United States,
            Fundación Friedrich Ebert, Santo Domingo.
Larson, Eric M., and Teresa Sullivan
1987   "'Conventional Numbers' in Immigration Research: The
            Case of the Missing Dominicans." *International Migration
            Review* 21 (4): 1474–97.
Lasch, Christopher
1977   *Haven in a Heartless World: The Family Besieged.* New
            York: Basic Books.
Leahy, P. J., and S. Castillo
1977   "Making It Illegally: 'Wetbacks' in the Social and Economic
            Life of a Southwestern Metropolitan Area." Paper pre-
            sented at the Annual Meeting of the Society for the Study of
            Social Problems.
Levine, Barry
1987   *The Caribbean Exodus.* New York: Praeger.
Light, Ivan
1972   *Ethnic Enterprise in America.* Berkeley and Los Angeles:
            University of California Press.
Lomnitz, Larissa
1977   *Networks and Marginality: Life in a Mexican Shantytown.*
            New York: Academic Press.
López, José Ramón
1973   "La caña de azúcar en San Pedro de Macoris, desde el
            bosque virgen hasta el mercado." *Ciencia* 2 (3).
Lowenthal, Abraham
1972   *The Dominican Intervention.* Cambridge, Massachusetts:
            Harvard University Press.

1981   "Changing Patterns in Inter-American Relations." *The Wash-ington Quarterly* 4 (1): 168–77.

Lozano, Wilfredo

1985a   *Proletarización y campesinado en el capitalismo agroex-portador*. Santo Domingo: Instituto Technológico de Santo Domingo.

1985b   *El reformismo dependiente*. Santo Domingo: Taller.

Mahler, Sarah

1988   "The Dynamics of Legalization in New York: A Focus on Dominicans." Paper presented to the Conference on Do-minican Migration to the United States, Fundación Frie-drich Ebert, Santo Domingo.

Maingot, Anthony

1989   *Emigration and Development in the English-Speaking Ca-ribbean*. Working paper no. 4, Commission for the Study of International Migration and Cooperative Economic Devel-opment, Washington, D.C.

Maldonado-Dennis, Manuel

1980   *The Emigration Dialectic*. New York: International Publish-ers.

Mann, Evelyn, and Joseph Salvo

1984   "Characteristics of New Hispanic Immigration to New York City: A Comparison of Puerto Rican and Non–Puerto Rican Hispanics." Paper presented at the Annual Meeting of the Population Association of America, Minneapolis, Minne-sota.

Mann, Michael

1986   "A Crisis in Stratification Theory? Persons, Households/ Families/Lineages, Genders, Classes and Nations." In Rose-mary Crompton and Michael Mann, eds., *Gender and Stratification*, 40–56. Cambridge, England: Polity Press.

Marshall, Adriana

1973   *The Import of Labour: The Case of the Netherlands*. Rotter-dam: Rotterdam University Press.

1983   *Immigration in a Surplus-Worker Labor Market: The Case of New York*. Occasional Papers 39, Center for Latin Ameri-can and Caribbean Studies, New York University.

1987   "New Immigrants in New York's Economy." In Nancy Foner, ed., *New Immigrants in New York*, 77–101. New York: Co-lumbia University Press.

Marshall, Dawn

1987   "A History of West Indian Migrations: Overseas Opportunities and 'Safety-Value' Policies." In Barry Levin, ed., *The Caribbean Exodus*, 15–31. New York: Praeger.

Marshall, Gloria
1964   "Women, Trade and the Yoruba Family." Ph.D. dissertation, Columbia University.

Martella, Maureen
1989   "A Review of Labor Market Theories Applied to Contingent Work." Department of Sociology, Temple University. Mimeo.

Martin, John Bartlow
1966   *Overtaken by Events: The Dominican Crisis from the Fall of Trujillo to the Civil War*. New York: Doubleday.

Massey, Douglas, Rafael Alarcón, Jorge Durand, and Humbert González
1987   *Return to Aztlán: The Social Process of International Migration from Western Mexico*. Berkeley and Los Angeles: University of California Press.

Meillassoux, Claude
1981   *Maidens, Meal, and Money: Capitalism and the Domestic Community*. Cambridge, England: Cambridge University Press.

Mesa-Lago, Carmelo
1983   "Social Security and Extreme Poverty in Latin America." *Journal of Development Economics* 12: 83–110.

Mines, Richard
1981   *Developing a Community Tradition of Migration: A Field Study in Rural Zacatecas, Mexico and California Settlement Areas*. Monograph Series No. 3. La Jolla, California: Center for U.S.–Mexican Studies, University of California, San Diego.

Mitchell, Christopher
1987   "U.S. Foreign Policy and Dominican Migration to the United States." Manuscript.

Morales, Rebecca
1983   "Transitional Labor: Undocumented Workers in the Los Angeles Automobile Industry." *International Migration Review* 17 (4): 570–96.

Moreno Ceballos, Nelson
1984   *El estado dominicano: Origen, evolución y su forma actual, 1844–1982*. Santo Domingo: Alfa y Omega.

Morokvasic, Mirjana
1984   "Birds of Passage Are Also Women. . . ." *International Migration Review* 18 (4): 886–907.

Moya Pons, Frank
   1974   "Nuevas consideraciones sobre la historia de la población dominicana: Cuevas, tasas y problemas." *Estudios Dominicanos* 111 (15).
   1981   *Dominican National Identity and Return Migration.* In Occasional Papers 1, Center for Latin American Studies, University of Florida, Gainesville.

Myrdal, Gunnar
   1957   *Rich Lands and Poor.* New York: Harper and Row.

Nakano Glenn, Evelyn
   1984   "The Dialectics of Wage Work: Japanese American Women and Domestic Service, 1905–1940." In Lucie Cheng and Edna Bonacich, eds., *Labor Immigration Under Capitalism: Asian Workers in the United States Before World War II.* Berkeley and Los Angeles: University of California Press.

Nash, June
   1976   "A Critique of Social Science Roles in Latin America." In J. Nash and H. I. Safa, eds., *Sex and Class in Latin America,* 1–21. New York: Praeger.

Nelson, Nici
   1978   "Female Centred Families: Changing Patterns of Marriage and Family Among Buzaa Brewers of Mathare Valley." *African Urban Studies* 3: 85–104.

Nutini, Hugo, and Timothy Murphy
   1970   "Labor Migration and Family Structure in Tlaxcala-Puebla Area, Mexico." In W. Goldschmidt and H. Hoifer, eds., *Social Anthropology of Latin America: Essays in Honor of Ralph Leon Beals,* 80–103. Los Angeles: Latin American Center, University of California.

Nutter, Richard
   1986   "Implications of Return Migration from the United Kingdom for Urban Employment in Kingston, Jamaica." In Russell King, ed., *Return Migration and Regional Economic Problems,* 198–212. London: Croom Helm.

O'Connor, James
   1973   *The Fiscal Crisis of the State.* New York: St. Martin's Press.

Oficina Nacional de Estadísticas (ONE)
   1983   "Datos del censo de nivel barrios y parajes." Unpublished paper. Santo Domingo: ONE.

Oficina Nacional de Planificación (ONAPLAN)
   1981   "La situación del empleo en Santo Domingo y Santiago en

noviembre de 1979: Resultados de la encuesta especial de
mano de obra." Santo Domingo: ONAPLAN.
1983   "El proceso de urbanización, en la República Dominicana."
         Santo Domingo: ONAPLAN.
Oppenheimer, Valerie K.
1973   "Demographic Influence on Female Employment and the
         Status of Women." In Joan Huber, ed., *Changing Women
         in a Changing Society*. Chicago: University of Chicago
         Press.
Papademetrios, Demetrios, and Nicholas Di Marzio
1986   *An Exploration into the Social and Labor Market Incorpora-
         tion of Undocumented Aliens in the New York Metropolitan
         Area*. Staten Island: Center for Migration Studies.
Patterson, Orlando
1978   "Migration in Caribbean Societies: Socio-Economic and
         Symbolic Resources." In William H. McNeill and Ruth S.
         Adams, eds., *Human Migration: Patterns and Policies*. Bloo-
         mington: Indiana University Press.
Pedraza-Bailey, Silvia
1985   *Political and Economic Migrants in America*. Austin: Uni-
         versity of Texas Press.
Peña, Javier, and Miguel Parache
1971   "Emigración a New York de tres comunidades: Jánico,
         Baitoa y Sabana Iglesias." Thesis, Universidad Católica
         Madre y Maestra.
Pérez, Glauco
1981   "Dominican Illegals in New York: Selected Preliminary
         Findings." Paper presented to the Center for Inter-Ameri-
         can Affairs, New York University.
Pessar, Patricia
1982   "The Role of Households in International Migration: The
         Case of U.S.-Bound Migrants from the Dominican Repub-
         lic." *International Migration Review* 16 (2): 342–62.
1986   "The Role of Gender in Dominican Settlement in the
         United States." In June Nash and Helen Safa, eds., *Women
         and Change in Latin America*, 273–94. South Hadley, Mas-
         sachusetts: Bergin and Garvey.
1987   "The Dominicans: Women in the Household and the Gar-
         ment Industry." In Nancy Foner, ed., *New Immigrants in
         New York*, 103–29. New York: Columbia University Press.
1988   *When Borders Don't Divide: Labor Migration and Refugee*

Movements in the Americas. Staten Island: Center for Migration Studies.

Petras, Elizabeth

1981 "The Global Labor Market in the Modern World Economy." In Mary Kritz, Charles Keeley, and Silvano Tomasi, eds., *Global Trends in Migration: Theory and Research on International Population Movements,* 44–63. Staten Island: Center for Migration Studies.

1988 *Jamaican Labor Migration: White Capital and Black Labor, 1850–1930.* Boulder, Colorado: Westview Press.

Petras, James

1975 "The Latin American Middle Class." *New Politics* 4 (6): 74–85.

Philpott, Stuart B.

1978 "The Implications of Migration for Sending Societies: Some Theoretical Considerations." In Robert F. Spencer, ed., *Migration and Anthropology,* 9–20. Seattle: University of Washington Press.

Piore, Michael

1979 *Birds of Passage: Migrant Labor and Industrial Society.* Cambridge, England: Cambridge University Press.

Poinard, Michel, and Michel Roux

1977 "L'émigration contre le développement: Les cas portugais et yougoslave." *Revue Tiers-Monde* 18 (January–March): 21–53.

Population Associates International

1986 "Impacts of Immigration on Local Labor Markets: The Case of New York." National Commission for Employment Policy. Mimeo.

Portes, Alejandro

1978a "Migration and Underdevelopment." *Politics and Society* 8 (1): 1–48.

1978b "Towards a Structural Analysis of Illegal (Undocumented) Immigration." *International Migration Review* 12 (4): 469–84.

1979 "Illegal Immigrants and the International System: Lessons from Recent Illegal Mexican Immigrants to the U.S." *Social Problems* 26 (4): 425–38.

1983 "International Labor Migration and National Development." In Mary Kritz, ed., *U.S. Immigration and Refugee Policy: Global and Domestic Issues,* 71–91. Lexington, Massachusetts: D. C. Heath.

1985   "Latin American Class Structures: Their Composition and
              Change During the Last Decades." *Latin American Re-
              search Review* 20 (3): 7–39.
Portes, Alejandro, and Robert Bach
1985   *Latin Journey: Cuban and Mexican Immigrants in the
              United States.* Berkeley and Los Angeles: University of Cali-
              fornia Press.
Portes, Alejandro, and Luis Guarnizo
1990   *Tropical Capitalists: U.S.-Bound Immigration and Small-
              Enterprise Development in the Dominican Republic.* Wash-
              ington, D.C.: Working Papers, Commission for the Study of
              International Migration and Cooperative Economic Devel-
              opment.
Portes, Alejandro, and Alex Stepick
1985   "Unwelcome Immigrants: The Labor Market Experiences
              of 1980 (Mariel) Cuban and Haitian Refugees in South Flor-
              ida." *American Sociological Review* 50 (4): 493–514.
Portes, Alejandro, and John Walton
1981   *Labor, Class and the International System.* New York: Aca-
              demic Press.
Poster, Mark
1978   *Critical Theory of the Family.* New York: Seabury Press.
Ramírez, Nelson, Pablo Tactuk, and Minerva Breton
1977   *La migración interna en la República Dominicana.* Santo
              Domingo: Alfa y Omega.
Rapp, Rayna
1978   "Family and Class in Contemporary America: Notes To-
              wards an Understanding of Ideology." *Science and Society*
              42 (3): 278–300.
Ravelo, Sebastián, and Pedro Juan del Rosario
1986   "Impacto de los dominicanos ausentes en el financiamiento
              rural." Manuscript, Universidad Católica Madre y Maestra.
Reichert, Joshua
1979   "The Migrant Syndrome: An Analysis of U.S. Migration and
              Its Impact on a Rural Mexican Town." Ph.D. dissertation,
              Princeton University.
1981   "The Migrant Syndrome: Seasonal U.S. Wage Labor and
              Rural Development in Central Mexico." *Human Organiza-
              tion* 40 (1): 56–66.
Reimers, Cornelia
1983   "Labor Market Discrimination Against Hispanic and Black
              Men." *Review of Economics and Statistics* 65 (4): 570–79.

Reubens, E.
1980 "Review Article of William Glaser's *The Brain Drain.*" *International Migration Review* 14 (3): 434–35.

Rhoades, Robert
1978 "Foreign Labor and German Industrial Capitalism, 1871–1978: The Evolution of a Migratory System." *American Ethnologist* 5 (3): 553–73.

Roberts, Bryan
1978 *Cities of Peasants: The Political Economy of Urbanization in the Third World.* Beverly Hills: Sage.

Roberts, Kenneth
1981 *Agrarian Structure and Labor Migration in Rural Mexico.* Working Papers in U.S.-Mexican Studies, no. 30. La Jolla: University of California at San Diego.
1985 "Household Labour Mobility in a Modern Agrarian Economy: Mexico." In G. Standing, ed., *Labour Circulation and the Labour Process*, 358–81. London: Croom Helm.
N.D. "Household Labor Mobility in a Modern Agrarian Economy." Manuscript, Department of Economics, Southwestern University.

Rodríguez Nuñez, Pablo
1984 "La economía agraria, la pobreza y la población en la República Dominicana." *Forum* (Santo Domingo) 12: 17–68.

Roseberry, William
1983 *Coffee and Capitalism in the Venezuelan Andes.* Austin: University of Texas Press.

Rothenberg, J.
1977 "On the Microeconomics of Migration." In A. Brown and E. Neuberger, eds., *Internal Migration: A Comparative Perspective*, 183–205. New York: Academic Press.

Rouse, Roger
1986 "Migration and the Politics of Family Life: Divergent Projects and Rhetorical Strategies in a Mexican Migrant Community." Paper presented at the Annual Meeting of the American Anthropological Association, Philadelphia, Pennsylvania.

Rubbo, Anna
1975 "The Spread of Capitalism in Rural Colombia: Effects on Poor Women." In R. Reiter, ed., *Toward an Anthropology of Women*, 333–57. New York: Monthly Review Press.

Rubenstein, Hymie
1983 "Remittances and Rural Underdevelopment in the English-

Speaking Caribbean." *Human Organization* 42 (4): 295–306.

Rubin, Lillian
1976   *Worlds of Pain: Life in the Working-Class Family.* New York: Basic Books.

Safa, Helen I.
1981   "Runaway Shops and Female Employment: The Search for Cheap Labor." *Signs* 7 (2): 418–23.

Safilios-Rothschild, Constantina
1984   "Role of the Family in Development." In Sue Ellen Charlton, ed., *Women in Third World Development*, 45–55. Boulder, Colorado: Westview Press.

Sahlins, Marshall
1972   *Stone Age Economics.* Chicago: Aldine-Atherton.

Sassen-Koob, Saskia
1978   "The International Circulation of Resources and Development: The Case of Migrant Labor." *Development and Change* 9 (4): 509–45.
1980   "Immigrant and Minority Workers in the Organization of the Labor Process." *Journal of Ethnic Studies* 1: 1–34.
1981   *Exporting Capital and Importing Labor: The Role of Caribbean Migration to New York City.* Occasional Papers 28, Center for Latin American and Caribbean Studies, New York University.
1984   "Notes on the Incorporation of Third World Women into Wage Labor through Immigration and Offshore Production." *International Migration Review* 18 (4): 1144–67.
1986   "New York City: Economic Restructuring and In-Migration." *Development and Change* 17 (1): 85–119.

Schmink, Marianne
1984   "Household Economic Strategies: Review and Research Agenda." *Latin American Research Review* 19 (3): 87–101.

Secretaría de Estado de Agricultura
1978   "Plan de desarrollo: La Sierra." Santo Domingo: Secretaría de Agricultura.

Selby, Henry, and Arthur Murphy
1982   *The Mexican Urban Household and the Decision to Migrate to the United States.* Occasional Papers in Social Change 4, Institute for the Study of Human Issues, Philadelphia.

Shadow, Robert D.
1979   "Differential Out-Migration: A Comparison of Internal and International Migration from Villa Guerrero, Jalisco (Mex-

ico)." In Fernando Camara and Robert Von Kemple, eds., *Migration Across Frontiers: Mexico and the United States.* Albany: Institute for Meso-American Studies, State University of New York at Albany.

Sharpe, Kenneth
1977   *Peasant Politics: Struggle in a Dominican Village.* Baltimore: Johns Hopkins University Press.

Singelman, Joachim
1978   *From Agriculture to Services: The Transformation of Industrial Employment.* Beverly Hills: Sage.

Sjaastad, L. A.
1962   "The Costs and Returns of Human Migration." *Journal of Political Economy* (7): 80–93.

Sjoberg, Gideon, and Roger Nett
1968   *A Methodology for Social Research.* New York: Harper and Row.

Smale, Melinda
1980   *Women in Mauritania: The Effects of Drought and Migration on Their Economic Status and Implications for Development Programs.* Washington, D.C.: Office of Women in Development, Agency for International Development.

Stack, Carol
1974   *All Our Kin: Strategies for Survival in a Black Community.* New York: Harper Colophon.

Stanback, Jr., Thomas M., and Thierry J. Noyelle
1982   *Cities in Transition: Changing Job Structures in Atlanta, Denver, Buffalo, Phoenix, Columbus, Nashville, Charlotte.* Totowa, New Jersey: Allanheld, Osmun.

Standing, Guy
1981   *Labor Force Participation and Development.* Geneva: International Labor Office.

Stansell, Christine
1986   *City of Women.* New York: Alfred A. Knopf.

Stark, Oded, and Robert Lucas
1988   "Migration, Remittances, and the Family." *Economic Development and Cultural Change* 36 (3): 465–82.

Stepick, Alex
1987   "The Haitian Exodus: Flight from Terror and Poverty." In Barry Levine, ed., *The Caribbean Exodus*, 131–51. New York:. Praeger.

Stoddard, Ellwyn
1976   "A Conceptual Analysis of the 'Alien Invasion': Institutional-

ized Support of Illegal Mexican Aliens in the U.S." *International Migration Review* 10 (Summer): 157–89.

Tancer, Shoshona
1973   "La Quesqueyana: The Dominican Woman, 1940–1970." In Ann Pescatello, ed., *Female and Male in Latin America*, 209–30. Pittsburgh: University of Pittsburgh Press.

Thorne, Barrie, and Marilyn Yalom, eds.
1982   *Rethinking the Family: Some Feminist Questions*. New York: Longman.

Tienda, Marta, Leif Jensen, and Robert Bach
1984   "Immigration, Gender and the Process of Occupational Change in the United States, 1970–80." *International Migration Review* 18 (4): 1021–44.

Tilly, Charles
1978   "Migration in Modern European History." In William S. McNeill and Ruth Adams, eds., *Human Migration: Patterns and Policies*, 48–72. Bloomington: Indiana University Press.

Tilly, Louise A., and Joan W. Scott
1978   *Women, Work, and Family*. New York: Holt, Rinehart, and Winston.

Torres-Saillant, Silvio
1989   "Dominicans as a New York Community: A Social Appraisal." *Punto 7 Review* 2 (1): 7–25.

Ugalde, Antonio
1984   "La mujer en la fuerza laboral en Santo Domingo: Un estudio socio-demográfico." *Estudios Sociales* (Santo Domingo) 17 (55): 85–102.

Ugalde, Antonio, Frank Bean, and Gilbert Cárdenas
1979   "International Migration from the Dominican Republic: Findings from a National Survey." *International Migration Review* 13 (2): 253–54.

Ugalde, Antonio, and T. Langham
1980   "International Return Migration: Socio-Demographic Determinants of Return Migration to the Dominican Republic." Paper presented at the Caribbean Studies Association, Curaçao.

Urrea, Fernando
1982   *Life Strategies and the Labor Market: Colombians in New York in the 1970s*. Occasional Papers 34, Center for Latin American and Caribbean Studies, New York University.

U.S. Bureau of the Census
1983   *1980 Census of Population: Ancestry of the Population by State, 1980.* Supplementary Report. Washington, D.C.: U.S. Bureau of the Census.
1984   *1980 Census of the Population.* Vol. 1: *Characteristics of the Population.* Washington, D.C.: U.S. Bureau of Census.
Uzzell, J. Douglas
1979   "Conceptual Fallacies in the Rural-Urban Dichotomy." *Urban Anthropology* 8: 333–50.
Vedovato, Claudio
1986   *Politics, Foreign Trade and Economic Development: A Study of the Dominican Republic.* London: Croom Helm.
Vega, Bernardo
1981   *La coyuntura económica dominicana, 1980–1981.* Santiago: Universidad Católica Madre y Maestra.
Vega, Gustav, and Emmanuel Castillo
1980   "Economía y política: La nacionalización de la Ley 299." Santiago: Universidad Católica Madre y Maestra. Mimeo.
Veras, Rafael A.
1976   "Santiago y su proceso de desarrollo urbano." In *Santiago ante el futuro,* 27–42. Santo Domingo: Fondo para el Avance de la Ciencias Sociales.
Verdugo, Naomi
1982   "The Effects of Discrimination on the Earnings of Hispanic Workers: Findings and Policy Implications." National Conference of La Raza, Washington, D.C.
Vicens, Lucas
1982   *Crisis Económica.* Santo Domingo: Alfa y Omega.
Vilas, Carlos
1976   "La política de la dominación en la República Dominicana." In A. Cortén et al., eds., *Azúcar y política.* Santo Domingo: Taller.
1979   "Clases sociales, estado y acumulación periferica en la República Dominicana." *Realidad Contemporanea* 10–11: 31–58.
Vuskovic, Pedro
1982   "Economic Internationalization, Neoliberalism, and Unemployment in Latin America." *Contemporary Marxism* (5): 81–87.
Waldinger, Roger
1983   "Ethnic Enterprise and Industrial Change: A Case Study of

the New York City Garment Industry." Ph.D. dissertation, Department of Sociology, Harvard University.

1986a   "The Problems and Prospects of Manufacturing Workers in the New York City Labor Market." Paper prepared for the Worker Literacy Project of the City University of New York.

1986b   *Through the Eye of the Needle: Immigrants and Enterprises in New York's Garment Trades.* New York: New York University Press.

1987   "Changing Ladders and Musical Chairs: Ethnicity and Opportunity in Post-Industrial New York." *Politics and Society* 15 (4): 369–402.

Wallerstein, Immanuel

1974   *The Modern World-System.* New York: Academic Press.

Wallerstein, Immanuel, W. Martin, and T. Dickson

1979   "Household Structures and Process." Paper presented at the Colloquium on Production and Reproduction in the Labor Force, Fione, Italy.

Warren, Robert

1988   "Legalization Data and Other Statistical Information About Dominican Migration to the United States." Paper presented at the Conference on Dominican Migration, Fundación Friedrich Ebert, Santo Domingo.

Watts, Susan J.

1983   "Marriage Migration, a Neglected Form of Long-Term Mobility: A Case Study from Ilorin, Nigeria." *International Migration Review* 17 (4): 682–97.

Weiss, Wendy

1985   "The Social Organization of Property and Work: A Study of Migrants from the Rural Ecuadorian Sierra." *American Ethnologist* 12 (3): 468–88.

Weist, Raymond E.

1970   "Implications of International Labor Migration for Mexican Rural Development." In F. Camara and R. V. Kemper, eds., *Migration Across Frontiers and the United States.* Contributions of the Latin American Anthropology Group, vol. 3: 85–97, Institute for Mesoamerican Studies, State University of New York at Albany.

1973   "Wage-Labor Migration and Households in Town." *Journal of Anthropological Research* 29 (3): 180–209.

Whiteford, Michael

1978   "Women, Migration and Social Change: A Colombia Case Study." *International Migration Review* 18 (4): 236–47.

Wiarda, Howard
1970   *Dictatorship and Development.* Gainesville: University of Florida Press.
1975   *Dictatorship, Development and Disintegration: Politics and Social Change in the Dominican Republic.* Ann Arbor, Michigan: Xerox University Microfilms.
Wiarda, Howard, and Michael Kryzanek
1982   *The Dominican Republic: A Caribbean Crucible.* Boulder, Colorado: Westview Press.
Wilk, Richard, ed.
1989   *The Household Economy.* Boulder, Colorado: Westview Press.
Wolf, Eric
1966   *Peasants.* Englewood Cliffs, New Jersey: Prentice-Hall.
Wong, Bernard
1987   "The Role of Ethnicity in Enclave Enterprises: A Study of the Chinese Garment Factories in New York City." *Human Organization* 46 (2): 120–30.
Wood, Charles
1981   "Structural Change and Household Strategies: A Conceptual Framework for the Study of Rural Migration." *Human Organization* 40 (4): 338–43.
1982   "Equilibrium and Historical-Structural Perspectives on Migration: A Comparative Critique with Implications for Future Research." *International Migration Review* 16 (2): 298–319.
World Bank
1978   *Dominican Republic: Its Main Economic Development Problems.* Washington, D.C.: World Bank.
1981   "República Dominicana: Análisis del sector agrícola." Report prepared for the projects department of Latin American and Caribbean Regional Office, World Bank, Washington, D.C.
Yanagisako, Sylvia
1979   "Family and Household: The Analysis of Domestic Groups." *Annual Review of Anthropology* 8: 161–205.
Young, Kate
1978   "Modes of Appropriation and the Sexual Division of Labor: A Case from Oaxaca, Mexico." In A. Kuhn and A. Wolpe, eds., *Feminism and Capitalism,* 124–54. London: Routledge and Kegan Paul.
Yunén, Rafael Emilio
1985   *La isla como es: Hipótesis para su comprobación.* Santiago: Universidad Católica Madre y Maestra.

Zavella, Patricia
    1987   *Women's Work and Chicano Families.* Ithaca: Cornell University Press.
Zolberg, Aristide
    1978   "International Migration Policies in a Changing World System." In W. H. McNeill and R. S. Adams, eds., *Human Migration: Patterns and Policies*, 241–86. Bloomington: American Academy of Arts and Sciences.
    1981   "International Migrations in Political Perspective." In Mary Kritz, ed., *U. S. Immigration and Refugee Policy*, 3–27. Lexington, Massachusetts: D. C. Heath.

Index

Acosta, José, xvi
Age: of illegal immigrants, 171; of New York Dominicans, 75
Agriculture, 35, 39, 48, 200; exports, 11n, 26–29, 30, 34, 114n, 132; in Juan Pablo, 54, 100–125 passim, 132, 141, 145–146; labor in, 11n, 26–27, 29, 35, 55, 105–6, 109, 115–18, 125, 128, 145–46, 201; in Licey al Medio, 54, 127, 129; in Los Pinos, 127–28, 132; migration affecting, 98–99, 127–29, 131–32; and remittances, 70, 129–30; in Santiago de los Caballeros, 55; Trujillo's control over, 28–29, 30
Alba, David, xvi
La Aldea, 126
Almonte, Paul, xvi
Altruism, 134
La Amapola, 126
April Revolution, 32
Argentina, 66
Asians, in New York, 166
Austerity Law No. 1, Dominican, 41
Authoritarian politics, Dominican, 33–44, 48–49
Authority: household, 148–49, 158. *See also* Patriarchy

Báez Evertsz, Franc, 59n, 86
Balaguer, Joaquín, 31, 32, 33–45, 48–49, 111–12
Balance-of-payments problems, 35, 45, 70, 73–74
Bananas, 106
Banking, mortgage, 86
Basmajian, Gloria, xviii
Beans, 115, 132

Beautician classes, 90
Benamou, Catherine, xvii
Berthin, Gerardo, xvii
Between Two Islands, as term, 16–17
Blacks, in New York, 166–67, 168, 179–80
Blanco, Jorge, 45, 46
Bonao, 104
Bosch, Juan, 1, 32
Bourgeoisie. *See* Middle class
Bracero system, 10–11
"Brain drain," 66, 96
Bray, David, xvii, 107n
Brooklyn, New York City, 163
Brukman, Jan, xv
Budget, household, 148–50, 156–58; expenditures, 118, 119, 156–57; investment, 137–38. *See also* Consumption; Income

Cacao, 26, 28–29
Campesinos, 82, 92
Capital investment, 30, 34–35; foreign, 26, 30, 34, 49, 208; return migrant, 90, 94; rural, 103, 122–23, 125, 132
Capitalism, 135–36, 143–44, 152–53
Capitalist class, of Juan Pablo, 101–11 passim, 115–18, 121, 143–44, 145
Caribbean countries, 9, 38, 67; Cuba/Cubans, 9, 32, 155, 160n; Haiti, 12, 27. *See also* Dominican Republic
Castillo, Enmanuel, xvi
Castro, Max, xvi, 57
Cattle, 30, 54, 130; exports, 132; in Juan Pablo, 100, 101, 111, 112–14, 115, 116, 120–21; in Los Pinos, 128
CEA (Consejo Estatal de Azucar), 28, 46

Centro de Investigación (Universidad Católica de Madre y Maestra, Dominican Republic), xvi
Charity, in Juan Pablo, 122n
Chickens, 54
Children: emigrating, 24, 25, 68–69, 74–75, 139–44, 159; household care of, 151–52, 159n; of immigrants, 204–5
Chishti, Muzaffar, xvii
Cibao, 51, 54, 81, 126
Citizenship, U.S., by Dominicans, 207
Clarke, Nancy, xvii
Class, 4–5, 10, 15–16, 65–66, 199, 200; and consumption, 195–96, 197, 201; Dominican emigrant, 13–14, 16, 107–8, 109, 126–27, 157, 174, 195–97; in Dominican Republic (general), 18–19, 24, 33–34; and household dynamics, 137, 139; immigrant perception of, 195–97; in Juan Pablo, 101, 105–18, 122n, 124, 125, 143–44, 145; male pre-migration/immigrant, 157. *See also* Middle class; Peasants; Proletarians; Upper class
Clothing, imported from U.S., 124
Cocoa, 34
Coffee, 26, 28–29, 54; in Juan Pablo, 100, 101, 103, 105–6, 113–14, 115, 116
Colombian immigrants, 8, 194, 205
Commercial sector: in Juan Pablo, 122–25; New York immigrant, 89, 168; remittances and, 130
Congress, U.S., 11. *See also* Law
Consejo Estatal de Azucar (CEA), 28, 46
Construction: migrant housing, 91; in Santiago de los Caballeros, 55, 122
Consumption, 6–7, 14, 16–17, 201; class and, 195–96, 197, 201; household strategies with, 137–38; in Juan Pablo, 118; migrant vs. non-migrant household, 70, 72–74, 95, 96, 118; PRD government and, 45, 49; of return migrants, 86–87, 91, 92–93; in urban areas (Dominican), 36, 72–73
Cordero, Neuli, xvi
Craft sector, in Juan Pablo, 122–25
Crisis: in Dominican economy, 44–46, 92, 206; in Dominican politics, 31–33, 48
Cross-Beras, Julio, xvi
Cuba/Cubans, 9, 32, 155, 160n
Cultural capital, 173–74

Deforestation, Juan Pablo and, 104
de Janvry, Alain, 7, 107n
del Castillo, José, xvi

del Rosario, Pedro Juan, 128, 132
Democratic politics, 44–46, 49
Dependency theory, 4, 18, 107–8, 124
Development, 6–7, 48, 66, 98; Balaguer's policy of, 33–44, 45, 49; industrial, 6–7, 29–31, 33–44, 45, 48, 49; migration-dependent, 33–44; state, 29–31, 49
"Disarticulated economies," 7
Discrimination, 164, 205
Divorce, 156, 158
D'Oleo Ramírez, Frank, 59n, 86
Dollar, vs. peso, 46
Domestic service: in Juan Pablo, 124; paid vs. unpaid, 153–54
Domínguez, Virginia, xv
Dominican Republic, 18–50, 206–7; map of research sites, 53; New York City emigrants from, *see* New York City; research design with, 51–57, 61; return to, 14, 17, 21, 23n, 51, 80–97, 156–58, 160; and U.S. immigration policies, 11n, 12, 20, 31, 33, 42, 48; U.S. occupation of, 1, 26, 31, 32. *See also* Class; Economy; Migration; Politics; Rural areas; Urban areas
Dominican Revolutionary Party (PRD), 31, 43, 44, 49
Dore y Cabral, Carlos, xvi
Duarte, Isis, xvi
Duration of stay abroad, of return migrants, 82–83, 84
Duverge, Helmer, xvii

Economy: crisis in Dominican, 44–46, 92, 174, 206; Dominican development policies, 6–7, 29–31, 33–44, 45, 48, 49, 98; Dominican GDP, 34, 41, 45; household, 133, 134–47; New York City, 166–69. *See also* Consumption; Employment; Income; Investment; Market
Education, 49; and "brain drain," 66, 96; and Dominican employment demand, 96–97, 200, 201, 204; Dominican level of in New York, 75–76, 164, 171, 174–78; Hispanic level of in New York, 164–66; illegal immigrant level of, 171, 174–78; middle class and, 36–38, 204; return migrant level of, 81, 83–84, 90; Santo Domingo level of, 76, 77; and unemployment, 38, 39; U.S.-gained, 90
Edwards, Richard, 193
Egalitarianism, household, 93–94, 148–56, 202
Eggs, 54

Egypt, 9, 66
Electrical shortages, in Dominican Republic, 206
El Guano, 130n
El Salvador, 12
Emigration. *See* Migration
Employment: discrimination of females, 187–94; of Dominican males in U.S., 157, 168, 175–78, 179, 202; Dominican public sector, 44–45, 49; of educated Dominicans, 96–97, 174–78, 200, 201; ethnicity of, 179–82; of illegal immigrants, 6, 11, 83, 168, 169–86, 189, 190, 193, 195; in Juan Pablo, 122–23; in Los Pinos, 128; migrant household, 74, 75, 158–60, 193, 194, 202; migrant/non-migrant/return migrant households, 74, 75; before migration, 76–80; in New York City, 162–98; New York native-born, 166; of return migrants, 74, 75, 84–90, 93; vulnerability of immigrants in, 6, 11, 182–86, 193, 198; of women, 89, 93, 124, 144–56, 159–60, 175–78, 179, 186–95, 202. *See also* Labor; Occupations
Entrepreneurs, immigrant, 89, 168
Equilibrium theory, 4, 124
Erosion, in Juan Pablo, 104
Espinal, Rosario, xvii
Ethnicity, of employment, 179–82
Ethnographic research, 56–57, 60–63
Eusebio Pol, Noris, 56
Exchange rate policies, 34, 35, 46, 48
Expenditures, household: Dominican rural, 118, 119; U.S. immigrant, 156–57
Exports, 7, 47–48, 199–200; agricultural, 11n, 26–29, 30, 34, 114n, 132; state policy and, 28–34 passim, 45–49 passim, 199–200

Families: authority in, 148–49, 158; children emigrating from, 24, 25, 68–69, 74–75, 139–44; household distinguished from, 133n–34n; marital status after immigration, 156, 159–60, 163, 193–94, 202–3, 205–6; migrant, 12–16, 67–75, 141–44; single-mate/multiple-mate, 148; unification of, 10, 87–88, 159, 166. *See also* Children; Gender relations
Farmers, 39; in Juan Pablo, 54, 101, 102, 103, 108–9. *See also* Agriculture
Fathers, Juan Pablo, 140–44
Females, 166, 201–2; discrimination in employment, 187–94; in domestic service, 124, 153–54; Dominican in U.S., 136, 146–47, 148–58, 159–60, 175–78, 186–95; emigration numbers of, 19; employment of, 89, 93, 124, 144–56, 159–60, 175–78, 179, 186–95, 202; gender roles in Dominican Republic, 93–94, 145–48, 150–52; head of household, 56, 68, 149, 156, 159–60, 163, 194–95, 202, 205–6; household roles of, 93–94, 135–36, 145–56, 193, 194; Juan Pablo emigrant wives, 144–47; and Juan Pablo land, 103n; in Licey al Medio agro-industry, 54; Los Pinos working-class, 127; New York labor-force participation rates, 163; return migrant, 89, 93–94, 156–58; in Santiago de los Caballeros, 68, 156; undocumented, 171, 175–78, 179, 189, 190, 193, 195; U.S. education of, 90
Fernández-Kelly, María Patricia, xv, 155, 160n, 187n
Financing: industrial, 34. *See also* Budget, household; Investment
Florida, Dominican population, 23
Foner, Nancy, xvii
Food: imports, 35, 46, 48, 132; prices of, 29, 35; production of, 29, 115, 131–32; riots, 45. *See also* Agriculture
Foreign investment: in Dominican Republic, 26, 30, 34, 49, 208; in Third World economies, 7
Foreign labor: in Dominican Republic, 27. *See also* Migrants
Forests, Juan Pablo and, 104

García, Anna, 155, 160n
García, Elena, xvi
Garcia, Ziamara, xvi
Garment industry labor, 89, 160n, 168n, 190, 191
Gender relations: household, 12–16, 93–94, 135–58 passim, 193, 194, 202; return migrants and, 93–94, 156–58. *See also* Females; Males
Generations: in Juan Pablo migrant households, 139–44; U.S. second, 204–7
Georges, Eugenia, xvii, 126–28, 130–31
González, María, xvii
Goody, Jack, 134n
Gordon, Andrew, 151n, 157n
Goris, Aneris, xvii
Government. *See* State policy
Grasmuck, Sherri, 56, 62
Greece, 66
Greenpoint, Brooklyn, New York City, 163

Gross domestic product (GDP), Dominican, 34, 41, 45
Guarnizo, Luis, 90n
Gurak, Douglas, xvii, 194n, 205
Gutiérrez, Carlos María, 30
Guzmán, Antonio, 44–45

Haiti, 12, 27
Hemispheric Migration Project, xvii
Hernández, Ana, xvii
Hernández, Ramona, 197n
Hispanics: in New York, 164–67, 179–82; wages of male-female, 188. *See also* Latin America
Historical structuralist perspective, 4–5, 6, 8, 12, 169–70
Household labor class, Juan Pablo, 107, 108–9, 110, 111, 118–20, 121, 123, 143
Households, migrant, 12–16, 67–75, 133–61; budgeting control, 148–50; defined, 68, 134n; egalitarian, 93–94, 148–56, 202; employment and, 74, 75, 148–56, 158–60, 193, 194, 202; female-headed, 56, 68, 149, 156, 159–60, 163, 194–95, 202, 205–6; gender relations, 12–16, 93–94, 135–58 passim, 193, 194, 202; generation relations, 139–44; Juan Pablo, 106–7, 108, 109, 110n, 117–18, 140–47; moral-economy view of, 133, 134–36; research with, 56–57; social-solidarity view of, 138; survival strategy view of, 133, 136–38, 142–43; in U.S., 148–56
Housework: domestic service, 124, 153–54; gender roles and, 151–52, 153–54
Housing, in Dominican Republic, 86, 91, 201
Huyck, Earl, xvi

Ideology: and household dynamics, 137, 138, 139, 143–44, 154–55; migration, 14, 17, 150–51
Illegal immigrants, 11, 21, 23; employment of, 6, 11, 83, 168, 169–86, 189, 190, 193, 195; research with, 59, 61; return migration by, 83; vulnerability in workplace, 6, 11, 182–86, 193
Immigrant: U.S. definitions, 12. *See also* Migrants
Immigration. *See* Migration
Immigration Act (1965, 1976), U.S., 10, 11
Immigration and Naturalization Service, 11

Immigration Reform and Control Act (1986), U.S., 11
Imports, 45; food, 35, 46, 48, 132. *See also* Foreign labor
Import-substitution policies, 30–31, 33, 35, 38, 48, 200
Income: Dominican erosion in, 46, 96; Dominican-U.S., 46, 47; of female-headed households in U.S., 156, 206; household roles with, 134–35, 138, 148–50, 158, 202; inequality in distribution of, 6, 38, 41, 43, 129–31, 199; in Juan Pablo, 109, 114–15, 117, 118, 145; in Los Pinos, 128; middle-class Dominican, 38–39, 40; migrant/non-migrant household, 71–72, 118; "off the books," 178–79; pooled, 149–50, 202; return migrant, 81, 87–90; U.S. immigrant, 148–51, 156, 163, 167, 179, 186, 188–89, 194; U.S. native, 46, 47, 163; U.S. public assistance, 194–95. *See also* Remittances; Wages
Individuals: migration theory and, 4. *See also* Migrants
Industrial sector: development in, 6–7, 29–31, 33–44, 45, 48, 49; garment, 89, 160n, 168n, 190, 191; Licey al Medio, 54; New York employment in, 5–6, 163–70 passim, 174–82 passim, 188, 190, 191; Santiago de los Caballeros, 55; skill downgrading in, 205; in sugar, 26, 34; and trade policies, 30–31, 33, 35, 38, 48
Inflation: demand-pull, 70; Dominican, 41, 45; international, 45
Informal sector, 6; Dominican, 38, 39, 41; New York, 178–79
Infrastructure, Dominican, 34, 208
Institute for Price Stabilization (INESPRE), 35
International economy. *See* World market
International Labour Organization, 9, 39
International Money Fund, 45
Investment: household strategies with, 137–38; petty-capitalist international, 207–8. *See also* Capital investment
Italian-born New Yorkers, 203

Jackson Heights, New York City, 163
Jamaica, 8, 20–21, 66, 86n
Jerez, Claudio, xvi
Jobs. *See* Employment
Job satisfaction: and class, 196; and gender, 189, 202
Joseph, Gil, xvii

Juan Pablo, 99–106, 126, 132; class in, 101, 105–18, 122n, 124, 125, 143–44, 145; first emigrant from, 103; land tenure in, 100–102, 103–4, 110–22, 140–41; non-agriculture sectors in, 122–25; research, 52–54, 55, 56–57, 61, 62; sons emigrating from, 139–44; wives emigrating from, 144–47

Kessler-Harris, Alice, 196
Kikuyu social relations, 136
Kinship: and household dynamics, 137, 138, 139, 140–44, 153–54. *See also* Families
Kritz, Mary, 194n

Labor, 5, 8–13, 208; agricultural (general), 11n, 26–27, 29, 35, 55, 201; agricultural in Juan Pablo, 105–6, 109, 115–18, 125, 145–46; agricultural in Los Pinos, 128; Balaguer regime and, 35–37, 38–39, 49; democratic politics and, 44–46; household division of, 151–53; imported to Dominican Republic, 27; industrial, 5–6, 163–70 passim, 174–82 passim, 188, 190, 191, 205; informal-sector, 6, 38, 39, 178–79; international division of, 3–8, 65, 95–97, 199; Juan Pablo, 105–6, 107, 108–9, 115–18, 121; labor-force participation rates of Dominicans in New York, 163–64, 166; reserve army of, 187n; return migrant, 81, 84–90; scarcity, 5–6, 169; service-sector, 5–6, 35–36, 79, 163–64, 178, 205; undocumented, 6, 11, 83, 168, 169–86; urban (Dominican), 38–39. *See also* Employment; Labor surplus; Occupations; Underemployment; Unemployment
Labor surplus, 5, 6–7, 8, 27, 66, 75–80; "apparent" vs. "hard-core," 66; household, 138–39, 144; Juan Pablo and, 107–8, 124, 144; as migration motivation, 65, 108, 144
Laite, Julian, 16
Landreau, Anita, xviii
Landreau, John, xvii
Land tenure, 26, 27, 29, 30, 54, 131; Juan Pablo, 100–102, 103–4, 110–22 passim, 140–41; research about, 62
Land use. *See* Agriculture
Laos, 20–21
Larkin, Mary Ann, xvii
Larson, Eric M., xvii, 22, 23n, 59n, 80, 81
Larson, Magali Sarfetti, xvii

Latin America, 38, 67. *See also* Caribbean countries; Mexico
Law: Dominican agrarian, 111–12; Dominican industrial, 34–35; U.S. immigration, 10–11, 20; U.S. labor, 182. *See also* Illegal immigrants
Legalization: of illegal immigrants, 11, 193. *See also* Law
Licey al Medio, 126; agriculture in, 127, 129; remittances received in, 129n; research, 52, 54–55, 56, 57
Living standards: migrant/non-migrant household, 72–73, 121. *See also* Class; Consumption; Income
Long, Jane-Ellen, xviii
Los Angeles, 6
Lower East Side, New York City, 163
Luepnitz, Deborah, xvii

McLuhan, Marshall, 64
Males, 166; emigration numbers of, 19, 59n; employment in U.S., 157, 168, 175–78, 179, 202; and gender differences in employment, 188–89, 190, 191, 193, 202; gender roles in Dominican Republic, 93–94, 145–48, 150–52, 156–57; gender roles in U.S., 148–58; generation relations, 139–44; household roles of, 93–94, 135–58; Juan Pablo, 139–44, 145–47; New York labor-force participation rates, 163; research with, 59; return migrant, 93–94, 156–58; Santiago de los Caballeros emigrants, 68; undocumented, 171, 175–78, 179, 189, 190. *See also* Patriarchy
Manufacturing sector. *See* Industrial sector
Map, of Dominican research sites, 53
Marcelo, María, xvii
Marital status: after immigration, 156, 159–60, 163, 193–94, 202–3, 205–6. *See also* Gender relations
Market: Dominican, 18, 26–29; Third World country, 6–7. *See also* Agriculture; Commercial sector; Industrial sector; Labor; World market
Marshall, Adriana, xvii, 167
Marshall, Dawn, xvii
Martin, John Bartlow, 33
Martínez, Victor, xvi
Marxism, 15, 134
Meillassoux, Claude, 135
Men. *See* Males
Merchant-capitalist class, of Juan Pablo, 101–11 passim, 115–18, 121, 143–44, 145

Methodology, research, 60–64
Mexico, 66; migrant household gender relations, 143n; migration to U.S. from, 7, 10–11, 21, 67; return migration to, 82–83
Middle class, 30, 33–34, 35–36, 49, 201, 204; attitude toward migrants in, 82, 91, 92; and Balaguer regime, 33–34, 35–39, 40, 44, 49; and consumption, 195–96, 197, 201; Dominican male immigrants and, 157–58; and education, 36–38, 204; emigration overseas by, 13–14, 174; and gender relations, 154–55, 157–58; and Guzmán regime, 44, 45; immigrant identification with, 195–97, 201; of migrant households, 95, 174; New York life-styles esteemed by, 93; proletarianization in U.S., 16; of return migrants, 82, 86–87, 92, 160; salaries of, 38–39, 40. *See also* Capitalist class
Migrants, 1–2, 4, 49–50, 63–64; class composition of Juan Pablo, 107–8; duration of stay abroad, 82–83, 84; employment of, 74, 75, 157, 158–60, 162–98; gender relations of, 12–16, 93–94, 135–36, 137, 138, 144–58; motivated by family unification, 166; motivated by household politics, 146–47; motivated by socioeconomics, 14, 46, 68–69, 94–95, 108, 121, 141–44, 166, 200, 201; motivated by state politics, 1–3, 43–44; naturalization of, 207; perception of material circumstances by, 195–97, 201; return, 14, 17, 21, 23n, 51, 80–97, 156–58; social networks of, 12–16, 197, 203, 206; sons from Juan Pablo, 139–44; wives from Juan Pablo, 144–56. *See also* Households, migrant; Illegal immigrants; New York City
Migration, 1–3, 13, 19–25, 44–46, 49–50, 79–80, 206–8; circulating, 87; duration of, 82–83, 84; research and, 51–52, 59, 61, 63; return, 14, 17, 21, 23n, 51, 80–97, 156–58, 160; rural-overseas, 66–67, 98–132, 200; rural-urban, 6, 7, 24, 35, 38, 43, 48, 55, 69–70; state policies and, 8–12, 19, 20, 31, 33–44, 48, 49, 199–200; step-, 24, 70; theories of, 4, 18, 107–8, 124; urban-overseas, 7–8, 24, 43, 59–60, 65–97. *See also* Migrants
Minifundios, 54, 131
Mitchell, Christopher, xvi-xvii, 103n
Modernization. *See* Development
Modernization theory, 4, 15, 107–8

Modes of production, migration influencing, 15–16
Moral economy, household as, 133, 134–36
Mothers: and child care, 151–52, 159n; emigrant children declared by, 24, 25
Multinational firms, in Dominican Republic, 49

National Catholic University of Santiago (UCMM), 56
National Institute of Child Health and Development (NICHD), xv–xvi
National Science Foundation, xvi
National Statistics Office, 55
Naturalization, of Dominicans, 207
Nelson, 136
Neoclassical economics, 134, 137, 169
New Jersey, Dominican population, 23
New York City, 31, 203–4; age of Dominicans in, 75; attractiveness of life-styles in, 93; consumption by migrants in, 91, 195–96, 197; educational level of Dominicans in, 75–76, 164, 171, 174–78; employment in, 162–98; household budgeting of Dominicans in, 148–50; politically motivated migrants in, 43; population of immigrants in, 162, 163; research on, 51, 57–60, 61, 63–64; second-generation Dominicans in, 204–5; time of migrant stay in, 83
New York Research Program in Inter-American Affairs (New York University), xvi
New York State, Dominican population, 23
Nicaragua, 12

Occupations, 36, 37, 39, 49; of Dominicans in New York, 163–66, 172, 174–78; of female immigrants in U.S., 187–88; of Hispanics in New York, 164–66; of illegal immigrants, 171, 174–78; of immigrants in New York, 163–66, 167–69, 172, 174–78; before migration, 78–79, 171, 172; of return migrants, 81, 85–86
Oficina Nacional Estadística, Santo Domingo, xvi
Opitz, Wolfgang, 22, 59n
Organization of American States (OAS), 32
Overseeing, in Juan Pablo, 114–15
Ownership: agricultural land, 26, 27, 29, 30 (*see also* Land tenure); in Third World economies, 7. *See also* Investment

Passports, Dominican, 19, 103n
Patriarchy: in Dominican Republic, 93–94, 140–43, 146–47, 148; and households, 135–36, 148, 149, 150, 157; in U.S., 148, 149, 150
Patronage, in workplace, 184–86
Peasants, 131; associations of, 120, 125; Juan Pablo, 102, 120, 125; Los Pinos, 127; in Peruvian mining industry, 16. *See also* Farmers
Pérez, Glauco, xvii, 193
Personalism, in workplace, 184
Peru, 16
Pessar, Patricia R., 11n, 56, 61, 62, 193
Petroleum, 45, 206
Petty-capitalist class: in Juan Pablo, 106, 107, 108, 110–11, 115–18, 121, 143, 145; U.S. and Dominican, 207–8
Los Pinos, 126–28, 130–31, 132
Piore, Michael, 13
Plantations, sugar, 26–27
Pol, Noris Eusebio, xvi
Political parties, Dominican, 19, 31, 32, 43, 44, 48–49
Political refugee, U.S. definitions, 12
Politics (Dominican), 19, 28–31, 32, 49–50, 65; authoritarian, 33–44, 48–49; crisis in, 31–33, 48; democratic, 44–46, 49; household, *see* Gender relations; migrants motivated by household, 146–47; migrants motivated by state, 1–3, 43–44; in migration policies, 8–12, 31, 33, 41–43; and world market, 48. *See also* State policy
Pons, Frank Moya, xvi
Population: of Dominican immigrants to U.S., 19–24, 59n, 162, 163; Dominican Republic, 27; of Dominicans residing abroad, 22–23, 59n, 67–68; Dominican urban, 43; illegal immigrants, 59n; Juan Pablo, 54, 100, 103–4, 123; Licey al Medio, 54; of naturalized Dominicans, 207; New York City immigrant, 162, 163; of return migrants, 68; Santiago de los Caballeros, 55
Portes, Alejandro, xv, xvii, 90n
Portugal, 66
Power relations, household, 134–36, 138, 141, 158
PRD (Dominican Revolutionary Party), 31, 43, 44, 49
Prices, 45; export, 29, 45, 46, 114n; food, 29, 35; land, 120
Proletarians: Balaguer regime and, 41; Dominican immigrant, 16, 196; Domini-

can informal, 38, 41; Juan Pablo, 107, 108–9, 110, 111, 112–13, 116, 118, 120–21; in Peruvian mining industry, 16; Los Pinos, 127; PRD government and, 49
Property values: Juan Pablo, 118–22. *See also* Land tenure
Protectionism, 34
Public assistance income, in U.S., 163, 194–95
Public-sector employment, Dominican, 44–45, 49
Puerto Plata, 105
Puerto Rico: Dominican emigrants to, 22, 207; migrants from, 7, 194, 196

Quatro Quarenta, 91n
Queens, New York City, 163
Quota system, U.S., 10, 12

Ramírez, Margarita, xvi
Rapp, Rayna, 133n–34n, 154
Ravelo, Sebastián, 128, 132
Reformist Party (PR), Dominican Republic, 31, 32, 44, 48–49
Reichert, Joshua, xvi
Reid Cabral, Donald, 32
Remittances, to migrant households, 70–75, 87, 90n; in rural areas, 109, 117, 118, 121, 123, 128, 129–31, 132
Repression: Dominican governmental, 41, 43, 61; of illegal workers, 184
Research, 51–64; chart of, 52; ethnographic, 56–57, 60–63; methodological notes, 60–64; participant-observation in, 60–61; survey, 55–56, 57–59, 60, 61–63
Return migration, 14, 17, 21, 23n, 51, 80–97; and duration of stay abroad, 82–83, 84; fragile conditions of, 86–94; gender politics and, 156–58; to middle class, 82, 86–87, 92, 160
Rice, 30, 115, 132
Riots, food, 45
Roberts, Kenneth, 136–37
Rodríguez, Hugo, xvi
Rouse, Roger, 147n
Rumbaut, Ruben, xvii
Rural areas, 35, 43; Dominican emigrants from, 23–24; occupations in, 39; out-migration from, 66–67, 98–132, 200; return migrants from, 81–82; underemployment in, 38, 131; urban immigrants from, 6, 7, 24, 35, 38, 43, 48, 55, 69–70. *See also* Juan Pablo

Salaries. *See* Income; Wages
San José de las Matas, 126, 128, 130, 132
Santiago de los Caballeros: households involved in out-migration, 67–75; Juan Pablo business relations with, 101, 102, 103, 105, 122, 125; middle class in, 36; remittances received in, 71–75; research, 52, 55, 56, 57; return migrants in, 81–85, 86–87; unemployment in, 55, 77, 79
Santiago province, 52
Santo Domingo: educational level in, 76, 77; employment before migration in, 77, 79; food riots, 45; income distribution in, 41, 43, 130n; informal sector in, 39; middle class in, 36; return migrants in, 81; unemployment in, 38, 39, 77, 79
Santos, Gil, xvii
Sassen-Koob, Saskia, xvii, 66, 169
Savings: of male immigrants, 157–58; rural, 121–22, 125, 132; of U.S. sponsors, 159
Scarcity, labor, 5–6, 169
Sección, 54, 99
Secondary sector, New York, 5–6, 178–82
Self-employment, immigrant, 89, 167–68
Semi-proletariat: Juan Pablo, 107, 110, 111, 112–13, 116, 120–21, 123; Los Pinos, 127
Service sector, 5–6, 35–36, 79; Dominican immigrant labor in, 163–64, 178, 205; Juan Pablo, 122–25; New York, 163–64, 168–69, 178; remittances and, 130; and wage deterioration, 205
Sex. *See* Females; Gender relations; Males
Sharecropping, Juan Pablo, 111–14, 120–21
Sierra, 54, 99, 104, 113
Skill level: of illegal immigrants, 171–72, 174; in manufacturing sector, 205; of return migrants, 86, 89. *See also* Occupations
Snowball research techniques, 58n
Social networks: defined, 13; migrant, 12–16, 197, 203, 206. *See also* Families; Households, migrant
Social-solidarity view, of households, 138
Socioeconomics: and immigrant gender relations, 154–55; migration motivated by, 14, 46, 68–69, 94–95, 108, 121, 141–44, 166. *See also* Class; Employment
Sons, emigration from Juan Pablo, 139–44
South Bronx, New York City, 163

South Korea, 66
Sponsors, in U.S., 159, 180–83, 206
Stack, Carol, xv
Standing, Guy, 138–39
State Department, U.S., 12
State policy, 8–12, 199; Dominican, 47–48, 199–200; Dominican development, 29–31, 33–44, 45, 48, 49; Dominican emigration, 9–10, 11n, 19, 41–44; Dominican employment, 44–45, 49; Dominican trade, 28–38 passim, 45–49 passim, 199–200; of receiving societies, 10–12, 20, 31, 33; of sending societies, 9–10, 11n, 19, 33–44, 199; U.S. immigration, 10–12, 20, 31, 33, 42, 48. *See also* Law
Step-migration, 24, 70
Sudan, 9
Sugar, 11n, 26–29, 30, 34, 45, 46; exports, 26–29, 132, 199–200; in Juan Pablo, 101
Sullivan, Teresa, 23n
"Super-exploitation," in employment, 6, 193
Surveys: in Juan Pablo, 101, 103; research by, 55–56, 57–59, 60, 61–63
Survival strategies, household role in, 133, 136–38, 142–43

La Tabacalera, 93
Tamboril, 126, 128, 129, 130–31
Tariffs, 30, 34, 35, 48, 200
Tavárez, Julia, xvi, 57
Tax exemptions, industrial, 30, 34
Tejeda, Manuel, xvii
Temple University, xvi
Third World: capitalist development in, 15; labor conditions in, 6–7, 65; migration from, 4, 7–8, 9, 65–66. *See also* Dominican Republic
Time spent abroad, by return migrant, 82–83, 84
Tobacco, 28–29, 54, 55, 93
Torres-Saillant, Silvio, 197, 197n
Trade. *See* Commercial sector; World market
Trujillo Molina, Rafael L., 28–32; emigration restricted under, 9, 19, 103n; export agriculture under, 24, 28–29, 30; research and, 61; state development under, 29–31, 47–48
Tunisia, 9

Ugalde, Antonio, 52
Underemployment, 38, 200–201; in rural

areas, 38, 131; in Santiago de los Caballeros, 55; Third World, 6, 7, 65
Undocumented migrants. *See* Illegal immigrants
Unemployment, 38, 200–201, 204; migrant household, 128; before migration, 76–77, 95; PRD government and, 44, 49; of return migrants, 74, 81, 86, 89, 94; in rural areas, 116, 131; in Santiago de los Caballeros, 55, 77, 79; in Santo Domingo, 38, 39, 77, 79; Third World, 6, 7, 8, 65
Unions: in Dominican Republic, 41, 44; in U.S., 183, 186, 189–93, 196, 197, 205
United States: Caribbean vs. other Latin American migration to, 67; clothing imported from, 124; consumerism in, 196; Dominican employment in, 157, 158–60, 162–98; Dominican gender roles in, 110, 136, 146–58; Dominican Republic occupied by, 1, 26, 31, 32; gender stereotyping in labor market of, 187–88; immigration policy, 10–12, 20, 31, 33, 42, 48; income for return migrants from, 87–90; Juan Pablo investments in, 125; after occupation, 32–33, 48; population of Dominican immigrants in, 19–24, 59n, 162, 163; in research design, 57–60; second-generation immigrants in, 204–7; wages in, 46, 47, 163. *See also* Migration; New York City
Upper class, and labor transfer, 65
Urban areas: households of migrants from, 67–70; illegal immigrants from, 171; import-substitution policies subsidizing, 35; middle class in, 33–34, 36; out-migration from, 7–8, 24, 43, 59–60, 65–97; return migrants in, 81; rural migration to, 6, 7, 24, 35, 38, 43, 48, 55, 69–70; underemployment in, 38, 55; unemployment in, 38, 39, 55, 76–77, 79. *See also* New York City; Santiago de los Caballeros; Santo Domingo

Ureña, Carlos, 102
Ureña, Osvaldo, xvi
Ureña, Rosa, xvi
Uzzell, J. Douglas, 203

Vargas, José, xvi
Vedovato, Claudio, 28
Visas, 12, 33; abusers, 171–74
Vulnerability, in workplace, 6, 11, 182–86, 193, 198

Wages: in Dominican Republic, 39–47 passim, 105–6; minimum, 41, 42, 44, 179; Third World, 7; U.S. distribution of, 204–5; of U.S. immigrants, 150–51, 163, 167, 179, 186, 188–89; of U.S. natives, 46, 47, 163; women's vs. men's, 187n, 188–89, 191–92. *See also* Income
Waldinger, Roger, xvii, 166, 167n, 168n
Warren, Robert, 22, 59n
Washington Heights, New York City, 163
West Indies Sugar Company, 28
Whites: decline in/"white flight," 6, 166, 167n; in New York, 166, 167n
Wives, Juan Pablo emigrant, 144–47
Women. *See* Females
Wood, Charles, 134–35
Working-class consciousness, 16, 196. *See also* Proletarians
World Bank, 38
World market, 5, 18, 49, 199; balance-of-payments problems, 35, 45, 70, 73–74; exchange-rate policies, 34, 35, 46, 48; foreign investment in Dominican Republic, 26, 30, 34, 49, 208. *See also* Exports; Imports
World-systems perspective, 18

Yoruba of Nigeria, 135
Yugoslavia, 66
Yunén, Rafael, xvi

Zacarias, Georgina, xvi

Compositor: Huron Valley Graphics
Text: 11/13 Caledonia
Display: Caledonia
Printer: Maple-Vail Book Mfg. Group
Binder: Maple-Vail Book Mfg. Group